KV-448-862

CONTENTS

Modern Sea Angling

(Previously published as *Sea Angling: Modern Methods, Baits and Tackle*)

Alan Young is the *nom de plume* of a well-known angler and journalist. He has also written *Bass: How To Catch Them, Sea Fishing Baits* and *Sea Angling for Beginners.*

Pan Anglers' Library

Modern Sea Angling

Alan Young

(Previously published as *Sea Angling: Modern Methods, Baits and Tackle*)

Pan Books London and Sydney

First published 1971 by Barrie & Jenkins Ltd
as *Sea Angling: Modern Methods, Baits and Tackle*
This revised edition published 1974 by Pan Books Ltd,
Cavaye Place, London SW10 9PG
2nd printing 1977
© Alan Young 1971
ISBN 0 330 23902 3
Printed and bound in Great Britain by
Cox & Wyman Ltd, London, Reading and Fakenham

ACKNOWLEDGEMENTS

I wish to express my sincere appreciation of the helpful information given to me by the individuals and organizations mentioned below in connection with the 'Where and When to Fish' chapter.

Scotland
J. A. Kerr Hunter Esq, Hon Sec, Scottish Federation of Sea Anglers.
The Scottish Tourist Board: The Scottish Council of Physical Recreation

Northern Ireland
James O'Kane Esq, Hon Sec, The Causeway Coast SAC
W. R. Murphy Esq, of Belfast: The Northern Irish Tourist Board

Republic of Ireland
Des Brennan Esq, Angling Officer, Inland Fisheries Trust: The Irish Tourist Board

England and Wales
The Clerk of the Seaham UDC
W. Samuelson Esq, Hon Sec, Sunderland SAA
J. Swales Esq, Hon Sec, Whitby SAA
The Director of Publicity, Scarborough
Hon Secretary, Filey Brigg AS
The Entertainment and Publicity Manager, Bridlington
F. A. Allenby Esq, Hon Sec, Humber SAC
The Clerk of the East Suffolk and Norfolk River Authority
The Secretary, Cromer Advertising Association
The Director, Great Yarmouth and Gorleston-on-Sea Publicity Dept
The Town Clerk, Southwold
The Town Clerk, Walton-on-the-Naze
The Publicity Officer, Southend-on-Sea
The Entertainments Manager, Herne Bay
The Publicity Manager, Margate

The Publicity Manager, Ramsgate
The Publicity and Entertainments Manager, Deal
The Publicity Manager, Dover
The Publicity Officer, Folkestone
The Publicity and Public Relations Officer, Hastings
The Clerk of the Council, Newhaven
The Director of Entertainment and Publicity, Worthing
The Clerk of the Council, Littlehampton
The Publicity Manager, Bognor Regis
The Information Officer, Ryde
The Hon Sec, Isle of Wight AS
The Clerk of the Council, Ventnor
The Publicity Officer, Bournemouth
The Publicity Officer, Poole
The Hon Sec, Swanage and District AC
The Publicity Officer, Swanage
The Publicity Manager, Weymouth
R. G. Smith Esq, Jersey
The Secretary, States of Jersey Tourism Committee
The Town Clerk, Bridport
The Publicity and Public Relations Officer, Torbay
The Secretary, Salcombe Town Association
Allen Higginson Esq, Hon Sec, Plymouth SAC
The Clerk of the Looe UDC
Wing Cmdr G. E. Ranson, East Looe
The Penzance Corporation
The Clerk of the Council, Isles of Scilly
Press and Publicity Officer, Newquay UDC
Newquay AA
The Publicity Officer, Ilfracombe
John V. Cope Esq, Hon Sec, Ilfracombe and District AA
Mrs P. J. Harris, Hon Sec, Watchet and District SAA
The Clerk to the Watchet UDC
The Information Officer, Tenby
B. Mills Esq, Competition Sec, Milford Haven SAC
The Isle of Man Tourist Board
Wales Tourist Board
Publicity and Information Officer, Llandudno
Clerk of the Rhyl UDC
The Director, Publicity Dept, Blackpool

AUTHOR'S NOTE

Figs 1a and 1b are produced to define the terms necessarily used in some cases of identification.

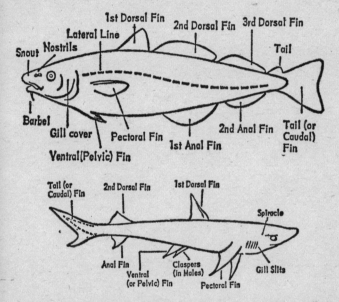

The rods referred to throughout the book as light, medium and heavy are described under 'Tackle'.

To avoid constant repetition of the words 'piers, groynes, breakwaters, jetties, etc', the word 'projection' has been used to cover everything which juts into the sea from which a man can fish, except rocks and other natural features.

CHAPTER 1

Sea Angling: A General Survey

Sea angling is a new sport compared to freshwater fishing, and there is no literature of the sea comparable to the whole libraries of volumes that deal with the practical details or abstract delights of angling for salmon, trout and the numerous species of coarse fish.

There is no fifteenth-century 'Treatyse of Fysshynge with an Angle' for sea anglers, nor did any Walton arise from their ranks to paint the picture of sea-fishing pleasures for the benefit of posterity – for the very good reason that so far as is known there were no sea anglers in that age nor in the two and a half centuries which succeeded it. Twenty titles would cover the sea-fishing books written before 1939.

Sea angling steadily increased in popularity in the years following the war, and in the past five years or so it has experienced what the population experts call an 'explosion'. This has given rise to many books on the subject and though most are mainly practical I am pleased to see that some have been written that get away from the instruction and – to quote my earlier paragraph – 'paint the picture of sea-fishing pleasures'.

However much may be written, practical or otherwise, it is well to remember that a wealth of knowledge and experience is held by sea anglers who do not write, and if they are prepared to talk it is advisable to listen, for so much of the success of sea angling depends on local knowledge of marks, tides and baits that none can afford to neglect them.

Movements of fish

Many people who do not fish, and a great number of freshwater anglers, think that it is only necessary to cast a line into salt water to haul out a fish. This is not true, even of the humble pouting and dab, and he who would catch bass or tope, flounder or pollack, must know where to fish – and the sea is vast.

The movements of fish are governed by two considerations which override all others: food, and the propagation of their species. Sea water contains chemical salts which feed the vast array of animal and vegetable plankton, some of which are microscopic, and some tiny but visible creatures. Some species of marine life which help to build up the enormous aggregate body of plankton are still microscopic in size when they have attained maturity. Other components of plankton are the larval forms of many species of crustaceans and molluscs – for example, crabs and mussels – which spend a certain part of their lives as minute and almost helpless organisms totally unlike the creatures they eventually become. Plankton cannot move of its own volition, but is carried by currents, and its depth is determined by the light which gives it life. On dull days and at night it is found at or near the surface; on bright days it is deeper down.

Plankton feeds many species of fish directly, but all fish life is dependent upon it directly or indirectly, for it feeds many molluscs, crustaceans, worms and insects which form the food of fish.

Some fish live on other fish; some subsist mainly on crustaceans and molluscs; others explore the areas washed by the tides in search of the creatures disclosed by the action of the waves. The sea is a constant battleground. The fry of herrings, for example, feed on plankton; mackerel chase the herring fry; and larger predators chase the mackerel. Some species of fish, themselves inoffensive and content to live on lower forms of life, are always subject to attack by creatures larger than themselves.

Anglers study their different habits, and deduce from the accumulated knowledge where fish of different species are to be found. Where food is, there will be the angler's quarry, and whether it be on the edge of a sandbank five miles off shore or a narrow gut at the seaward end of an estuary where the tide runs out like a millrace, every part of the sea has some particular appeal or lack of appeal to some particular inhabitant of it.

Anglers resident on the coast know the best marks for fish of different kinds. Those who visit it only occasionally will be well advised to listen to anglers who know the area, for haphazard fishing is the cause of much loss of time and temper. Marks differ with different states of the tide, and again on whether the tides are neaps or springs, while they alter once more with the change of water temperature as the year progresses. Such intricate details can be learned only on the spot through years of experience, and newcomers can save themselves much tribulation by taking advice. Experiment is good and desirable, but a week's fishing holiday is not the time for it. Professional fishermen are not always willing to impart their knowledge of fishing marks to casual visitors. The experienced amateur sea angler is the best source of advice.

Even those who live by the coast cannot afford to be hidebound, for marks can differ from year to year, and even from week to week. A strong gale or some act of Man can alter the coastline, sometimes by the veriest trifle – an extra yard on a sand spit, a sunken boat; or a new groyne – and these may be sufficient to change the direction of currents, and with a change of currents comes a change of feeding grounds.

The other factor which governs the distribution of fish, the propagation of the species, is more concerned with the 'when' than the 'where' of fishing, though places are affected in the wide terms of offshore and deep water. Some species of fish come into shallow water to spawn, some ascend estuaries, and some leave their normal habitat in shallow water to spawn in the deeps, and these movements, differing with the species and groups of the same species, occur in well-defined cycles. There is, for example, a migration of black bream from Mediterranean latitudes to our southern coasts in summer. In October cod come in from the deeps, while mackerel are found inshore in late summer and autumn.

Sporting fishing

If the sole object of angling were to catch fish, one might as well discard the rod and use a net, or lay down a line with a hundred hooks. Something more than mere numbers is required, and that something is to be found by using a rod with tackle suitably designed for the quarry expected.

A century ago the books of Philip Henry Gosse started a craze for collecting flora and fauna from the sea shore and rock pools, and as a result the people of England invaded and 'discovered' the sea coasts. As holidays by the sea became more and more popular, so some of the male members of these Victorian families, tiring perhaps of the search for insignificant creatures on shore, accompanied commercial fishermen in their boats, and engaged in fishing for sport. They used the heavy handlines and weights employed by their mentors, and when sea angling with rods from rocks and piers developed as a pastime, an unfortunate legacy of heavy lines and weights led to the use of very heavy rods which persisted for many years.

The development of lines with high breaking strains and small diameter (monofilament, braided nylon, Terylene, etc) has done much to correct this. The resistance they offer to the current is slight, and light weights can be used. This means lighter rods and reels.

Sporting tackle can be defined as tackle which will enable the average weight fish of the species sought to exercise its strength in such a way that some skill is necessary on the part of the angler if the fish is to be caught.

Unfortunately, other factors in sea fishing often make the ideal impossible, and there are many places and conditions which demand tackle much heavier than is necessary for the fish. The force of the tidal currents around pierheads, in estuaries, and along beaches often necessitates the use of leads of 4 or 6 oz, while in some places even a 2 lb weight will scarcely hold the bottom. On piers crowded with anglers, one must fish as the others are doing, for on light tackle a fish could weave around other lines and cause considerable annoyance and confusion. When one is fishing from a point high over the water, fish have to be hauled up, and the line must support their dead weight. When fishing is being done from the beach with a ledger or paternoster, the line is subjected to severe wear by the action of waves, sand and shingle. All these factors prevent the use of light lines which would be adequate for catching the fish if the factors did not exist.

Sometimes it is a case of fishing with comparatively heavy tackle or not fishing at all. When this is so, one must make the best of it, but the aim of every angler whose object is sport rather than numbers should be to fish as lightly as possible in the conditions which obtain. It is not often that conditions conspire to prevent the use of float or drift line tackle, or a light ledger or paternoster, from some point of vantage in any particular vicinity.

I define sporting fish as those which possess the strength and spirit to give a keen fast run on feeling the hook, and to fight matters out to a finish. The chief sporting fish under this definition found in British waters are bass, coalfish, garfish, halibut, mackerel, mullet, pollack, sharks (blue, mako, porbeagle and thresher) and tope. Flounders and turbot can be added to the list for although they do not give a long run they fight in a series of plunges which exercise the angler's skill. In order to provide sport they must be hooked on tackle proportionate to their strength.

Skates, rays and congers are sporting fish in a different category. They do not habitually run, but their strength, weight and sustained resistance make them formidable antagonists. Since they do not exhaust themselves by making dashes for freedom the principles of light angling cannot be applied, and though some sense of proportion can be observed they demand a heavy rod and stout tackle.

Boat or beach

Generally speaking, boat fishing off most parts of the British coasts is more profitable in size, variety and number of fish caught than beach or pier fishing. It has its drawbacks, however: bad weather can drive the fisherman to the beach or keep him there; it is relatively expensive; and a great many people suffer from sea-sickness in small boats.

Beach and pier fishermen can therefore be numbered in thousands against the hundreds of boat fishermen, and the former have many compensations, not least being the fact that bass, flounders and mullet, all sporting species, are inshore fish.

Boat fishing

Some anglers start their sea fishing careers in boats. Some take to boat fishing after an apprenticeship on the beach; and others are satisfied to fish always from the land.

Boat fishing has, superficially, many advantages over beach fishing, but all these are cancelled out by bad weather. Often boats are unable to put out, and this happens most frequently in the winter, when the quality of the fishing at many places is at its best. The angler who is firmly wedded to boat fishing and disdains flirtation with beach and rock fishing must perforce suffer many days on which he cannot fish at all.

Boats are expensive, but most people can afford at least an occasional boating expedition, and many clubs have their own boats. Every newcomer to angling should give boat fishing a trial, once he has got used to his tackle and knows how to play a fish.

Deep sea angling

Deep sea angling is only a comparative term, applied to the sport of fishermen who go a mile or more out to sea, where deep water is to be found. This deep water is still on the shallow Continental Shelf, and can be called deep only in comparison with the coastal shallows.

In these waters the angler can fish for big skates and rays, and for tope. There are also many rocky areas or sandbanks within a few miles of the shore which are the established feeding grounds of pollack, flatfish, gurnard, etc, and marks such as these are a favourite objective of boat anglers. They are generally fished on the side sheltered from the flow of the tide. Rocky areas harbour coalfish and pollack; and old wrecks are often the homes of large congers.

Precautions. Every season a few anglers are drowned in boating accidents, some of which could have been avoided. Anyone going out in a boat, with or without a professional boatman, should satisfy himself that certain safety precautions have been taken. A *Code of Conduct and Safety at Sea for Angling* has been issued by the National Anglers' Council. It is reproduced in Appendix I. It is a counsel of perfection, but perfection and some fussiness are better than being adrift for hours in bad weather with the chance of fatalities.

Beach fishing

Beach fishing has many attractive features, for it is possible to combine considerable movement with one's fishing. It is necessary to learn to cast before fishing from the beach, but a long cast is not always necessary or desirable. If the beach is a sandy one with a gentle slope it will probably harbour flat-fish at most times of the year, and codling in the winter. Paternosters or ledger tackle can be used, and here again the strength of the tackle is governed by the current.

On a beach where the shingle drops suddenly to a considerable depth, long casts are inadvisable, for many species of fish, including bass, come close to the foot of the ridge, for it is there that food is to be found.

On the gently sloping beach gumboots or thigh waders are an advantage, for they gain another two feet or so of depth. On shingle beaches with a sharp drop they are dangerous, for in moments of excitement it is easily possible to step into deep water, and shingle does not provide a firm foothold.

When the paternoster or ledger has been cast out, the rod can be placed against a forked rest stuck in the beach, but as a general rule for all fishing it is better if the rod is held in the hands all the time. Many fish can be missed if there is too long a delay between bite and strike.

If a big fish is hooked from the beach and played to exhaustion, care should be exercised in bringing it in, for the pull of the waves on its bulk is considerable. It is best to wait until a good breaker lifts the fish, and then bring it in on top of the wave.

Testing a beach

It may happen that information about angling at some spots is not available from any source. If an angler wishes to fish a lonely beach (and he may prefer such a place to more popular areas near towns) he will probably have to discover its fishing possibilities for himself. A study of the shore at low water will enable him to pick out places which, because of some extra depth, the presence of mud or sand, and the absence of weed and rock obstruction, should be worth fishing.

This is particularly applicable to areas which slope very gently downwards. Here even the smallest depression may make a difference to the catch. Some years ago I spent a considerable time near a part of the Bristol Channel where the tide went out for more than a mile. I could gain no information about its fishing value, but I was certainly not going to leave it unfished on that account. For a week or two I pegged out, every day, a long line, furnished with two dozen hooks on snoods, baited with different baits. By trying this line at different likely-looking spots on the beach. I was able to select two or three places which later gave me the best of what rather poor sport was available.

If one is resident at such a place this is worth trying, but careful notes of position, baits, tide and results must be kept.

The tide usually comes in gently on such beaches, and it is possible to use light ledger and paternoster weights. It is also possible to gain a couple of feet of depth by wading, but one must make sure that one's line of withdrawal is clear of snags, holes or patches of soft mud.

Harbour fishing

Harbours may be almost enclosed by stone piers or they may be simply areas of water sheltered from wind and tide by a break-water or jetty. Fishing can be done from the structure itself, from flights of steps, and from other points of vantage. The depth of water, the nature of the bottom and the locality of the town determine the types of fish which may be found, but in a hypothetical harbour which has a mud bottom, rocks near the seaward extremity, and a small river running into it, one may expect to find flounders, pouting, whiting, freshwater eels and (near the rocks) conger eels, all feeding on or near the bottom. School bass, mullet and small pollack may be found higher in the water.

Paternostering, ledgering and float fishing can be practised, and near the harbour entrance there will often be enough current to make drift lining possible. The absence of strong currents makes it possible to use very light weights and tackle with the paternoster and ledger.

Beginners are strongly advised to start their fishing careers in a harbour, for here they will learn to handle their gear in easy conditions, and to get the feel of a fish at the end of their lines. Harbour fishing usually provides only small fish, but occasionally a two-pounder takes the bait and causes some excitement. Because the fish are comparatively small they should not be despised, for they provide good sport if the tackle is light enough, and it is often possible to fish in harbours when the outer seas are unapproachable.

Pier fishing

Pier fishing is an intangible business, for in some places it may provide the best fishing in the district; in others it can be mediocre; and in some it offers little but crabs. But even in the worst fishing areas really good fish are sometimes caught from piers, and it is this element of the unknown and the possible which brings anglers day after day to the pier.

The majority of pier anglers fish with paternoster or ledger tackle, and the weights they use are determined by the force of the current. Heavy weights in fishing are an abomination, but if one has to use them they must do their job. If an attempt is made to use lighter weights than are necessary, the line will drag and foul those of other anglers, with regrettable results.

If there are only a few people fishing, and there is a little room to manoeuvre, it is possible to catch good fish with float tackle. If no drop net is available, it will be necessary to use 12 lb or heavier line. Bass like to explore the structure and piles of piers, so the float tackle can simply be lowered straight down and allowed to travel where the current takes it. If the water is not more than 14 ft deep it is a good idea to start fishing 2 ft from the bottom, and gradually reduce the depth until the fish are found.

If a really good fish is hooked and played out, it may be impossible to lift it without risking a broken line. If there is a drop net on the pier (and some pier authorities provide them), the fish should be held until someone lowers the net. When this is below the surface the fish is drawn over it and the net is lifted. While the net is being raised no line should be recovered in case the fish drops back again. If no drop net is available, try to work back along the pier, towing the fish, until it can be beached.

Rock fishing

Rock fishing provides excellent sport in many parts of the country, and in Scotland fishing for coalfish in this way can almost be called a national pastime.

Off promontories and headlands there is usually a very definite sweep of current, which aids drift lining and float fishing, two methods which are generally better than paternostering, for the bottom in the vicinity of rocks is often foul, and weights and hooks get caught up. Bass and pollack are often caught in this way, and mackerel in their season. Bass and wrasse can also be caught, in quieter areas, from rocks. Prawns are a nuisance to carry and keep alive, but they should not be dismissed on this account. If it is possible to get them alive to the fishing point they are killing bait for bass in all forms of rock fishing.

Average catch

I have noticed time and time again that newcomers to sea angling, and those who do not fish at all, have an exaggerated idea of what the sea has to offer.

It may be well to consider the sea fish of interest to anglers. Dabs and poor cod are weighed in ounces. One pound would be a fair weight to put down as an *average* for pouting, mackerel, soles, whiting, gurnard and mullet. This figure is a little high for some species and a little low for others, while it may not apply at all to such favoured spots on our coastline as Cornwall and South Devon. Subject to the same qualification, the average weight for bream and codling is about 2 lb, flounders can be put at 1 lb and plaice and pollack at 4 lb. The last-named is the only species so far mentioned, which touches the 10 lb mark, and a 10 lb pollack is an exceptional specimen.

It is difficult to arrive at an average for bass, but many anglers who have fished industriously and exclusively for them for years have never succeeded in catching one of more than 6 or 7 lb. The angling correspondent of a national newspaper wrote in 1951, 'Only one bass in a 100 weighs more than 7 lb. Only one bass in 500 is a 10 pounder, and anything over 12 lb is a fish in a thousand.'

That disposes of the light and medium weight fish commonly caught. Thornback skate occupy a position on the borderline and a great many of this species weighing between 8 and 12 lb are taken.

In the heavy class the commonest species are skate and tope, and here 10 lb is only a trifle, but neither species is so numerous as to make its capture a foregone conclusion, and for every time an angler catches a 60 lb skate or a 30 lb tope he has probably had a dozen blank or 'small fry' days.

Bull huss and cod can be counted as fairly common fish which run over the 10 lb mark. Lastly, there are congers. Plenty of ten-pounders are caught, but, as with skate and tope, their capture calls for special tackle and methods.

To sum up, the angler who wants to catch 10 lb fish, must be satisfied with thornback rays, cod and huss or he must fish specifically for skate, tope or conger. Two or three times in a lifetime, perhaps, he may catch a double-figure bass or pollack.

This review is intended to be encouraging rather than discouraging. Real discouragement comes from expecting too much. If sea angling is undertaken with these points in mind, the angler will experience some satisfaction with small catches, and when the big fish does one day come to gaff or net, it will be appreciated as it should be.

For freshwater anglers

The freshwater angler who restricts his activities to coarse fishing has at least to suffer a twelve-weeks' close season. If he lives in a big city or a thickly populated area, he may have to travel far to reach waters which he can fish as an individual, for during the height of the season club waters are often fully occupied at weekends by match fishermen. The weather, too, can put a further curb on his fishing hours, for prolonged droughts or heavy rain can render rivers unfishable. Trout fishermen have to endure an even longer close season, and although their waters are unlikely to be so crowded, their fishing can also be adversely affected by the weather.

These points show that a freshwater angler would get more fishing and more fun if he had a second string to his bow, or perhaps a more fitting metaphor would be 'a spare tip to his rod'.

An increasing number of freshwater anglers, who spend much of the year fishing in lake, river and canal, now go in for sea fishing on their annual holidays and on occasions when they would like a change; several freshwater angling clubs now have thriving sea-fishing sections. These individual fishermen and club members will already know the ropes about sea fishing, but for those freshwater anglers who know little or nothing of it, the following notes may be of use.

Freshwater anglers can, of course, fish in the sea for any species of fish by any method, providing they have suitable tackle, but if they do not want too sudden and drastic a change in their mode of fishing, grey mullet are undoubtedly the fish they should seek. Fishing for grey mullet is described later in this book, but it may be well to add here that the very lightest tackle can be used with advantage, providing the fish, when played out, can be reached with a landing net, and providing there are no snags in the water. Mullet can be caught with roach tackle, but it is then impossible to exercise very much control over their direction. They are cunning fish, and attempt to twist the trace round anything available. Very fine traces can be used if one is fishing from the steps of a stone jetty, or from a boarded-in wooden jetty, but if the structure from which one is fishing stands on piles, stronger tackle must be used, for a mullet's first move will be to dash into and around the piles.

Bass fishing from the beach calls for normal sea tackle, but these fish ascend estuaries where they can be caught by ordinary float or ledgering methods.

Wrasse will also appeal to freshwater anglers in the early stages of their sea-fishing experience.

There are two other factors which may appeal to freshwater anglers. Anglers' wives are long-suffering women who put up philosophically with the absence of their husbands at weekends. The countryside in which men fish may have few amenities to offer women and children. It is very different by the sea. Providing the weather is reasonably good, even the smallest resort on our coast can provide interest, food, drink and amusement for a family, who will probably regret departure time as much as the angler.

The other advantage lies in the catch. Most freshwater fish are returned to the water to conserve the stocks. This is unnecessary in the sea, providing the fish are above the minimum size limit for the species. A few sorts of freshwater fish are welcome on the table, but no one will dispute the statement that really fresh sea fish are good eating and an acceptable gift to one's neighbours.

The majority of anglers for coarse fish are members of one or more clubs. The formation of a sea-fishing section of a freshwater angling club is, I think, the best way of tackling this problem. The advantages are many. Coach parties to the selected spot on the coast can travel at the cheapest rates. Secretaries of sea-angling associations, prepared as most of them are to help an individual, are even more willing to help a newly-formed section. Bait and boats can be arranged for. Above all, members will not feel so lost and isolated when among their friends as they might if they tackled a new sport alone.

Holiday angling

Every summer thousands of people get a world of satisfaction and enjoyment from sea fishing. They are not anglers (for I do not here refer to freshwater fishermen on holiday), but they enjoy catching fish, and there is every reason why they should continue to enjoy themselves in this way.

Some go whiffing for mackerel, a sport which, in spite of the heavy tackle used, is exciting for those who do not often visit the coast, while a few hours in an open boat on a summer's day is the finest cure for any ills, physical or mental, induced by a year in factory or office. The boatman usually provides the necessary tackle, so the sport can be described as 'readymade'.

Others hire rods and tackle from local tackle dealers or from the stewards of angling clubs, most of which clubs have a rule under which visitors can join for a week or a fortnight for a subscription of a small sum. This is an excellent investment, for the visitor is assured of good advice, supplies of bait, the use of club boats and, where they exist, the amenities of club rooms. Where there is no club it is often possible to hire a fishing outfit from a tackle dealer. Most dealers will give their customers some advice on where to go and what to do, but I have seen some whose sole object is to exploit the holidaymaker, who wanders off to fish in an impossible place with impossible bait.

Where there is a pier, the visitor's best course is to fish from it with pasternoster tackle, but unless he knows how to cast it will be safest to lower the tackle straight down, where it will stand a good chance of catching any fish which comes along.

On rocky shores where there is no pier, wrasse fishing usually offers sport which can be thoroughly enjoyable.

On sandy beaches where there is no deep water inshore, and no pier, boatmen often cater for visiting anglers and take them out bottom fishing. Tackle (either rod or handline) is provided by the boatman. Charges for hiring a boat and boatman for fishing vary considerably. Some are extremely cheap, some moderate (and fair to both sides), and some can only be described as iniquitous. Boatmen in one resort usually make the same charge, and the variations occur between different resorts.

Another form of angling which should appeal to the holiday-maker is boat fishing in an enclosed harbour with float tackle. This can be a family affair, and no boatman is necessary.

Notes for beginners

The newcomer to sea angling will naturally look for some information about how to cast in a book on the subject. Unfortunately this is one of the things which cannot be learned from a book, for the only way to learn to cast is to cast. The beginner is advised to watch experienced anglers casting from the beach, and to get a slow-motion demonstration from any kindly person prepared to give it. He can then take his own rod, reel, line and weights – but no hooks – and retire to a field, a deserted beach or some similar situation, and learn to cast. The beginner must curb impatience, for however keen he may be to get a baited hook out, he must first learn to control his gear. A common fault is to try to cast great distances at the first attempts. Be content with 15 or 20 yards to begin with. When this distance has been thoroughly mastered, without over-runs, and with some accuracy, the range can be extended. When he is sure of himself for casts of 30 or 40 yards he can go to the beach and make his first real attempts at paternostering or ledgering.

In the early stages it is not advisable to cast from crowded piers or beaches, for if anything goes wrong with the cast, it is better that lead and hook should fly in the empty air than twist themselves around an onlooker's neck.

Whenever you cast, in any method of fishing, glance down at the reel to see that the reel line runs clear to the first ring. It can easily get caught up on some obstruction.

When playing a fish, keep the line between rod and fish taut. If a bass, garfish or mackerel swims towards you, this may be impossible, but it can sometimes be done by ignoring the reel and recovering line with the left hand.

If there are no snags, let a hooked fish complete its first dash with only the check or tension to hold it. This dash will exhaust much of its energy, and it can then be treated according to its size and strength. If a hooked fish makes for a danger spot – piles, rocks, etc – extreme pressure can be put on it by holding the rod sideways to the pull of the fish. Except in such an emergency the rod tip should be kept well up.

Do not kill fish you do not want. Return them alive to the water.

Try not to get in a rut. Do not let the first form of fishing you try remain your only one. Experiment with beach, rock, pier and boat fishing for different species of fish. Eventually you will come to like one more than the others, but give them all a trial.

Never put out to sea in a boat without an experienced boatman. He need not be a professional: many anglers are experienced boatmen. This applies to estuaries as well as the open sea, for tidal currents in estuaries can be tricky.

When you have a particularly successful catch, make a note of conditions – tide, weather, time, bait, fishing depth, etc – and watch for a recurrence of similar conditions.

Man has still much to learn about the inhabitants of the sea. Do not follow blindly all precepts. If you have plenty of time for fishing devote some of it to experiment on different marks, and with different combinations of bait and tackle.

Whatever happens, the beginner should not be discouraged. 'Bird's nests' from over-runs, trouble with weed, bait-consuming crabs, and a dozen other tribulations are the common lot of all

24

anglers, experienced or otherwise; and they are part of the whole scheme of things in angling, providing contrast, so that when the rare day comes when everything goes right there is a standard by which such pleasures can be measured and appreciated at their true worth.

CHAPTER 2

Tackle

So many different patterns of every item of tackle are now available that it would be an impossible and, indeed, a useless task to refer to them all, and I make no attempt to do so. I shall refer only to basic arrangements of tackle, leaving the reader to make what adjustments and modifications he pleases. When, later in the book, I deal with the different species of fish, I mention lines, hook sizes, etc, recommended to deal with them. These should be regarded only as a guide to the appropriate strength of tackle. For example, I have throughout regarded a 12 lb bs line as a useful standard line for a wide variety of bottom fishing, but if this were reduced to 10 lb or increased to 14 lb it would matter little. No angler can be expected to have in his possession a multiplicity of tackle which could meet exactly every given situation, and a great deal must be left to personal preference and to 'making do' with such tackle as can be afforded.

Rods

A fishing rod is an implement designed to play a definite part in a combination of tackle which includes reel, line and weight. The duty of a rod is to assist in casting, and to lessen the strain put on the line by a fish. It has been said that a fish in water can exert a pull of about one-third of its weight. In theory, therefore, a 15 lb fish could be caught on a 5 lb bs *handline*. When that line is used in conjunction with a sufficiently supple rod, it is capable of dealing with a strain of considerably more than 5 lb, for the pliancy of the rod takes up a large proportion of the 'pull' of a fish. It follows, therefore, that there must be a balance between rod, reel, line and weight. If a light rod is used with a heavy line and weight, it will soon buckle under the strain. If a rod is so stiff that it cannot be bent with a pressure of 10 lb, then a 10 lb bs line used with it would be no more than a handline, for it would get no help from the rod.

Some sort of fumbling success can be achieved with ill-balanced tackle if it is being lowered from a boat, but when it comes to casting – and the all-round sea angler has much casting to do – it will be found that rods simply fail to do things for which they were never designed. It is impossible to cast a 1 oz weight on a 30 lb line from a stiff rod. It is just as impossible to cast a 6 oz weight on a 5 lb line from a light spinning rod. If, therefore, the rod is wrong – e.g., too heavy and stiff – an angler finds himself perforce using a 30 lb line and a 4 oz weight to catch fish weighing only half a pound.

It is clear from this that one rod will not be suitable for all the many different methods of sea fishing for quarry ranging from half a pound to 50 lb in weight, but three rods, suitably chosen, should answer all reasonable requirements.

Throughout this book I refer to three rods: light, medium and heavy, which are roughly to the specifications given below. Each of them can be bought in split cane, tubular steel, hollow fibre-glass and solid fibre-glass. Fibre-glass is now a favourite material, for it takes no ill effects from salt water and thus needs far less attention than do split cane and steel. This applies to the rod itself, and not to its fittings. Solid fibre-glass is rather stiffer in action and decidedly heavier than hollow fibre-glass, but it is also considerably cheaper, and the newcomer to sea angling may well elect to use solid fibre-glass until he has found out what sort of fishing he intends to do regularly.

The light rod should be capable of casting weights up to 1 oz; the medium 1 oz to 3 oz; and the heavy 4 oz to 8 oz. These weights refer to casting. If tackle is being lowered from a boat slightly heavier weights can be used in all cases. Twenty years ago there was little choice of sea rods in the light and medium classifications, and many anglers made do with freshwater spinning rods or bottom rods for the first, and pike or salmon rods for the second, in spite of the disadvantages which this entailed, the worst of which was the small diameter of the rod rings. British rod manufacturers have more than filled the gap, and there are now scores of rods in each class from which to choose.

The light rod I have in mind can be 7 ft or 7½ ft in length. I use a tubular fibre-glass one, but I do not claim that it has any advantages over cane or steel. It is used for light casting, light spinning, drift lining and float fishing.

The second can be 9 ft to 10 ft in length. It can be used for all types of fishing where weights of not more than 3 oz are required.

The heavy rod should be strong but not too stiff, with a length of about 8 ft, though if an angler decides that beach fishing is to be his future an 11 ft or 12 ft rod to the same specification will be more useful for distance casting. In beach work a long rod also helps to keep the line out of the breakers.

With the light rod, every type of fishing can be done from a boat where the currents do not call for heavy weights and where catches are not expected to exceed 8 lb in weight. It is ideal for float fishing and drift lining from projections, rocks and boats. It is suitable for light ledgering and paternostering from beaches where long casting and heavy weights are not necessary. It can deal with all the common species of fish except big skates and rays, congers, tope and sharks, and 'outsize' bass, pollack, coalfish and dogfish. Even these may be captured if they can be brought to landing net or gaff without having to raise them from the water or drag them ashore.

The medium rod is perhaps the best single rod. It is a little long for boat work, but not impossibly so. Reasonably long casts can be made from beaches. It is suited to float fishing and drift lining, and, though not ideal, can be used as a spinning rod. It has considerable strength and can deal successfully with fish up to 30 lb in the water. It is too strong to give fish such as mackerel a chance to show their sporting qualities – but it still catches them.

The heavy rod is, naturally, for heavy fish such as congers, skate and rays. It must also be used when tides call for heavy weights. Much depends on the area in which fishing is done. Off Dover breakwater, for example, anything may turn up, and although hundreds of small fish are caught on terminal tackle suited to their capacity, it is always anchored to a heavy weight to withstand the tide, and connected to a suitably heavy line. Bringing a half-pound pouting in on such tackle may not seem very 'sporting' fishing, but the situation dictates the tackle and anglers on the breakwater enjoy their fishing as much as the most advanced exponents of light tackle fishing.

Reels

Reels fall into three main groups – centre-pin, multiplying and fixed-spool.

Centre-pin reels
These are available in a very wide price range and the cheapest
are very cheap indeed. Cheapness should not be the criterion in
buying a reel, for it is essential that these implements should do
their job at all times. The diameter should not be less than 4 in
for any sort of sea work. With these reels a good deal of practice
in casting is necessary to prevent over-runs, for the line has to be
controlled (with fingertip, thumb or brake) to prevent line
continuing to run off (and back on to the reel again in the
opposite direction) when the speed of the lead slows down.
Some of the more expensive types of centre-pin reels have an
automatic drag which reduces the chances of over-runs.

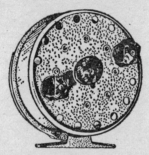

FIG 2. A centre-pin reel (Grice & Young Seajecta de Luxe)

Nearly all these reels have a 'check' operated by a knob on the
back plate. When 'on', a tooth engages a cog wheel which prevents line being drawn off freely.

Some of these reels are beautifully made precision instru-
ments with various aids to casting and to playing fish incorporated in them. The better the reel the more attention it needs
– drying, washing, oiling, etc. Partially for this reason many
anglers still use the old-fashioned Scarborough reel – of large
diameter, usually made of walnut wood with a brass star back.
They are simple to operate and there is no complicated mechanism to become clogged with sand. The large diameter (7 in or
more) in which they are available makes for quick line recovery.

Multiplying (or multiplier) reels
These are the supreme casting reels, used by the majority of

anglers who regularly fish from the beach and by all competitors in long-distance casting competitions, amateur or professional. Much practice is needed before even short-distance casts, without over-runs, can be made almost without thinking about them, but once this dexterity has been achieved the reels are most pleasant to use.

FIG 3. A multiplier reel (Grice & Young Tatler III)

They are geared to recover line at ratios of anything between 2:1 and 5:1, according to the make, which means that, for example, a 2½:1 reel makes 2½ turns of the drum for every turn of the handle. This is a great advantage when recovering line from a considerable depth, or when drawing tackle over weedy or rocky ground, for with a quick rate of recovery there is less chance of the hook or lead fouling the bottom. Quick recovery pays dividends, too, when a hooked fish swims towards the angler.

Instead of or in addition to a check mechanism, a multiplying reel is fitted with a screw which can increase or decrease the tension at which line is drawn off. When a fish is being played the tension can be adjusted to suit the strength of the fish.

Although primarily designed for casting, multiplying reels are excellent ones for boat and pier fishing.

Many models have attachments to minimize the chance of over-runs. There are dozens of models available in various sizes.

Fixed-spool reels

In their early days fixed-spool reels were designed for ultra-light bait or lure fishing for trout. Since then they have been developed for other purposes including sea angling. There are now available models which have the necessary large line capacity and in which the intricate working parts are enclosed so that sand and salt water cannot penetrate. Even so, it is advisable to take down these reels at frequent intervals and clean and oil them in accordance with the instructions which accompany them.

When casting, line flies off the reel like cotton off the end of a cotton reel. There is practically no friction to slow it down, providing that the reel is properly filled with line, i.e. to within 1/16 in of the rim. Over-runs are impossible. Distance casting becomes

Fig 4. A fixed-spool reel (K. P. Morritt 'Intrepid' surfcast)

simple: accuracy in placing the bait or lure needs practice. Playing a fish, too, is more complicated than with other types of reel (see *Pumping* below).

Fixed-spool reels recover line on a multiplying basis, the ratio differing with the models. They have an adjustable slipping clutch which releases line when a fish exerts a heavier pressure than the tension is set for. When a fish is taking line against the clutch it is useless to try to wind in. Turning the handle in these circumstances does not recover line: it merely puts a twist in it with every turn of the handle.

Fixed-spool reels can be used in any fishing method but they are pre-eminently spinning and casting reels. Regular beach casters, skilled in the use of multiplying reels, are inclined to look down on anglers who use fixed-spool reels. In the hands of a real expert the multiplier can achieve greater distance than the fixed-spool, but the big fixed-spool reels designed for sea fishing can get all the length that is required for 90 per cent or more of all beach casting. Only in very special circumstances is the extra length likely to be important. It is thus the better beach reel for those who fish only occasionally and who have no time or no inclination to master the casting techniques of the multiplier.

The main objection to the big fixed-spool reels for sea work is their weight. Plenty of lighter models are available which will do for light casting, float fishing, etc, but unless they are known to be made to withstand sea water they should be taken down and cleaned after every fishing excursion.

Pumping
Sea fishing often calls for the recovery of line against heavy pressure. It may be caused by a heavy fish, a mass of seaweed or even by the lead weight in a strong current. It is naturally tied up with the strength of rod and line: a light rod will jib at a pull which a heavy one would take easily. You can always feel when too much strain is being put on the reel – when the line becomes so taut that it can be reeled in only with considerable effort.

If you continue to reel in, the line forces its way through the looser coils already lying on the reel and prepares the way for a good tangle. Far too much strain, too, is put on the reel mechanism. In these circumstances pumping is the answer. This is done by (1) lowering the rod to the horizontal, (2) holding the line fast, (3) raising the rod to the vertical, (4) lowering the rod quickly and reeling in the line recovered. In other words the fish is drawn up a few feet at a time by rod and line only – not by the reel.

This method is most advisable with all types of reel. It is *essential* with fixed-spool reels, and is necessary in that case whenever the pressure is greater than the tension setting.

Casting Check
No matter what type of reel you are using, look down at it immediately you have completed a cast to see that the line runs without obstruction to the first ring. Loose coils of line can easily

twist around the reel or some part of it. Make this an automatic habit.

Trying out reels
When you buy a reel which is more complicated than the simple centre-pin type, give it a thorough testing to discover what its gadgets are for before you fish with it. Do not be content to sit in an armchair, read the directions and fiddle with the knobs. Set up rod, line, reel and weight and see how every part of the reel acts. This is especially true of fixed-spool reels and multiplying reels. It is more than annoying, when you have a good fish on, to press the wrong button and lock the line or move a lever which takes off brake, tension or check.

Lines

Until recent years flax lines were used for most forms of sea angling, but the products of the laboratory have put them out of court except in special circumstances.

Nylon monofilament
Great advances have been made in the nature, sizes, reliability and choice available of this substance. It is now used by a majority of anglers for a great many forms of fishing.

Some advantages are:

1. It is available in strengths from 1 lb bs to 120 lb bs.
2. Most makes can be bought in continuous lengths up to 200 yards. Some makes can be bought up to 1,000 yards.
3. A choice can be made of supple or stiff monofilament.
4. It is practically imperishable and takes no harm from salt water.
5. Its diameter in relation to its breaking strain is low compared with most forms of plaited line. This means that it is far less affected by the current than the thicker lines and that lighter weights can therefore be used with it, thus reducing the weight of the whole equipment.
6. It is ideal for fixed-spool reels and can be used well on centre-pin reels.
7. It is reasonably cheap.

Some disadvantages are:

1. It stretches considerably. This means that with a long line out, a strike must be heavy in order to drive the hook home.
2. Although it can be used with multiplying reels it is inclined to come up in coils (especially in the heavier sizes) and be a nuisance.
3. If it is subjected to heavy strain it loses its strength. The strain has to be really heavy before this happens, but if, for example, the terminal tackle is caught up in rocks and a break has to be made, much of the line may be rendered useless by the strain put on it before the break occurs. This may in part be obviated by using traces lighter than the line itself, but even that is not a complete guarantee. Partially for this reason many anglers who fish always over rocky ground (off the Yorkshire coast, for instance) still use 'cuttyhunk' – the old flax lines.

Continued friction against the rod rings will wear and weaken monofilament, so for casting and spinning many anglers use 20 ft or so of stronger line than the main line to connect the main line with the end tackle. This length takes up most of the wear and tear of casting, and it can be replaced when worn by a new length. If this is not done, the worn part of the main line will have to be cut off continually, gradually reducing its length.

Any monofilament which is knotted or kinked should be discarded.

Monofilament stored for a long time may lose its strength.

Braided Terylene

This is a first-class line for almost all sea angling purposes. It is very fine in diameter in relation to breaking strain; it is water resistant; and it is practically inelastic. It is the ideal line for use with multiplying reels. It can be obtained in strengths up to 120 lb. All this applies to other proprietary brands of lines braided from man-made fibres – the American *Dacron*, for example.

Metal lines

These lines have not so far been much used by British anglers, but those who do use them consider them to be superior to any other form of line within their considerable limitations. The proprietary brand is *Monel*, in strengths from 8 lb to 100 lb in

America. Medium strengths (mainly 12 lb) are available in this country.

Their use is restricted. They cannot easily be cast and must therefore be lowered from boat or pier. Unless carefully handled they will kink, and when that happens the angler is in bad trouble. They put heavy wear on the rod rings and these must be of expensive wear-resistant type, while the end ring must be of the roller kind where the line runs over a revolving hard-metal drum. This means a special rod.

Once the knack of using them is learned their advantages are apparent. Chief of these are their extremely fine diameter for their breaking strains and their complete inelasticity. The first means that less weight is required to hold bottom than with other lines. The second means that the slightest touch from a fish – even that of a 4 oz pouting – is immediately communicated to the rod.

I suggest that anyone trying them out for the first time does so with an ordinary revolving drum reel, so that reel complications can be avoided. They are normally used with multiplying reels. They *cannot* be sensibly used with fixed-spool reels.

Care of lines

Monofilament and braided Terylene lines are described as rot proof. They probably are, but no line should be left coiled on a reel for too long. From time to time, run off monofilament lines and rewind them. Braided lines collect incrustations of salt, and they should be run off and washed in fresh water. A line winder is a useful thing to have. Lines can be run off on to it and left to dry: they relieve the line from the small tight coils of the reel. Incidentally, and this affects reels rather than lines, monofilament that has been wound on to a reel under extreme pressure should always be run off as soon as possible. If this precaution is neglected the reel drum may be damaged as the line contracts.

Weights

Weight, leads, sea leads, sinkers – they all mean the same thing. They are that part of the tackle that sinks it to the bottom or, in the case of float fishing, to the required depth. Americans use the one word 'sinker', and since that covers all purposes it is a sensible one. It is coming into use in this country, but since most catalogues of tackle still refer to weights and leads I have continued to use those words in this book.

Weights can be divided into three groups:

1. Light weights for float fishing, drift lining and spinning, the last named being preferably anti-kink leads.
2. Heavier weights to hold the bottom.
3. Weights that still hold the bottom but whose shape offers the minimum resistance to the air and which are thus the best for casting.

Fig 5 shows some of those in Group 1.

(*a*) is the Jardine or spiral lead. The line is wound through the brass wire and around the grooves and through the wire at the other end. The wire should then be closed up. Available in sizes from 1 in to 3 in. Used for float fishing and drift lining and, when bent, as an anti-kink lead for spinning.

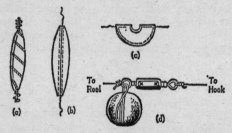

FIG 5. (*a*) Jardine or spiral lead (*b*) Pierced barrel (*c*) Foldover or half-moon lead (*d*) Hillman anti-kink lead. (See text for details)

(*b*) is the pierced barrel lead. Obtainable in weights from a few drams to 8 oz. In the smaller sizes it can be used for float fishing and drift lining, with a split-shot stop or a swivel beneath it to maintain its position on the line. In the heavy sizes it can be used as a bottom weight or as a ledger weight, though it is not ideal for this purpose as the hole is likely to get clogged with sand, preventing the free run of the trace.

(*c*) Foldover or half-moon anti-kink leads. Obtainable in sizes from ¼ in to 1½ in. For float fishing, drift lining and spinning.

(*d*) is a spherical Hillman anti-kink lead. The wire attachment that fits into a groove in the sphere enables it to be attached to a swivel instantaneously. The line and swivel have been illustrated to show where the swivel should come. If the swivel is put on the reel-line side of any anti-kink lead the line *will* kink.

Fig 6 shows some general bottom leads.

(*a*) is a grip lead, useful for holding the bottom on sand, mud and fine shingle. A lead of similar shape without the central hole or the knobs is known as a watch lead. Obtainable in sizes up to 8 oz. These are not good casting weights but have their uses in pier and boat work.

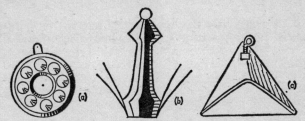

FIG 6. (*a*) Grip lead (*b*) Spiked anchor (*c*) Capta lead. (See text for details)

(*b*) The spiked anchor lead. A bad caster, but a good lead to hold the bottom. Normally for boat use.

(*c*) This is the patent Capta lead, with a swivel incorporated in the top. Its flat base holds the bottom well on sand, mud and fine shingle, but it should not be used on foul ground. The swivel makes it a useful ledger lead.

Fig 7 shows three leads in Group 3.

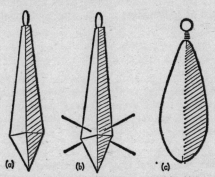

FIG 7. (*a*) Torpedo lead (*b*) Armed torpedo lead (*c*) Pear-shaped lead with swivel (Arlesey bomb). (See text for details)

(*a*) The torpedo, is the ideal casting lead, offering a minimum of resistance to the air. Obtainable in sizes up to 8 oz.

(*b*) is the torpedo lead with wire arms which, when set roughly at right angles, help to hold the bottom on sand.

(*c*) The pear-shaped lead casts reasonably well though not so well as the torpedo. It can be bought with an ordinary ring, or, as in the drawing, with a swivel fitted at the top for ledgering.

Fig 8 is a weight that does not fall into any of the three groups. It is a mackerel lead used for whiffing, and as they

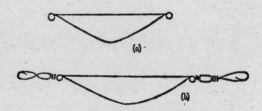

FIG 8. (*a*) Mackerel lead, for whiffing (*b*) Fitted with quick-release swivels. (See text for details)

weigh 8 oz or more they do not enter into the sporting fisherman's tackle. Whiffing, however, is the quickest way to catch mackerel for bait, with one of these leads on a handline armed with a dozen or so feathered or fish-skin baited hooks.

Swivels

Swivels are essential parts of nearly all arrangements of tackle for sea fishing, for they minimize line twist. Casting, spinning and the action of tidal currents all cause the line to spin round. Swivels can never entirely stop this but they can prevent hopeless tangles.

Fig 9 shows the actual sizes of barrel swivels, the type most commonly used. Although strong, there is a limit to the strain which any swivel can stand, and care should be taken to use those

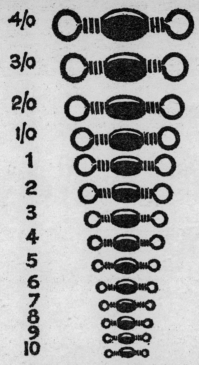

FIG 9. Barrel swivels: actual size

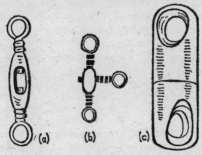

FIG 10. (a) Box swivel (b) Three-way swivel (c) Heavy duty sea swivel.

of sufficient strength to match the rest of the tackle. They must do their job properly and they should be examined from time to time to see that they are turning freely.

Fig 11 shows various types of quick-release swivels. They are particularly useful for attaching and detaching leads quickly, as

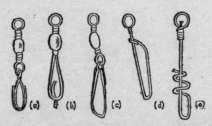

FIG 11. Quick-release swivels, mainly used for attaching weights, though they have uses in several arrangements of tackle. (*a*) Link (*b*) buckle (*c*) snap (*d*) spring (*e*) spiral. All available in a range of sizes.

the tide changes and more or less weight is needed. They have many other uses, some of which will be seen in the illustrations of arrangements of tackle.

Hooks

Good hooks are a vital part of the sea angler's equipment, and if he finds he has to economize, let it be on something other than hooks. The difference in cost between a first-class hook made by a reputable firm, and an untrustworthy one made by no one knows whom, is too small to be an appreciable saving.

Hook sizes are confusing, for all makers do not follow the same system of numbering, and different types of hooks of approximately the same size do not necessarily have the same commercial numbers. By the courtesy of Messrs S. Allcock & Co Ltd, now part of Norris Shakespeare Ltd, I am able to reproduce actual hook sizes from 10 to 5/0 (Fig 12); 6/0, 8/0, 10/0 (Fig 13); and sizes 1 to 6 in extra long-shanked hooks designed for sea anglers (Fig 14). Throughout this book the hooks to which I refer will be the size of hooks shown in these three figures. My suggestions of hook sizes for different purposes are to be considered only as a guide, for the size of bait

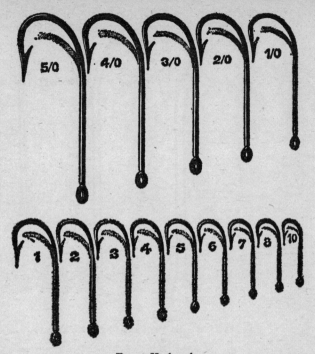

FIG 12. Hook scale

used has to be taken into consideration. Generally speaking, I prefer short-shanked hooks to long, for the only advantage of the latter seems to be the ease with which fish can be unhooked.

Hooks are made in several 'bends' or patterns. Those in Figs 12 and 14 are Kirby bend; those in Fig 13 are Limerick bend. Both patterns are good ones for sea fishing.

Some 'Mustad' hook illustrations are reproduced, by permission, in Fig 15. The swivelled conger hook in this particular brand ('Mustad') is an efficient one, but there are others on the market which, while sufficiently strong for their purpose, have poor hooking qualities owing to the thickness of the hook point.

The short-shanked 'Sea Master' with its exaggerated bend

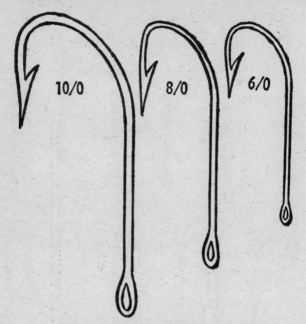

FIG 13. Hook scale continued: Limerick bend

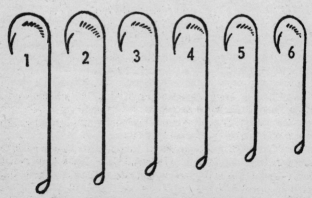

FIG 14. Extra-long-shanked finned whiting hooks

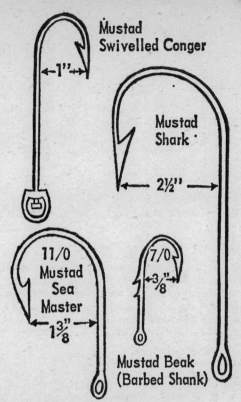

Mustad
Swivelled Conger

←1″→

Mustad
Shark ·

←——2½″——→

11/0
Mustad
Sea
Master

←1 3/8″→

7/0

←3″→
  3/8

Mustad Beak
(Barbed Shank)

FIG 15. Some hooks for special purposes

is one I like for single-hook bottom fishing. The size shown is a
very large one but they are obtainable in smaller sizes. Note that
the shark hook has a 2½ in gape. For comparative purposes, the
10/0 shown in Fig 13 has a 1⅛ in gape.

The 'Mustad Beak' is shown in only one size, but is available
in the entire range. The two 'beaks' on the shank help to hold
worms and other soft baits in position: Americans call these
hooks 'bait holders'.

The angler ties ringed hooks to monofilament or wire, but

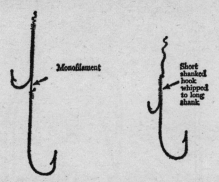

FIG 16. Pliant Pennell tackle   Rigid Pennell tackle

Either tackle can be made up with any sizes of hooks

many sizes and patterns can be bought already mounted on 6 in to 12 in looped snoods of wire or monofilament.

Pennell tackles (Fig 16) are useful for fishing with worms. They consist of two hooks mounted one above the other on opposite sides of the trace.

Landing nets

In fishing for such fish as mackerel and grey mullet, nets with a diameter of 18 in or so, designed for use in freshwater, are adequate. For bigger fish the largest net it is possible to buy is not too large. Its diameter should be limited only by one's ability to handle it without difficulty.

Gaffs

Wherever and whenever possible I prefer to use a net to a gaff, and it follows that I use a gaff only for the heavyweights. Gaffs must be very strong, and a point to look for when buying one is the way in which the hook is attached to the handle. It *must not* be able to slip round the shaft whatever pressure is applied.

Arrangements of tackle

Paternosters

The paternoster is one of the oldest rigs in sea fishing and is as popular today as it ever was. It can be used for nearly every species of fish except the heavyweights, and it has been adapted to the modern refinements in tackle.

Fig 17 illustrates the basic principle of the paternoster. I have purposely refrained from giving measurements, snood length, hook sizes, weight of lead, etc, for these are capable of scores of variations, depending on the quarry sought, the state of the tide, the depth being fished, the force of the current and the nature of the bottom.

Even at the slackest of slack water there is some current in the sea, and the theory of paternoster fishing is that while a lead of sufficient weight holds the line to the bottom, the hooks

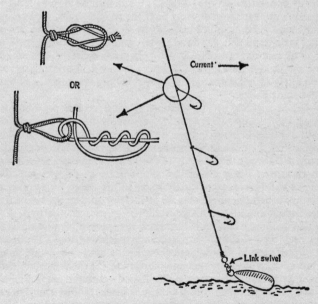

FIG 17. Three-hook paternoster. Whatever the length of the snoods they should be spaced so that they cannot tangle with each other

on their snoods stream out in the current, the line between rod-tip and weight being kept as taut as possible.

I have illustrated a 3-hook paternoster, but unless I am fishing for small fish I prefer to use only one hook, set at the height on the line at which I hope to catch the particular species I am seeking.

If one is fishing for anything which may come along, the three-hook paternoster is probably the best type, particularly if the snood of the lowest hook be sufficiently long to allow the bait to lie on the bottom. If the current is strong, it may be necessary to pinch a piece of lead on the lowest snood in order to achieve this object.

The amount of weight necessary to keep a paternoster and its line anchored depends on the strength of the current. At times a weight of 6 oz or more is necessary. At others a $\frac{1}{2}$ oz weight will suffice. The strength of line depends on the weight, and the rod must suit the line, so the whole tackle in paternoster fishing is really dependent on the weight. This should be kept as light as possible, but it must do its job. If the weight drags, more must be added. The snoods to the hooks should be proportionate to the weight of fish expected. For example, in whiting fishing 4 lb bs snoods are sufficient. If big bass are expected, something nearer 10 lb is necessary. The finer the snoods the more fish you are likely to hook, though in general fishing you must expect to lose some hooks.

When making up a paternoster, consider the position the hooks will occupy in the sea. If you are fishing from a boat the paternoster will hang down as near the vertical as the current will allow and the hooks will fish almost as far above the bottom as they are set above the lead. If the same paternoster is cast out from a pier, the angle of the line may be 45 degrees and the hooks will be correspondingly lower in the water. If it is fished from a beach the angle may be as little as 20 degrees below the horizontal and all the hooks would be close to the bottom.

To arrange a simple paternoster, tie the requisite number of loops in the reel line at the desired positions above the lead. Looped snoods can be attached by passing the snood loop through the loop on the line, threading the hook through its own loop before drawing tight. Snoods without loops can be attached with a half-blood knot (see insets to Fig 17). Three-way swivels can be used, if preferred, to loops in the line.

A popular type of paternoster uses one, two or three booms or

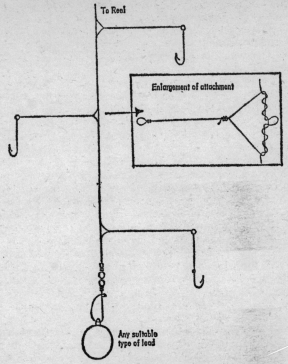

FIG 18. Three-boom paternoster

stretchers, usually made of stout wire. The simple form is shown in Fig 18. The snoods are attached to the ends of the booms, which should be sufficiently far apart to avoid snood entanglement. It is obviously difficult to cast with them and they are best used when it is possible to fish straight 'up and down'.

There are many sorts of boom, varying in length from 3 in to 12 in. Fig 19(*a*) shows the Clement boom, with porcelain ringed eyes. Fig 19(*b*) is one of many types of revolving boom. Fig 19(*d*) is a simple rig used for generations by professional fishermen, mainly for cod. They use it with a hand-line and very stout snoods and a heavy weight, but it can be easily made

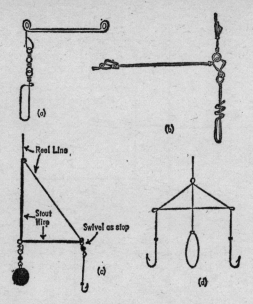

FIG 19. Some types of booms (see text)

to a much lighter pattern. With a supply of brass or stainless steel wire and a pair of pliers you can make up booms of any required length, strength or pattern.

Fig 19(c) shows how the ledger principle (see below) can be used with paternoster tackle. An infinite variety of rigs can be worked out on these lines, but I suggest that the beginner be satisfied with the most simple arrangements until he has gained experience.

It is possible to buy booms made of celluloid, or similar semi-transparent materials. They are flat and relatively broad. The theory is that the fish cannot see them, but I believe that a fish can see anything. I have tried them out and have found they have no advantages over wire snoods, while in a strong current their flat surface offers unnecessary resistance. Fish do not seem to be worried about masses of ironmongery. One has only to see some of the successful tackle employed by professional handliners to realize the truth of this.

48

Trace tackle

This consists simply of a weight at the end of the line and a trace (usually 2 ft or more in length) attached to the line above the weight (Fig 20). It should be used only when the current is

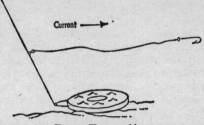

FIG 20. Trace tackle

strong enough to flow out the trace. Ordinary paternoster snoods can be attached higher up the line if desired. This arrangement is often wrongly referred to as ledger tackle, but it does not conform to the principle of ledger fishing (see next section).

Ledger tackle

Ledger tackle is used for bottom or near-bottom fishing and possesses an advantage over paternoster tackle in that a fish can take and move off with a bait without feeling resistance from the weight. This is because the line runs through the ring of the weight or of the swivel if one is incorporated in the weight (Fig 21). Any type of weight can be used as a ledger weight.

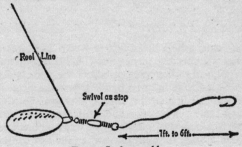

FIG 21. Ledger tackle

A stop, usually a swivel too large to pass through the ring of the weight, is tied to the trace at the required distance from the hook. The reel line is threaded through the ring of the weight and attached to the swivel-stop. When a cast is about to be made the weight rests on the stop. When hook, bait and weight reach the water the weight sinks to the bottom. The angler then makes the line nearly taut. When a fish takes the bait it can draw off line through the ring without resistance from the weight.

Ledger tackle is of use only for bottom-feeding or near-bottom fish. Crabs are often a nuisance, but they can be circumvented by fixing a piece of cork, big enough to give buoyancy to hook and bait, a few inches from the hook. This raises the bait out of the way of crabs, but leaves it sufficiently low to interest bottom feeders.

The ledger principle can be used with any tackle; fine, medium or heavy, according to the quarry sought and the force of the current. It is a good method for all flat fish and for bass-fishing from the shore. It can be used from a boat for skate-fishing. A modification of the tackle, designed for tope fishing, is described in the chapter on tope.

The length of line beyond the stop can be short or long according to circumstances. A short length means that the bait will be on or very close to the bottom. A long one – 6 ft or so – is known as a flowing trace. The bait, at the end of its long trace, is picked up and swirled about in the current in a way likely to attract the attention of any fish that is not actually grubbing along the bottom.

A flowing trace – one of 3 ft or more – should never be used unless the current is sufficiently strong to stream it out. It will get hopelessly tangled in the changing slight currents of slack water.

Floats and float fishing

Most non-anglers think that a float is used to indicate a bite, and dictionaries support this definition. This is not quite true. A float is employed to support the bait at the correct depth, and the fact that it also indicates a bite is a secondary consideration. If one considers the matter it will be seen that, unless a float is used, a bait can never be offered to a fish at any set depth higher than a few feet from the bottom, unless one is immediately above the fish – in a boat, for example – when the line can be held at the desired depth.

The height between the weight on a paternoster and the highest hook on it must be less than the length of the rod, or the hook will meet the rod rings while an unmanageable length of line still hangs free. Ledger tackle fishes only on or near the bottom. Drift line tackle fishes at varying depths, but these are not accurately known. Only a float can determine depth.

There are dozens of patterns of floats, but they all fall into two main categories, adjustable floats and sliding floats.

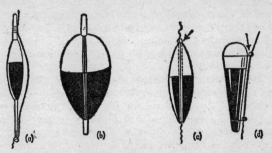

FIG 22. (a) Fixed float (b) *Fishing Gazette* float (c) and (d) Sliding floats (see text)

Adjustable floats embrace the majority of types used in fresh-water fishing, but they can be used in salt water where the depth being fished is less than the length of the rod. 'The depth being fished' means the depth at which the angler wishes to present the bait, not the depth of the water. For example, in float-fishing for bass it is often desirable to fish at a depth of only 5 or 6 ft, so an adjustable float can be used. Adjustable floats can be moved up or down the line and set in different positions, but the line cannot run through them. I use them wherever possible, since they are more reliable than sliding floats, which do not always work as they should. For light work, such as mullet, wrasse and mackerel fishing, and for harbour fishing, a freshwater float with a cylindrical body (Fig 22(a)) is as good as any. For heavier work in a current the *Fishing Gazette* float (Fig 22(b)) is ideal. Both types can be obtained in several sizes.

Sliding floats are made in such a way that, when a cast has been made, the float slides up the line until it reaches a stop. When a fish is being reeled in, the float slides down the line until it reaches the swivel, lead or a specially designed lower stop. If, for example, it is desired to present the bait at a depth of 18 ft, a stop is made on the line 18 ft from the hook, above the float. When the cast is completed, hook and weight sink, drawing the line through the float until the latter reaches the stop, when it supports the bait at the required depth.

Stops are made by attaching something to the line which will pass through the rod rings but not through the ring of the float. A piece of stiff nylon knotted round the line, with its ends trimmed to about one-eighth inch is a common stop. For heavy work I prefer three-quarters of an inch of bicycle valve rubber with half its length cut open. Thread the rubber on the line when assembling the tackle, with the cut end towards the hook. The stop is adjusted at the required position by pushing a small piece of matchstick into the rubber. This holds it firmly against the line. The open ends prevent the whole thing sliding through the float rings. An advantage of this method is that it can be easily moved up or down the line as the height of the tide changes.

In some sliding floats the line passes through the centre of the float (Fig 22(c)), and in others through two rings at the side of the float (Fig 22(d)). The arrows in Fig 22 indicate the stops. In order to minimize the chances of operational mishaps, the rings in the second type should stand well out from the float, so that the line does not touch the bodywork. Sliding floats which have projections at the top should be avoided, as these sometimes foul the line in casting.

The size of float used for any particular fishing depends on the tackle. The float has to support the bait, the weight, the trace, any swivels used, and such portion of the line as lies below it. With light tackle the weight is the only one of these which really counts. It is necessary, therefore, to choose a float which is sufficiently buoyant for its purpose, *but* (and this is a point not as widely known as it should be) it should have only just sufficient buoyancy to keep it from being submerged by the waves. Unless its buoyancy is almost counteracted by the weight beneath it, it will offer so much resistance when a fish takes the bait that the fish may be frightened off. If there is considerable difference between the buoyancy of a float and the weight it supports, and the float cannot be changed, it is better to add more weight than to leave things as they are.

In float-fishing the line between reel and float should float,

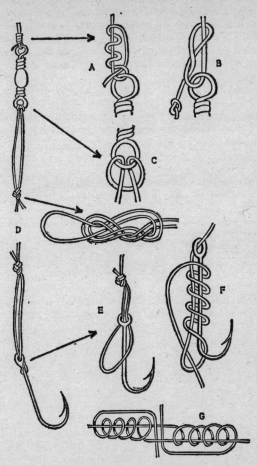

FIG 23. Knots: (a) shows the method of attachment of nylon monofilament to swivel using three turn half blood knots (b) flax or braided
line attachment to swivel (c) method of attaching trace loop to swivel
(d) formation of cast loop using blood bight knot (e) hook attachment on
cast loop (f) method of attachment where eye of hook permits only a
single thickness of line or trace to pass through (g) four turn blood knot
for joining two lengths of monofilament

for if it sinks the effect of a strike is completely deadened. Lines for this purpose should be of Terylene or monofilament.

Most floats are painted green and red. I paint or enamel the top halves of all my floats orange, as I find this colour shows up most clearly. In sea fishing I do not think the colour of the submerged portion of the float is of any importance.

Knots

The knots shown in Fig 23, and the method of attaching wire traces to hooks or swivels (Fig 24) can be used to make up every combination of tackle needed.

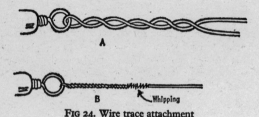

FIG 24. Wire trace attachment

CHAPTER 3

Lures and Baits

Lures

Metal and plastic lures such as spoons, spinners, pirks, plugs, artificial fish and feathered lures are slowly becoming more popular among anglers for specific purposes. A study of any tackle catalogue or a look round the show cases of a well-stocked tackle dealer will show that the variety of these, in pattern, size and colouring, is bewilderingly wide. A brief mention of some basic types follows, but two lures that have been popular for more than fifty years are discussed first. These are the rubber eel and the mackerel spinner.

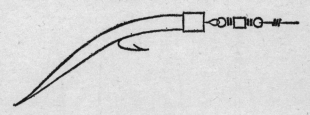

FIG 25. Rubber eel

Rubber eels
These can be bought in a wide range of colours – red, white, green, brown, gold, amber, black, aluminium, etc – and in sizes from 4 in to 7 in. They can easily be made at home with a length of rubber tubing, a hook and a swivel. It is impossible to lay down any 'best' size or colour for sand eels. Every locality has its favourites, but the wise angler carries a selection.

It is essential that the tail of a rubber eel should wriggle in the current. Some of the commercial eels are too stiff. After some use in salt water the rubber tends to stiffen and crack. When this happens the lure is useless and should be discarded.

Rubber suitable for making these imitation sand-eels can be bought at chemists' shops. This is medical rubber tubing used for joining glass tubes together. Cut off the required length, leave the front part intact and cut away the 'tail' portion as in Fig 25.

Some good plastic eels are now available.

Rubber eels are cast into the sea and slowly recovered, or trailed behind a boat. Many species of fish have been caught on them, but they are particularly used against pollack, coalfish and bass.

Mackerel spinners

Fig 26(*a*) shows one pattern of this very popular and successful lure. They can be obtained in slightly different shapes, and with single, double or treble hooks. I think the single hook is by far the best. The usual length, without hook, is about 1½ in. As its name implies it is mainly designed for mackerel fishing, being cast or trolled in the upper layers of the water when mackerel are about. Garfish are also often caught on these lures.

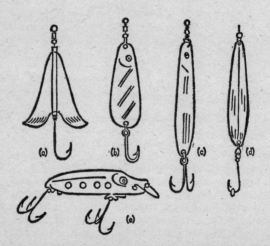

FIG 26. Some artificial lures: (*a*) Mackerel spinner (*b*) Spoon (*c*) Plastic fish (*d*) Pirk (*e*) Plug. (See text for details)

Spoons, spinners, etc

Spoons and spinners of many patterns are now being used
by sea anglers, especially when bass are feeding on brit near the
surface. The boat is allowed to drift close to or through the
shoal, and the anglers cast their lures among the feeding fish.
Much experiment has been done along these lines in areas where
bass gather off the south-east corner of Ireland.

When fishing from a boat, lures of almost any type can be
used, but in casting from the shore the lure must not be too
heavy. A solid metal spoon, for instance, would sink too quickly
to the bottom and be caught up. The best types for this purpose
are light lures such as the Abu 'Krill' (Fig 26(*c*)) and the long,
thin, curved pirks (Fig 26(*d*)). These are cast into the breakers
where bass may be feeding, and where they may be allowed to
wash around in the ebb and flow until they eventually come
ashore. Heavier and well-weighted lures can be cast far out
where the shore is steep-to, retrieved and re-cast. This is the
method adopted by the American surf-casters on the Atlantic
coast, their quarry being the striped bass, a relative of the
European bass. There is, as I write, a suggestion that striped
bass be introduced to British waters.

Emphasis seems to have been laid on bass in this section, but
lures of all types can be successfully used, well-weighted, a few
feet above the bottom for many of the bigger predators. A spoon
specially adapted for flounder fishing is described in Chapter 6.

Plugs

Fig 26(*e*) shows a typical plug, but there are many kinds, including two- and three-jointed patterns. They are cast out and
as line is recovered the metal plate fixed in the head of the lure
causes it to dive and wobble. They are extremely popular in the
United States for sea fishing, but they have been neglected in
British waters. Articles in the angling Press show that some sea
anglers use them, but they are few in number. A limiting factor
may be their high cost compared with the less elaborate metal
lures. They are complicated to make at home, whereas many
simple lures can be made up with a sheet of copper or some
metal oddments and a few hooks and swivels.

Feathered lures

These are sometimes called flies but they must not be confused
with the flies used in freshwater fishing. They are often crude,

57

being no more than a bunch of chicken feathers whipped to a hook, but trailed or jigged in the water they represent small fish. It is customary to have half-a-dozen or more feathered hooks on a line, each attached by a short snood, the theory being that the numbers create the impression of a shoal of small fish, which is more likely to attract attention than a single lure.

They have been used for generations in Scotland and the north-east of England and in recent years they have become increasingly popular in southern waters.

Possibly more important are the experiments being made with single-feathered hooks, of large size, which are proving successful against several species of fish.

They are experiments that may with advantage be extended, for in the United States, particularly off the Pacific coast, remarkable catches have been made with feathered lures of all sizes

FIG 27. A feathered lure

and many colours, fished at every depth. In that area more than 30 species are regularly caught by this method.

A friend of mine in California, who did much of the experimental work in those waters, has sent me a collection of the feathered lures he uses. They are in outrageous colours, and of all sizes, but they work. Fig 27 is a black and white reproduction of one of these. The original, tied on a 1/0 hook, is a brilliant chrome yellow and 4 in in overall length.

Soleskin lure

Lures made from soleskin are effective and long lasting. The skin should be cut from the white side of the fish and folded while still damp. The hook is then bound in. The skin stiffens as it dries (Fig 28).

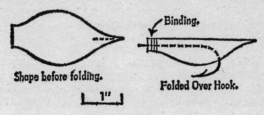

FIG 28. Soleskin lure

Spinning flights

Fig 29 shows one of many spinning flights. They are made in sizes to take fish of any size from small sprats to small herrings. They are used in the same ways as artificial lures. When biggish fish are being used it is best to secure them with thread in addition to the hooks.

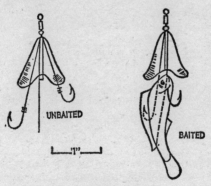

FIG 29. Spinning flight

Baits

Lugworms, ragworms, crab, mussels and strips or pieces of fish are the baits most commonly used, and over the years these have proved successful with most species of 'anglers' fish in almost every combination of season, tide and weather. These five are discussed below in some detail. Mention is also made in this chapter of many other baits. Some of them are excellent but scarce; others are ideal for certain limited methods of fishing; while some are inferior, to be used only when no more attractive baits are available.

The price of bait seems steadily to increase. During the season it must be ordered in advance from seaside bait sellers or tackle shops. A study of the classified advertisements in any periodical covering sea angling will show you where to get worms by rail or post. Both these sources mean pre-planning and are no good to the man who suddenly finds he has time to go fishing. Preserved baits are always available and the deep-frozen ones are a great advance, but neither are quite as good as fresh bait. The angler who can gather his own therefore has a distinct advantage.

Lugworms

Lugworms first pass a larval stage among the plankton, but as they assume their true worm shape the common species settles

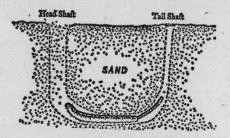

FIG 30. A lugworm in its tube

down to life on shore between the tide lines. They live by swallowing sand and extracting from it any organic matter it contains, and they survive in the greatest numbers in sand with a slight admixture of mud. Pure sand does not contain enough organic matter to enable them to subsist, while pure mud is a substance with which their digestions are incapable of dealing.

They burrow into the sand of their choice, making a U-shaped tube by cementing the sides with a sticky substance which they secrete. One upright of the U is the head tube; the other the tail tube. The horizontal part of the U can be called the living quarters. Once the worm is established in its home it stays there. It cannot turn round and its life is spent moving up the head tube to take in sand and reversing up the tail tube to defecate sand from which all organic matter has been extracted. These two constantly recurring movements furnish a clue to the position of lugworms, for on wet sand behind an ebbing tide will be seen small heaps of worm casts and, a few inches away, depressions the size of a five pence piece, marking respectively the tail and head tubes.

Digging: A broad-tined fork is probably the best digging implement. When digging for individual worms (necessary where they are scarce) first note the head and tail shafts of the selected worm, and take out a fork's width of sand to a depth of 4 or 5 in immediately over them. Then move the fork a few inches back; dig straight down as deep as possible; depress the fork handle almost to ground level and lift. The worm should come up complete (Fig 31).

In places where lugworms are found in such numbers that the whole beach is thickly spotted with their casts there is no need for individual worm digging. They can be brought up with a fork anywhere, though it is perhaps more efficient to dig a trench, sorting the discarded sand after each turn of the spade or fork.

Storing: Lugworms can be kept alive for a day or two in damp sand in a plastic box or basket. They do not survive long in metal containers, though a tin with a handle is a convenient receptacle for collecting them as they are dug up.

Do not put lugworms in the same container as ragworms.

Baiting: Lugworms vary in size from 3 to 10 in.

The tail, less in diameter than the rest of the body, contains nothing but sand and should be nipped off (for general purposes) just before the worm is put on the hook. This releases a

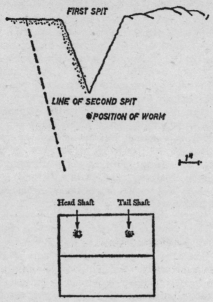

FIG 31. Digging lugworms: First spit, 4 to 5 in deep. Second spit as deep as possible

quantity of blood and orange-coloured mucus (lugworms are a messy bait) and considerably reduces the bulk of the creatures. Some people find this messiness objectionable, but the matter is easily wiped off the fingers and I have no doubt the smell of it is attractive in the water. The taint may also serve to counteract the scent of tobacco on fingers.

For float fishing and drift lining I usually leave the sandy tail on. The bait looks more natural, and a fish taking a moving bait in a tideway does not need to be attracted by scent.

Two or more small worms or one large one can be put on single hooks: Pennell hooks are useful for large ones.

A device for stopping a worm from sliding down the shank of a single hook is shown in Fig 32.

Lugworms do not travel well and are not sent out alive to the same extent as ragworms. See, however, the section on preserved baits at the end of this chapter.

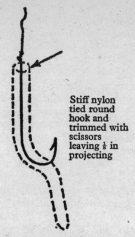

Stiff nylon
tied round
hook and
trimmed with
scissors
leaving $\frac{1}{8}$ in
projecting

FIG 32. Lugworm on hook

Lugworms are naturally best used over the sandy areas from which they come, and they regularly account for most species of flatfish, pouting, whiting and codling. Bass, skates, rays and wrasse are often caught with them.

The Dungeness black lugworm and the Deal yellow-tail are two famous local varieties of lugworm. They are regarded as the best of all baits in their respective areas and are sent out by bait merchants.

Ragworms

The name ragworm is applied generally by anglers to a number of species of *Nereis* which live in the mud of harbours and estuarial foreshores. They are all characterized by the possession of very numerous lateral outgrowths, or plates, each of which is fitted with bristles, which allow locomotion on or within soft mud.

FIG 33. Ragworm

The only distinction recognized by anglers is between the smaller ragworms and the king rag, the latter being 12 to 18 in long.

The most commonly used species of ragworm is reddish bronze in colour and from 3 to 5 in in length. They are an extremely popular bait on the south and west coast, and thousands are dug every week and despatched to coastal towns where they cannot be found locally.

Ragworms are plentiful, but their habitat is circumscribed, and they can subsist only in mud or a mud-sand mixture in which mud predominates. They prefer mud of a certain consistency, neither too soft nor too hard. A good guide is that one's gumboots sink to the ankles in mud most favoured by these worms.

They are naturally prolific in the shores of muddy estuaries and in muddy creeks and it is mainly to feed upon them that flounders, bass and several other species of fish penetrate the estuaries with the tide. They are thus the ideal bait for most forms of general fishing in those areas, and they are possibly the best bait for use with the baited spoon.

Collecting: The presence of ragworms may be indicated by small holes in the mud, but there are no wormcasts. Approach should be soft-footed, for heavy vibrations will send worms downwards.

They can be dug with a fork.

King Rag. This term has been applied to a species of ragworm which can grow to 12 in or more in length. They are found in defined localities, mostly between Suffolk and Dorset. They are popular and killing baits in the areas in which they are found, and there is a demand for them (filled by bait merchants) in many parts of the country from which they are absent. It is debatable whether they are better than local baits in these areas.

White Ragworm. This worm, known in some areas as the sand-ragworm, is white or light-coloured but otherwise looks like the ragworms of the mud. It is a useful bait and whenever possible supply should supplement the more common worms so that a change can be made if sport is slow.

Rock Ragworms. These are fragile worms that live in shaly or soft rock. They are not tough enough to stand up to much handling or casting but they serve in an emergency. With them can be coupled other worms of similar appearance that can usually be found under stones between the tide lines.

Hermit-Crab Ragworms. A fair proportion of hermit crabs, especially those which have chosen whelk-shells as a home, share the shell with a whitish form of ragworm. This will be found in the point of the shell. It is another useful stand-by bait.

Swimming Ragworms. One small type of ragworm (*Nereis pelagica*) emerges from the mud in spring in order to propagate its species. The lateral plates on its tail-half increase in size, enabling it to swim and giving it a bloated appearance. The worms swarm in thousands in the surface waters of harbours and in quiet reaches of estuaries, where they are preyed upon by shoals of small pollack and similar fish. They can be caught in a fine meshed hand net and make good bait, on drift line or float tackle, for the fish which feed upon them.

Storing: Any old tin with a handle can be used for collecting ragworms on the shore, and if they are required for immediate use they can be kept in it. If they are not wanted for some hours they should be transferred to a wooden or plastic box and kept moist. If it is the intention to keep a good supply available for several days they should be put into a wooden bait box, water-proofed with some damp mud. Many of the plastic boxes and containers now available can be adapted to temporary or semi-permanent bait boxes.

Use on the Hook. For normal use, put the hook through the worm behind the head. For flatfish, use a Pennell tackle or hook the worm a couple of times so that no loose ends are dangling.

King ragworms are usually cut into pieces for use in general fishing, though whole ones can be used when big fish are expected.

King rags and some of the larger ordinary ragworms are capable of nipping a finger and drawing blood. Handle them carefully.

Other worms

There are scores of species of marine worms besides lugworms and ragworms. Hungry fish do not discriminate, nor need the angler. Any kind that can be kept on a hook is likely to be attractive.

Crabs

It is safe to say that practically every fish that feeds on or near the bottom will eat crab meat. Some of them will take whole crabs especially if these are in the peeler stage (see 'Shore Crabs' below). The shore (or green) crab is the commonest British species and is easily collected because of its habit of lying up in weed, pools, etc, when the tide recedes, but any other type of crab – there are edible, fiddler, hermit, masked, sand and spider crabs – will be acceptable. Their names and appearance do not matter to the angler unless he is interested in that sort of thing. *Every crab is good bait.*

Mr Barry Atkinson, in an article in *The Angler* (September 1955) analysed the food of sea fishes from an examination of the stomachs of many hundreds, co-ordinating his own experience with reports from other anglers and from scientific bodies. Species whose *primary* food supply included crabs were bass, cod, dabs, flounders, gurnard, haddock, common skate and thornback rays. Crabs also appear lower down the list of food eaten by many other species. The crabs found in a fish's stomach are nearly always hard-backs.

Peeler crabs: The common shore crab, or green crab, is a well-known creature to anyone who walks the shores between the tides. They are numerous on all coasts.

They start life as floating plankton, and after a series of changes they become complete, though tiny, crabs. Their shells do not grow with their bodies, and from time to time they find it necessary to shed them. Just before this happens the flesh becomes detached from the shell, and the carapace looks dull and lifeless, and it can be easily removed. A shore crab in this state is known as a peeler crab (or, simply, 'peeler'), and it is then in the best condition for use as bait.

Soft backs. I have many times watched the shell-shedding process take place in the bait tub. Immediately after a peeler crab has struggled from its shell it appears to swell, and it becomes considerably bigger than its old shell. At this stage the skin of the back is parchment like, and the crab is known as a 'soft back'. Naturally enough these crabs, being completely defenceless, hide themselves away in nooks and crannies in the rocks, under seaweed, or in any place which will give them real or imagined sanctuary. Soft backs make good bait, but they are not as good as peelers.

Hard backs. This is the crab in its normal state. It is not generally regarded as good bait, but there is no doubt that a hard back will catch fish, particularly if it is being swirled

66

around by the action of the current and thus given a lifelike appearance. Crabs in this condition are the normal food of crab-eating fishes, for only rarely can they find peelers and soft backs, since crabs in that state hide themselves away until their shells harden. However, there is no doubt the softer crabs are better baits. They are raw flesh, easily seen and smelt. The dead hard back probably looks unnatural and, if motionless, may be thought by fish to be an empty shell.

Collecting: The British Museum (Natural History) displays the shells cast by a shore crab during the 38 months which elapsed between its capture (in its 'pre-crab' stage) and its death. There are seventeen of these, the smallest of which is about 3/16 in across, and the largest $2\frac{1}{4}$ in. It will thus be seen that a search of the shore may produce shore crabs of usable sizes from that of a 5p piece to some 3 in across, and that irrespective of size they can be in any of three conditions, peeler, soft back or hard back.

They are to be found in rock pools and under stones, but I have found them to be most numerous in long ridges of rock covered with seaweed at about the half-tide mark.

Baiting: Small peelers and soft backs can be used whole; larger ones can be cut in halves for bass, cod, etc, and into smaller

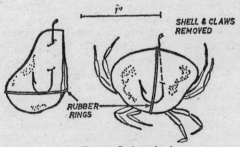

FIG 34. Crab on hook

portions for smaller quarry. It is usual to remove the legs and claws of a crab before using it for bait. This is, perhaps, advisable when portions are being used, but with small ones it is better to remove only shell and claws, since they then look more natural (Fig 34).

Crabs in all stages of development, used whole or in pieces, are difficult to keep on the hook. They can be tied on with wool or fastened with rubber rings.

Storing: Crabs can be kept for two or three days in any handy receptacle, such as a bucket, if a little damp seaweed is included. The receptacle should be covered to keep out light.

If they are to be kept for any longer period, a larger home – such as an old wash-tub – should be provided, and each crab should be allowed 12 sq in of floor space. The seaweed should be changed, and sprinkled with fresh sea water daily. Fish heads and guts, or pieces of fish, should be fed to the crabs if they are kept more than a week.

Overcrowding is the usual cause of failure to keep crabs.

Mussels

Mussels are a useful bait for nearly all species of saltwater fish, and they are expressly recommended for cod and haddock. Some authorities consider that dogfish dislike them, and they are on that account used by professional fishermen in areas where dogfish regularly rob the hooks. On the south and south-west coasts they are somewhat despised by anglers, for there ragworms, lugworms and peeler crabs are considered the pre-eminent baits, but in other areas they are rightly regarded as an excellent bait, and many of the specimen fish caught on the east and north-east coasts have been taken on mussels.

Mussels start life as part of the zooplankton, and from the larval stage they turn into young mussels. At this stage they are fairly active, using a form of foot to draw themselves into the area covered by the tides. Once they settle down they rarely move. A mussel 'settles down' by anchoring itself to its sur-roundings with a number of cables, formed of a mucus which quickly hardens in saltwater, and which is directed to its anchorage through a groove in the mussel's long tongue.

They are extremely prolific, and can be found in 'beds' on rocks, groynes, pier supports and similar hard objects which lie between the tides. In localities where there are only a few mussels, they can grow as much as an inch a year, but in their normal crowded conditions they usually take about six years to attain their standard length of 3 in.

Baiting: When opening a mussel for bait, first insert a knife blade at the broad end, and run it completely round the mussel between the edges of the shell. This severs the ligaments holding the two halves together, and the shell opens easily. Cut out the mussel carefully. Insert the hook through the gristly substance found at one end.

Mussels can be kept alive for many days in a sandbag (or similar container) holding a quantity of damp seaweed.

Pieces of fish
Whole fish and the skin of fish will be dealt with in due course, but mention must be made here of the age-old standby, a thin strip or a lump of fish as bait for bottom feeding fish. It is safe to say that any fish in the sea will serve as bait, but some, either on account of more attractive appearance or flavour, or because they remain longer on the hook, are better than others.

Mackerel is the best of them all, followed by pilchard, but chad, eels, garfish, herring, smelts, sprats and whiting are useful.

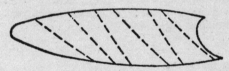

FIG 35. Half a mackerel, boned with fins and head removed

With small fish it is best to split them down the back, remove the backbone and cut the flesh into diagonal strips (Fig 35) with a sharp knife. The size of the bait depends on the quarry and the size of hook used. These points are discussed under the headings of the respective fish. Long thin strips, hooked at one end, are good in a current.

Bread
Bread crust is used as a bait for grey mullet.

Brit
The young of herrings, pilchards and sprats are known to fishermen as brit or sile, and to restaurateurs as whitebait. They swim in immense shoals, individual specimens rarely exceeding 2½ in in length. They form the principal food of mackerel during the summer and autumn months, and are eagerly sought as food by other species of fish.

Examination of the stomachs of freshly-caught mackerel will usually disclose brit, some of them perfectly-formed fish scarcely half-an-inch in length.

They are sometimes herded into harbours and bays by their enemies, and can then be scooped out with a fine meshed net. They rarely survive for use as live bait, but they are so slight in build that they are (if fresh) as good dead as alive, and they can be used in this way, hooked through the lip, on float or drift line tackle. They will not stand up to spinning or casting.

Chad
Chad are young red bream, and are used as baits in the south-west, where they abound. They can be used whole for trailing for big pollack and as a conger bait, or in pieces for bottom fishing.

Cockles
Useful bait for flatfish, pouting, etc, and for general harbour fishing with small hooks. They can be raked from the sandy mud of estuarine waters near the low tide mark.

Conger eels
See under *Sand eels*.

Cuttlefish, squid and octopus (Fig 36)
Cuttlefish, squid and octopus are all excellent baits for most species of sea fish, especially cod, conger and bass. The flesh is tough and stands up to any amount of casting. Unfortunately

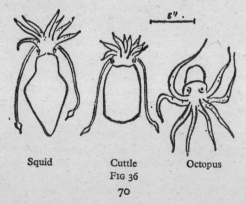

Squid   Cuttle   Octopus

FIG 36

they are not baits commonly come by, though it is possible sometimes to buy them from incoming trawlers; while squid are occasionally caught by anglers. Deep-frozen squid can be bought at many tackle shops.

In all cases the flesh must be absolutely fresh. If it cannot be used within twelve hours it is better to freeze it, salt it down or preserve it in a solution of formalin than to use it tainted.

Cuttlefish and squid sometimes take bait intended for other fish, and they should be gaffed or netted as they are brought to the surface. Before removing them from the water, wait until they have ejected the protective 'ink', which they can squirt several feet. It does not improve even an old suit relegated to fishing excursions. If any suitable stick lies to hand, the process can be hastened by squeezing their bodies against the boat or quayside.

The bag-like bodies of cuttlefish and squid should be opened, flattened out, and cut with scissors into suitably sized squares or triangles. A 2-in-sided piece is suitable for bass and cod, while half of one of these creatures is not too much for a big conger.

Cuttle and squid possess short tentacles which make good bait used as they are. In the case of octopus only the flesh of the tentacles need be used, cut into 3 or 4 in lengths. These may be better if skinned.

Earthworms
Lobworms and other earthworms are not recommended for general sea fishing, but they can be used as an emergency bait for mullet and wrasse.

Flatfish
Small flatfish of any sort make good bait for bass. Cod take them readily.

Gapers
I have never used gapers as bait, though they are recommended for cod, plaice and other bottom-feeding fish. There are three species, found respectively in muddy sand, stiff mud and clean

FIG 37. Gaper

71

sand. Their use either as food (gapers are the edible clams of America) or bait has not been much exploited in this country.

Groundbait

Groundbait is something of a misnomer in saltwater, for it is rarely used on the sea-bed. A weighted net bag containing fish guts (particularly those of oily fish such as mackerel, herring and pilchard), crushed crab and any other fish substance can be lowered from an anchored boat to the bottom, near the hook bait. This is called 'rubby-dubby'.

The same type of bag can with advantage be lowered a short way below the boat when float fishing or drift lining. Oil and small particles of fish drift off with the current and attract fish up the 'scent lane'. It can be supplemented by throwing in from time to time small chopped pieces of fish rubbish. The suspended net bag can also be used for the same types of fishing from piers and projections.

Hermit crabs

Hermit crabs are not often found on shore, but they can be caught in prawn nets (Fig 40); and they may be bought, by previous arrangement, from fishermen who set prawn and lobster pots.

The tail of a hermit crab is a good bottom bait.

Herrings

Herrings are oily fish, and are, therefore, good bait. They can be used whole or as fillets for tope or conger (small ones for pollack) and in pieces for other fish. They are obtainable during the winter when mackerel are off.

Kippers

Good bait for the larger bass which have taken to scavenging.

Limpets

See also *Slipper limpets*.

I wish I could recommend limpets as bait, for they are so easily gathered that an angler's bait troubles would be over if fish liked them. They can be used with some slight hope as bottom bait if nothing else is available. I have used limpets on two or three occasions on the west coast of Ireland, while awaiting supplies of better bait, but I have never caught anything with them.

Lobworms
See *Earthworms*. (In some localities lugworms are called lobworms.)

Mackerel
Whole mackerel, boned mackerel and half mackerel are standard baits for sharks, tope, conger and the bigger skate.

They have other uses as bait. Many fish rely on small fish for their food – brit, sand eels, sprats and similarly sized fish. A killing imitation of these can be made from the skin of a fish, and the texture and shininess of mackerel skin makes it ideal for this purpose. These lures are known as lasts or lasks.

To make lasts, the skin of a fish is cut from the sides with a sharp knife. It is then cut, preferably with scissors, into strips

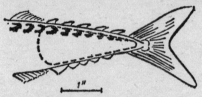

FIG 38. Mackerel tail

FIG 39. Last (or Lask) on hook

from 2 in to 3 in long and from ½ in to 1 in wide at the broad end. They can be rectangles, triangles or triangles with rounded corners – the popular shape.

To work successfully, these baits should wriggle in the current, simulating the movements of small fish. They should, therefore, be mere slivers of skin with very little flesh adhering to them. When mackerel are plentiful it is best to take only two lasts from each fish (one from each side) as in Fig 38. They are cut from the head towards the tail, and the skin side is predominantly silver.

The hook is inserted twice at the broad end of the last (Fig 39).

Maggots
Maggots are sometimes used in mullet fishing. A couple should
be hooked through the skin of the tail on a No 10 freshwater
hook. The tail of a maggot has two dark spots, which look to the
uninitiated like eyes, causing them to confuse the insect's ends.
Maggots can be bought from tackle dealers who cater for freshwater fishermen.

Mudworm
See *Ragworm*.

Octopus
See under *Cuttlefish*.

Paste
Paste made from bread or flour is used as bait for mullet. A
small quantity of the green, silky weed found on harbour
stones stiffens the paste and gives it a marine tang.

Pilchards
Pilchards are one of the best of baits, their only drawbacks being
a certain fragility and their limited distribution. If much casting
is to be done, it is best to tie this bait on with wool. If pilchards
are used whole (in tope and conger fishing, for example), a small
slit should be made in the belly to enable the juices to seep off
with the current and attract fish.

Pilchard oil
Pilchard oil is not a bait but it may make some baits more
attractive to fish, either because of its actual taste or because
the oil, gradually disseminating down current, forms a 'scent-
beam' up which fish move to its source. Its use is particularly
recommended when baits which have been preserved in salt or
formalin are being used.

Pilchard oil has an unpleasant smell, stains clothes per-
manently, and 'runs' easily. I keep my oil in a tightly-corked
bottle and put the bottle in a screw-topped jar. A useful sub-
stitute for pilchard oil is unrefined cod-liver oil. This is much
cheaper than pilchard oil and can be bought from large country
chemists. It is intended for veterinary use and not human con-
sumption.

Prawns

Live prawns are the best bait for bass and pollack in clear water. They can be used for both species on float or drift-line tackle from boats, piers, jetties and rocks.

Wrasse also take live prawns.

Dead prawns (shelled) are used for mullet and 'flats' and for harbour fishing. Boiled prawns can be used on spinning tackle.

The technique of hooking and fishing live prawns is explained in the section on bass.

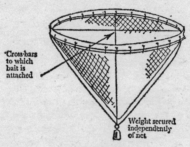

FIG 40. Prawn net

Prawns are caught by professional fishermen in pots and trawls, and can be bought in places where such fishermen operate. They can be caught by anglers in drop or scoop nets. A useful drop net for this purpose can be made from the rim of an old bicycle wheel or any strong ring of similar size (Fig 40). (See also Fig 80, Chapter 9, for a collapsible type.)

The net should be baited with fish-heads, crushed crabs, kipper, or any other fish scraps, and lowered to the bottom in still water from a harbour wall. It should be left for four or five minutes and then hauled steadily up.

Pools can be netted with a small-meshed net on a handle. This should be poked round the pool, particular attention being paid to clumps of weed and to the under surfaces of flat shelves of rock. Prawns can also be caught in the hand-net by pushing it along well-weeded walls of quays and harbours at low tide.

I put live prawns in a nylon net bag with damp seaweed. Prawns will remain alive out of water for an hour or so in such a bag, but it should be lowered into the water as soon as fishing commences. It should be examined at half-hourly intervals and dead prawns removed.

This method serves for a few hours' fishing, but it is no good if prawns are gathered on one day for use on the next. The best means of keeping them alive is to put them in a wooden box with two wire gauze sides, which can be lowered into the water at some secluded spot where it will remain covered at low tide. Whether it is there the next day or not will depend on how many children and other curious people there are around.

Ray's liver

The liver of various species of ray is a good bait for bass, but it is difficult to keep on the hook in its natural state. I wrap up a piece of liver in a piece of lady's hair net to make a bait the size of a golf ball.

Razor-fish

Razor-fish are extremely good baits for general fishing and particularly good for bass. They are tough, and stay on the hook through prolonged casting. Unfortunately they are scarce and difficult to gather, but are available deep-frozen.

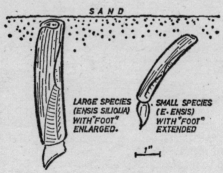

FIG 41. Razor-fish

Razor-fish live in sand in a vertical position, and when scared they go down with considerable rapidity. They do this by projecting a long 'foot' into the sand below them, into which blood is pumped until it swells into an irregular mass which forms an anchor. The shell is pulled down to the foot, and the process

76

repeated. If one seizes a razor-fish when the foot is enlarged, the creature cannot be extracted without breaking it and rendering it useless for bait.

Bait-pickers extract razor-fish from the sand with a hooked iron rod, but this is a professional job. It is just possible to dig them up with a spade, but the work is hard and disappointing.

Rockling

Two British species of rockling (Fig 42) can be found under stones along the coast at low water. These small fish are hardy and make reasonably good live bait for all predatory fish. They can also be caught by normal angling.

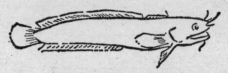

FIG 42. Five-bearded rockling

Sand eels

Sand eels are the ideal bait. They can be used dead on spinning tackle for bass, mackerel and pollack, or alive on float, drift-line or bottom tackle. Cut into pieces, they make good hook baits for bottom fishing, though they are rarely used in this way, for sand eels are not often available in such plenty as to make their use in pieces anything but a waste of good live or spinning bait.

There are two common species, the greater and the lesser, varying in size from 3 to 8 in, but the differences are slight and unimportant to the angler. These eels swim in immense shoals, and can be caught in fine-meshed nets. They are pursued by ravenous fish – bass, pollack, mackerel and the like – and they are often preyed upon by gulls, which indicate the position of the shoals. The eels find comparative safety by burrowing into sand and it is there that bait-pickers seek them, close to the low water mark. Professionals flick them out of the sand with a special knife, catching them in the disengaged hand, but this is a trick I have never learned.

In areas where sand eels are plentiful (Teignmouth, for example) the local angling club, or some of the boatmen, catch sand eels in seine nets. The considerable haul is kept in large floating boxes until required for bait. Where this is done it is usually possible to buy live sand eels.

A dead sand eel can be hooked on spinning tackle (Fig 43). If a live sand eel is being fished in a current the hook should be put through the lower lip. It is best to hook most live fish through the upper lip, so that they can continue to breathe naturally, but the hard spade-like projecting lower lip of a sand eel gives a better hold than the upper (Fig 44). In slack or nearly slack water it is better to pass the hook through the skin on the back behind the head (Fig 45).

FIG 43. Sand eel on flight

FIG 44. Lip-hooked sand eel

FIG 45. Back-hooked sand eel

Sand eels can be kept alive in a perforated box, preferably pitch-lined, lowered into the sea.

Small congers and freshwater eels can sometimes be found under rocks and stones behind an ebbing tide, and these, up to a length of 6 in, can be used for bait in the same way as sand eels.

Sandworm
See *Lugworm*.

Silver eels
See *Freshwater eels* (page 113).

78

Slipper limpets

During the 1914–18 War some slipper limpets were accidentally brought from America with ballast which was emptied into the sea off Hampshire. There have been other arrivals, but however they came they have now firmly established themselves and are spreading up the North Sea. They are a menace to oyster beds and efforts are being made to limit their further expansion. They have been used most successfully for bait. Accounts of fish caught on 'limpet bait' have almost invariably omitted the word 'slipper'. They can be bought frozen.

Smelts

These small silvery fish are frequently caught in large numbers by pier and harbour anglers. They are sometimes caught in drop nets designed for prawn fishing. They make useful baits for bass and pollack on float tackle and spinning tackle, or for the larger bottom feeders, particularly cod, on ledger tackle.

Soles

Skin from the white side of a sole can be made into lasts (Fig 39) or lures (Fig 28).

Sprats

Sprats are good winter baits. They can be used whole for bass, coalfish, cod, pollack and whiting, and in 1-in or smaller cutlets for lesser fish.

Squid

See under *Cuttlefish*.

Whelks

Whelks are used by professional fishermen on their cod-lines, but since their capture necessitates a boat and apparatus similar to the prawn drop-net, they are not a bait on which it is worth wasting time.

Winkles

Winkles are too well known to need description. Shelled, they make an emergency bait for bottom feeders.

Preserved baits

Lugworms, ragworms and a few other baits could always be

79

bought salted and dried, but deep freezing and modern preserving techniques have improved the situation. Many fishing
tackle shops keep baits in the deep freezer, and they can also be
bought preserved and packed in polythene envelopes. I have
found the first to be almost as good as fresh baits. Salted or
preserved baits are improved by the addition of pilchard oil.

Some of the baits that can be bought in these forms are
slipper limpets, cockles, mussels, strips of herring and mackerel,
king ragworms, ragworms, black and ordinary lugworms, razor-
fish, squid, sprats and sand eels.

Peeler crab can sometimes be found tinned.

Other baits
Fish on the feed do not discriminate much. If you cannot get
any of the recognized baits, use any creatures that you can find
under stones, in seaweed or in rock pools. Do not be bound by
habit.

CHAPTER 4

Bass and Bass Fishing

Anglers who fish the south-east, south and west coasts of England, Wales and Ireland have reason for self-congratulation, since these waters are the home of the bass, which satisfy every characteristic asked of a game fish. They run to a good size – fish of more than 20 lb have been taken in nets; they come within easy reach of the shore and pier angler; they can be fished for with almost every combination of tackle and methods from shores, piers and boats; they are wary and unpredictable in their

FIG 46. Bass

habits, but voracious and catholic in their tastes; and once hooked they put up as thrilling a fight as any man can desire. Hundreds of anglers now fish exclusively for bass. They have many blank days when anglers with a big bag of whiting or flats look at them with pity, but the time comes eventually when bass are 'on', and the long hours of waiting are amply atoned for.

Habits and distribution

Bass are members of the perch family and carry the characteristic spined dorsal fin. They are a dusky blue on the back, silver on the sides and white on the belly.

Fish up to 1½ lb are known as school bass or shoal bass. They remain in inshore waters throughout the year. The majority of mature bass caught range from 2 to 6 lb in weight: 6 to 8 lb fish are not uncommon, and while a number of fish over 10 lb are caught every year these can be considered exceptional bass.

The rod-caught English record bass (18 lb 2 oz) was caught at Felixstowe in 1943.

It is believed there is a seasonal migration of bigger fish (over 1½ lb), the fish coming close inshore (especially into estuaries) in May, leaving again in November; but the winter retirement is probably only to deeper and warmer water still fairly close to the coast. Angling records prove that big bass are caught inshore through the winter months, and although they only exceptionally remain in the vicinity of estuaries, there is reason to believe that much larger numbers haunt sandy bays in the cold months than is usually thought to be the case.

Bass are found in considerable numbers along the south and west coasts of England and Wales, and off the coasts of Ireland. They favour particularly the deep estuaries of rugged coasts. They are rarely caught north of Suffolk on one side and Anglesey on the other. Bass have been caught outside these limits – even in Scottish waters – but it would be a waste of time to fish specifically for these odd fish.

Bass come into shallow water in May, and throughout the summer months they are to be found close inshore. They are always searching for food. Their food consists primarily of shore and other crabs, sand eels, prawns and shrimps, but in addition they eat almost any living creature which comes their way – brit and other small fish, ragworm and lugworm, sand-hoppers, shore-hoppers, and anything else edible providing it is alive or very fresh. All this food, with the exception of brit, lives in the area between the tides, and bass therefore follow the tides in, often penetrating far up estuaries. They nose into rocks and weed patches in search of crabs; they inspect the waters around piles and jetties for prawns; they follow the tide over mud and sand flats ready to consume the numerous creatures which the incoming tide coaxes or washes from their low-tide hiding-places; they investigate wrecks, hulks, sunken pipes and any other surfaces on which weed grows. They seek their prey along the bottom and in mid-water, but if a shoal of brit or sand eels passes overhead they come to the surface and feed madly while the opportunity lasts. They swim in the breakers, sometimes in only a couple of feet of water, where the breaking waves and the undertow churn up sand and shingle to disclose food. They favour, too, the swiftest water, where the incoming or outgoing tide sluices through a narrow gut.

Gales send bass to deeper water, but as soon as the waves subside a little they return with ravenous appetites to seek the increased quantities of food made available by the action of the more than usually powerful waves.

On still, clear days bass rarely come into the beaches. This is generally attributed to their shyness, but it may also be that they know the gentle waves will not dislodge sufficient food to make their journey worth while.

Bass can be caught by day in summer, especially off lonely beaches, undisturbed by bathers and motor-boats, but they feed more freely at night. Dawn is the best of the daylight hours in which to seek them, and the next best time is the twilight of evening. In winter they seem to feed readily by day.

The best state of tide for bass fishing differs in different localities, and can be found only by inquiry or experiment. In many places the two hours before and after high tide are the best. In others the period from the second hour of a making tide is favoured. Anglers often use different marks in one comparatively small area at different states of the tide.

Float fishing

Float fishing is a widely practised method of fishing for bass, and it has much to recommend it, for there are no heavy weights to minimize the sporting qualities of the quarry, and it can be employed from a boat, from any projection into the sea and in certain circumstances from the shore.

From boats

When fishing from an anchored boat it must be decided at what depth the fish are feeding, and this – unless they can be seen near the surface – can only be found by trial. If the fish are feeding well down, and the depth is greater than the length of the rod, it is necessary to use a sliding float. If the required depth is not greater than the length of the rod, the much more reliable adjustable float can be used.

The tackle consists of the medium rod, a line, a float, a trace of 8 to 10 lb bs, and a short-shanked, No 2/0 to 1, hook tied to the end of the trace. A weight sufficiently heavy almost to counteract the float's buoyancy is attached to the trace 3 ft from the hook. Any type of reel which holds 100 yards of line or line and backing will do. The line can be of any strength, for in this type of fishing it is the delicacy of the trace which matters. Whatever line is used, it must float, and must if necessary be treated with one of the preparations designed for that purpose. If the line sinks between rod and float the effect of the strike is deadened.

The choice of position is generally governed by local knowledge of the marks, but the entrance to an estuary is usually good. Anchoring the boat just off the breakers and allowing the float to drift into them is a good method, but this is dealt with more fully under 'Driftline fishing'.

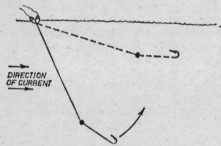

——— Position when float is travelling with current.
...... Position when float has been stopped for a few moments.

FIG 47. Float tackle

When all is ready the bait is lowered gently over the side, followed by weight and float. The tackle should not be cast out. It is allowed to float away with the current, and the angler should be ready for action from the moment the float is in the water. Some anglers let the line run off a free reel; I prefer to 'feed' line by drawing it off the reel (on check) with the left hand and paying it out. The float can be allowed to drift for 20 to 30 yards, after which it is slowly recovered. A pause should be made before starting to recover line. At the moment when the line is held, the current sweeps the bait up from its fishing level, and a fish is sometimes hooked at this moment (Fig 47).

The float can, of course, be allowed to drift more than 30 yards, but it is difficult to control the strike even at that distance. (The tackle would suit the light rod were it not that many yards of line have sometimes to be lifted from the water on the strike, imposing a heavy strain on the rod.)

Bass usually take a moving bait with a rush, and the float disappears in a moment, but in a weak current they may make the float bob a couple of times before taking it under. When the float is within 20 yds of the rod-tip, wait until the float goes down before striking. If it is beyond that distance strike as soon as the float bobs, for increased distance increases the time-lag between rod-tip and hook. The strike should be strong and firm, but not jerky.

Once the hook has been set, let go everything except the rod to enable the fish to make its first run restrained only by the check on the reel. Its size can then be estimated, and it can be played to the net slowly and cautiously or quickly and unceremoniously, according to its fighting capacity. Fish of 2 lb or over should be played right out before bringing them alongside and even then one should be prepared for a last-minute revival which may take the line under the boat or around the anchor rope.

From projections

Piers, groynes, jetties, breakwaters and similar structures which project into the sea are ideal stances for float-fishing. In all such places the current of the incoming or outgoing tide sweeps past, sometimes parallel with the beach, sometimes straight in and out, and sometimes at an angle. In all cases the tactics used are the same as those used in boat-fishing, and the float goes off with the current.

An angler will be most unpopular if he uses float tackle from a position crowded with other anglers using paternosters. The float fisherman has only limited control over his float, and none at all over the direction taken by a hooked bass; and if such a fish chose, as it well might, to head into the jetty and mix itself around half a dozen lines, the consequent tangle would be unsortable. Float-fishing and drift lining should be practised only when they will not interfere with the sport of others.

The tackle recommended for float-fishing from a boat will serve for fishing from projections *if* it is possible to use gaff or landing net, or if a drop net is available. If a hooked fish has to be drawn up through the air a much stronger trace is needed.

From rocks

Rocks, particularly those on headlands which are washed by strong tidal currents, are in almost the same category as projections, and the same tactics apply. It is, however, advisable in rock fishing to use a 12 lb bs trace (and a correspondingly heavier line), for though bass in the open sea make a running fight of it, some of those I have hooked over rocky sea-beds have dived to cover like pollack, and if these fish are not kept from the bottom they will sever the line.

A long-handled landing net saves a lot of wear on the line.

I urge anglers, particularly visitors to the coast, who go rock fishing to study carefully the times of the tides, the level which high water covers and their line of retreat to dry land.

In sheltered positions

There are many places around the coast which, owing to their configuration, remain quiet areas where the water is out of the main force of the current, and which merely increase in depth as the tide makes. Rings of rocks on the side of promontories remote from the run of the rising tide often provide such conditions, as, too, do some parts of break-waters and harbours. Bass visit these spots for a minute or two in their passage up-tide, and it is possible to catch them with the lightest of tackle.

FIG 48. Prawn on hook

I use the light rod with 8 lb monofilament line, Nottingham reel, a 5 in roach float and sufficient split shot to cock the float. I tie a No 4 short-shanked hook direct to the line.

The most killing bait for this type of fishing is undoubtedly a live prawn, hooked through the second segment of its shell (Fig 48).

Prawns are not always available, and I have found peeler crab acceptable. I have not tried other baits, but sand eels, rag-worm and lugworm are recommended by some experienced anglers.

A depth of 6 ft is ideal between float and hook. The tackle is cast very quietly into the water. It will generally move slowly in a circle with the gentle current, and the bait is most likely to be taken when the float is near, or even scraping, the sides of rock or wall. The angler should make no sudden movements, and should do his best to efface himself.

Where a beach shelves steeply, it is possible to cast a float tackle from the shore to a point just beyond the breakers. This is a very successful method of fishing during the winter months on days when the sea is neither too calm nor too tempestuous. The depth should be estimated so that the bait is just clear of the bottom. The weight is fixed 2 ft from the hook. The action imparted by the waves gives an attractive motion to the bait, and enables lasts, dead sprats and brit, pieces of fish and other normally inactive baits to assume a lively appearance. This compensates for the fact that live sand eels and small fish do not stand up well to repeated casting.

Drift lining

In my opinion drift lining is the finest of all methods of bass fishing, for, except in a strong current when a little lead has to be used, there is nothing but the line between rod-tip and hook.

The tackle can consist of the light rod, any sort of reel (I prefer a free-running centre-pin), at least 100 yds of monofilament or Terylene line, 8 to 10 lb bs, with a short-shanked hook whose size is determined by the bait. I use a short trace attached to the reel line by a swivel.

The best results are usually obtained from an anchored boat, or from rocks and projections past which the tide flows fairly strongly.

A good method is to anchor the boat 30 or 40 yards from the breaker line on a rising tide – in safe weather conditions, of course. The drift line is lowered over the side, the hook baited with any of the recognized bass baits. I use sand eels, if I have them. On the many occasions when I have not I use a fish strip, 5 in long and $\frac{1}{4}$ in wide, hooked at one end. This gets swirled about in the waves and presumably looks like a sand eel. Line is released, and the bait drifts into the breakers, where it can be held for a considerable time. If you have a boatman, he can drift the boat parallel to the beach. Float tackle can also be used in this way.

A method which is particularly useful in and at the mouth of an estuary, is to anchor the boat off a bass mark so that the current will take the drift line to the mark. Bass seem to be attracted to buoys and isolated rocks, and these are good marks for this purpose.

Spinning

In spinning for bass the medium rod can be used with a 10 to 12 lb bs line. One end of a 4 ft trace is attached to the line by a swivel, and the other end carries a quick release swivel (buckle, spring or link) so that lures can be changed quickly. I use a fixed-spool reel for this purpose.

The lures and spinners on the market are legion and any of them may catch bass. In addition to the artificials, any small dead fish (including sand eels) can be mounted on a spinning flight. Narrow strips of fish or squid can be used in the same way. I have a preference for rubber eels; the relatively new flexible imitation fish; and the strip of fish. If bass are about I fish hopefully if I can ring the changes on these three.

As I write a new form of artificial sand eel is being brought into production. Invented by Mr Alex Ingram, it is a replica of a sand eel made in soft translucent plastic. The hook sits a little more than half-way down the body and the remaining 'free' part of the eel has moulded fins that cause it to wobble. Trials by several anglers with prototypes in two sizes have demonstrated the value of these lures, and they are to be produced in a range of sizes.

Spinning can be done from beaches, rocks, projections and from anchored or drifting boats. When bass gather in hundreds near the surface to feed on brit or other concentrations of small fish, good catches can be made by drifting the boat alongside the shoal and casting into it, repeating the process by returning under power, well clear of the shoal, and starting another drift. Congregations of gulls are often an indication of such shoals. Finding feeding shoals of bass in the open sea is mainly a matter of chance, but there are certain areas – Splaugh Rocks off the south-east coast of Ireland, for example – where bass gather with some regularity to feed.

Hooks must be examined frequently when spinning from the shore, for the points get bent and blunted against pebbles and shingle, and barbs may be broken off.

Jigging

Although not true jigging in the cod-fishing sense, all the lures mentioned, baited or unbaited, can be used with the spinning tackle in any conditions where they can be lowered into fairly deep water. Instead of casting them out and retrieving them, they are dropped to near-bottom and fished by raising and lowering the rod tip. The current ensures that they do not move straight up and down and it imparts a more natural half-horizontal movement to the lure.

Ledger and paternoster

I have written about float fishing, drift lining and spinning for bass first because they are methods by which this magnificent sporting fish – in my opinion the equivalent of the salmon – can be hooked on relatively weightless tackle and can thus be allowed to show its true sporting qualities.

However, any angler who confined himself to these methods exclusively could fail to catch bass even when they were present to be caught in large numbers. He would certainly be less likely to catch the double-figure specimens which all bass fishermen dream of than would be the man who ledgered or paternostered for them.

Ledgered baits from the beach and ledgered or paternostered baits from projections and boats account for a high proportion of bass caught. Both methods demand weights that will hold the bottom and although this means a general increase of strength in line and rod it need not be carried to excessive lengths. The finer the line, the less pressure is put upon it by the current and a lighter weight can be used than with a heavier line. This is all a matter of degree, and in these types of fishing for bass I do not go below a 12 lb to 15 lb bs line. It must be worked out according to circumstances. The bait itself is another problem in current resistance. I use really large hooks (up to 4/0) and large offerings of bait – squid, hermit crab, peeler crab, worms and whatever may be available, usually in the form of a mixture threaded up the length of the shank – and this needs more weight than would, say, a single ragworm on a No 3 hook. This has to be considered in the general allotment of tackle, but these very generous baits will still be taken without trouble by a 2 lb bass and at the same time be attractive offerings to larger fish that might not be interested in a single worm. Another point that should be considered is that large hooks need more power to drive them home on the strike, and that the line to which they are attached must be sufficiently strong to exert this power.

Conservation

Ten years ago there was little commercial fishing for bass in the waters of the British Isles, except for some local netting carried out in south-west England. Bass are not popular with British housewives and they are rarely seen on the fishmongers' slabs. It is far otherwise in France, and there is a steady demand from that country for bass, and a good price is paid for them. English and Irish fishermen are catching and exporting bass of all sizes in considerable numbers. These fish, unlike most marine species, are very slow growers. Some examples taken from a long list compiled by Michael Kennedy show that an 8 oz bass was three years old; one of nearly 4 lb was nine years old; a 5¾-pounder was 14, and a 11¾ lb specimen had lived for 21 years. With such a slow growth rate the destruction of immature fish can only lead to a steady decline in the number of bass of sporting size.

A bass tagging scheme has been in operation for some years under the auspices of the Ministry of Agriculture, Fisheries and Food, the National Anglers' Council and the National Federation of Sea Anglers. Ministry scientists at the Lowestoft department have now (1973) collated the results and a formal request to the Ministry for a size limit for bass has been made.

The Republic of Ireland has already taken action, and on 5 September, 1969, the following statement was issued to the Press:

BASS FISHING

The Minister for Agriculture and Fisheries has considered the evidence given at the sworn public inquiries held at Dublin, Waterford, Cork and Galway in January, 1969, into the need for conservation of stocks of bass and the recommendations of the Presiding Officer in the matter. He has decided to make a bye-law providing for

(1) A minimum size limit of 14 in for bass measured from tip of the snout to the fork of the tail;

(2) A prohibition on the use of nets and weirs for bass fishing between 6 AM on Saturday and 6 AM on Monday as applies in the case of salmon;

(3) A complete prohibition on the netting of bass in Clonakilty and Rosscarbery Bays, Co Cork, which will be regarded as sanctuaries.

This bye-law covered a period of 5 years, but I have been told by the Irish authorities (in 1973) that it is likely to continue for several years.

CHAPTER 5

Cod and Cod Fishing

Cod and codling are the same fish (*Gadus callarias*, *G. morhua* (Linn)), Fig 56(*a*). Small fish of the species are called codling but the weight division between cod and codling differs with localities. In some places it can be about 4 lb and in others 8 lb, but since they are all cod it is not important.

They are cold-water fish found in the Atlantic north of the Bay of Biscay and in Arctic waters. In summer they usually feed in depths between 15 and 100 fathoms, but from about November onwards many come into shallower water. At this time there is usually an influx of heavy cod into the southern North Sea and the English Channel.

They are almost omnivorous and they gather in shoals wherever food is abundant. The food may be anything obtainable on or near the bottom, and a large part of their diet consists of crustaceans and squid. They follow shoals of herrings, sprats and whiting wherever these are to be found.

The world angling record is 78¼ lb, taken off Maine, USA, in 1960. The British record of 53 lb was taken off Start Point, Devon, in 1972. The Irish record of 42 lb was established at Ballycotton as long ago as 1921.

Some people write cod off as fish that give little sport and that are therefore not worth fishing for. The lucky anglers who can go wherever they want to in search of fish may be justified in this opinion, for it cannot be said that the cod fights magnificently, reels 500 yards of line off the reel or otherwise imitates a bass or a marlin. It is just a cod, but it provides sport for tens of thousands of anglers in this country, many of whom fish for nothing else. They are the mainstay of all sea angling throughout the year north of a line drawn through the Wash; and the winter fishing south of that line would be very thin were it not for the annual invasion of cod – many of them of great size.

The boat fisherman has the best of the cod fishing for he can move to known cod grounds or follow shoals of smaller fish on which the cod are feeding. The beach fisherman has to cast into relatively deep water in order to reach his quarry and he must know where to cast, but a combination of knowledge and casting ability can result in very large catches. Later in this chapter I list some of the big cod caught in one December: they were boat-caught specimens of more than 30 lb, but in the same period a beach angler on Orford Island, Suffolk, caught 280 lb of cod on lugworm bait in one session. The largest fish weighed 28 lb.

Methods

Since cod feed on or near the bottom, the normal tackle is ledger, trace or paternoster. In beach angling it is undesirable to have complicated ironmongery at the end of the line, and I find a single hook ledger with a short free line beyond the weight as good as anything. Boat anglers use all three methods success-fully. Much depends on the nature of the bottom and the flow of the current, but I generally favour a single hook paternoster, either boom or on a three-way swivel, arranged so that the bait is level with the weight when the tackle is at rest. If it is known that the cod in the vicinity are likely to be less than 3 lb or so (and cod shoals are usually made up of fish of similar size) it is possible to use 2- or 3-hook paternosters. If larger fish show themselves it is easy to change to a single hook.

Very few anglers spin for cod, but two types of artificial lure are employed against them. One is the jigger, a favourite in Scandinavian countries, and the other a pirk. The first is simply a heavy, boat-shaped piece of polished lead, armed with hooks. Many cod take these lures in their mouths in mistake for food, but where cod are densely packed more fish are foul-hooked than fairly caught.

The pirk is a different matter. These long, colourful lures can be dropped, baited or unbaited, among a shoal of cod and jigged up and down, or allowed to go down current for a few yards and then retrieved. Cod take a good grab at them, and few fish are foul-hooked.

A standard way of fishing is from a boat anchored over a known cod mark, but a pleasant way of spending a day is to drift with the tide with the bait tripping the bottom. In the cod areas cod will be the main catch, but whenever drifting is done there is always the exciting lucky-dip atmosphere of 'What's coming next?' Gurnard, flatfish, unusual rays – anything may take a fancy to the bait and provide variety.

In some areas it is possible to drift down several miles on part of a tide and then drift back again after the turn. This demands miles of clean bottom. More usual is the drift of half-a-mile or a mile along a known stretch and a return under power to the starting point for another drift.

Hooks and baits

Normally the hook is matched to the bait, but in cod fishing it is better to match the bait to the hook. No normal cod will expend much energy on chasing or seizing a single lugworm. Large hooks and plenty of bait is the rule, and if the bait is too small for, say, a 6/0 hook, use more of it – a dozen lugworms or a 'cocktail' of mussel and worms threaded up the shank. A 6/0 hook is nothing to a cod. It has a wide, all-engulfing mouth and on this account it is fatal to strike at the first touch. There is no hurry, and the fish should be allowed to get the bait well into the back of its mouth. The strike should be firm and hard, for these big hooks need some setting. This means, too, that it is no use trying to fish fine for big cod. The hooks must be set, and I use 20 to 30 lb line for the job.

In general cod fishing, the best baits are those popular in the locality – for example, mussels in the north and squid in the south, but there is no rule either for bait or method. Consider the following list. The information was gathered from four issues of a weekly angling periodical, and it gives details of a few of the top-weight fish out of more than a hundred of over 20 lb caught in that month. The favourite bait was squid, but plenty were caught on worm, mussel and fish strips.

$40\frac{1}{2}$ lb. Caught off the Kent coast on a home-made lure of white plastic, allowed to drift along the bottom with the tide and then slowly recovered.

40 lb. Isle of Wight. Squid on 6/0 hook.

37 lb. Isle of Wight. Squid and sprat 'cocktail' trotted along the bottom.

34 lb. Hurst Point. Herring-baited pirk.

32 lb. Medway estuary. Small whiting.

32 lb. Isle of Wight. Squid on trail with 6/0 hook.

31 lb. Needles. Ledgered squid. 8/0 hook.

$31\frac{3}{4}$ lb. Dover Breakwater. Twenty lugworms on a 2/0 hook.

30 lb. Isle of Wight. Squid-baited pirk.

28 lb. Newhaven. Half a herring.

A 24½ lb cod was caught off Southend with an elaborate bait consisting of 12 lugworms, two sprats and a whole small squid all impaled on a 9/0 hook. Five anglers off Ramsgate caught 300 lb of cod in a tide, best 20 lb, on mackerel and lugworm 'cocktails'.

All this shows that big baits on big hooks catch big cod – but they will also catch small ones.

North-east coast cod fishing

All the foregoing applies to cod fishing off the coast of nearly all parts of the British Isles, but off the north-east coast of England unusual physical conditions have led to a method of fishing for cod which has been in use for many generations.

Along much of that coast the sea bed consists of flattened rocks interspersed with countless gullies, all filled with tangles of dense seaweed. Cod seek their food in these and to catch them local anglers use long strong rods, Scarborough type reels of not less than 7 in diameter and cuttyhunk or similar lines with a minimum breaking strain of 50 lb, often 70 or 80 lb. A flattish, oval, 8 oz. lead with a hole bored through one end is attached to the reel line by a length of line weaker than that of the reel line. This is anything from a foot to 3 ft long, depending on the nature of the bottom, particularly the depth of the weed. A hook is attached paternoster fashion to the line above the junction with the lead-line.

This is cast out and allowed to fish by itself. When the angler sees the indications of a bite he takes up his rod, but without hurry. He rightly allows the fish plenty of time before striking.

Losses of leads are considerable, but this is part of the game and is accepted. There is no question of fine tackle and delicate handling, but the method works, and thousands of cod are caught every season, while the angler gains much satisfaction from his mastery of a casting apparatus that needs skill and practice.

CHAPTER 6

Flounders and Flounder Fishing

Flounder (*Platichthys flesus*). Local names: fluke; white fluke.
  See Fig 57(*a*).

Flounders are not an important fish commercially, for their
flesh is inferior to that of plaice or dabs, but they are highly
regarded by anglers for the spirited way in which they fight. A
flounder cannot make a long dash for freedom like other sporting
fish, but it can and does fight in a series of dives which, on light
tackle, have to be treated with caution.

Flounders, like other flat fish, emerge from the eggs as
normally shaped fish, but as they grow the whole of the cranium
turns until both eyes are on one side, while the body becomes
laterally flattened. Thus, when a flatfish lies on the bottom the
white underpart is one side of the fish and the coloured upper
part is the other. Normal fish in a similar position have the
dorsal surface uppermost and the ventral surface below. If a
flounder is held on edge by the dorsal fin, coloured side towards
one, the tail is on the left and the eyes on the right. Plaice, soles
and dabs also have their eyes on the right. Turbot and brill, held
in a similar way, have eyes on the left and tail on the right.

Flounders are the commonest of flatfish in British waters,
with the exception of dabs. They are to be found in some areas
on sand, but their favourite habitat is mud, and they are met with
in great abundance in muddy estuaries and creeks, which they
ascend with the tide in search of food. This food can be almost
anything alive – the whole gamut of the smaller shelled creatures,
ragworms, lugworms and any other living organisms which the
returning tide uncovers. Anglers fish successfully with any of the
recognized baits, but there is no need to go further than ragworms if these are available.

Flounders spawn in the sea, probably not far off shore. Even
in the same areas there seems to be a considerable difference in
the spawning times, but in general terms early fish may spawn

as early as March and late ones as late as June. In mid-spring therefore, the angler is likely to find fat flounders in first-class condition about to spawn; and skinny wrecks which have completed the spawning process. Not even a salmon shows the effects of spawning so plainly as does a flounder, and anglers who catch fish in this condition should return them alive to the water, for they are quite useless as food. Unlike the majority of salmon, flounders quickly recover from spawning, and a few weeks' rich feeding in an estuary will make them once again fish worth catching.

Although flounders can be caught almost anywhere around our coasts except where the bottom is rocky, the best place for them is the type of harbour or inlet which, at low tide, is a featureless mass of mud. Southampton Water, with its attendant creeks, is a fine example of good flounder 'country'. A boat is necessary to fish these large mud-flats, but there are many projections which make flounder fishing simple, while hundreds of these fish are accounted for yearly by shore fishermen. Flounders offer sport right into the brackish waters of estuaries, and even into the fresh water beyond, for they are remarkably adaptable in this respect.

Bottom fishing

Bottom fishing, either by paternoster, ledger or a combination of both, accounts for the majority of flounders caught by anglers, and if the current is slight and the water comparatively shallow, so that light weights can be employed, it is a sporting method of fishing. When weights of more than 2 oz have to be used, the corresponding increase in the strength of tackle reduces the sporting value of the fishing.

Paternoster and ledger tackle can be used with the medium rod. The line can be the standard 12 lb bs, with 9 lb bs trace and No 5 long-shanked hooks. In ledgering it is an advantage to have a second hook fixed to the line, paternoster fashion, 5 ft above the weight, for flounders are not exclusively bottom feeders, and they will readily take a bait which is well off the sea-bed. In spring and summer they often take food in the upper layers of the water.

They appear to hunt their food more by sight than scent, and baits on normal ledger tackle, or on the bottom hook of a paternoster, may well be hidden from their sight.

Flounders are deliberate takers, and a slow count of four should be allowed between bite and strike.

The baited spoon

The late J. P. Garrard, who wrote under the pen-name of 'Seangler', evolved a method of flounder fishing which has become very popular in recent years. This is done with a baited spoon. Spoons similar to those used for pike fishing, about 3 in long and 2 in across the widest part are the type used with most success, but they need modification. Three or four swivels should be joined together in place of the wire bar normally found on such spoons, and a single hook attached to the last swivel so that the bend is 1½ in from the end of the spoon. The chain of swivels is fastened only at the thin end of the spoon. (Fig 49).

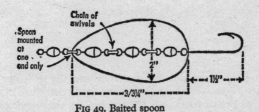

FIG 49. Baited spoon

Bait does not seem to be important as long as the hook *is* baited. In normal spinning the lure itself attracts the fish. In baited spoon fishing the spoon is an attraction, but flounders will not attack it. They will rise to investigate it and then take the bait on the hook.

Normally the baited spoon is fished *with* the current and slightly in advance of it, and this is best done from a boat travelling with the stream. It can, however, be used from projections and by casting. Considerable success has been achieved by anglers using the baited spoon in conjunction with a float.

The subject is a specialized one, and I suggest that anyone interested should read 'Seangler's' book, *Sea Angling with the Baited Spoon*.

Wander tackle

A Hampshire angler, Mr P. Wadham, invented wander tackle for flounder fishing. It is one of the best methods, since it accounts for large numbers of fish and enables them to exercise their fighting qualities to the full.

The tackle is illustrated in Fig 50. It is used with the light rod.

The hooks are baited with ragworm, lugworm or crab, and the tackle is cast out from an anchored boat, or from a flat shore, across a muddy creek or estuary, on an incoming tide. It is essential that the water should be comparatively shallow and that the bed should be clear of obstructions. The weights and hooks sink to the bottom and the line is slowly reeled in. The weights stir up the mud and attract the attention of feeding flounders. When a touch is felt, recovery should be halted, and a strike made after a pause of four or five seconds.

FIG 50. Wander tackle

This method cannot be practised with light tackle if the angler is perched high up on a pier, or on the bank of a deep creek, for the upward pull of the line lifts the weights off the mud. It can be used in these circumstances with the medium rod, a 12 lb bs line and a 2 oz spiral lead if the line is recovered very slowly, but the comparatively heavy weights reduce the sporting element, and the only advantage of this tackle over paternostering or ledgering is that the baits cover more ground and are on the move.

Flounders do not feed to any great extent at night, and though they are sometimes caught on bottom baits during the hours of darkness, the baited spoon and wander tackle methods are usually successful only in daylight.

CHAPTER 7

Mackerel and Mackerel Fishing

Weight for weight, no fish in British waters puts up a better fight for freedom than the mackerel, and it is doubtful whether foreign waters can produce its equal. Such a statement should need amplification, but those who have caught, say, 1 lb mackerel and 1 lb trout on similar tackle will know which is the better fish. Since this is so, mackerel are of immense importance to anglers, for they satisfy the requirements of true angling, being highly sporting fish which can be caught on light and unencumbered tackle.

Mackerel live between the latitudes of Norway and the Canary Islands, for the greater part of the year in the upper layers of the water. They spawn in the spring, anything from 10 to 50 miles from the coast, and their eggs sink to mid-water, where they hatch in from six to ten days according to the temperature of the water. Mackerel attain a length of a foot in three or four years, and at that age they are mature. In winter they seek deep and comparatively warm water; in spring, summer and autumn their movements are governed by the movements of brit, and, in the early part of the period, by the urge to spawn. These movements are of interest to the angler, for on them depend his opportunities to catch mackerel.

During the winter, mackerel congregate in immense shoals, probably in areas covered by the Atlantic Drift. In spring they move to their spawning areas, but late April and May see the arrival off-shore of two enormous shoals of mackerel, one of which moves up the Irish Sea and the other up the English Channel.

At this stage in their migration they are scarcely worth the angler's time, for unless their position is known he may spend days without seeing a mackerel. If his boat happens to meet one of the big shoals, his sport is assured.

In the period from June to September (extending into October in a mild autumn) the fish split up into smaller shoals, which come inshore. Some of these can still contain tens of thousands of fish. The mackerel season for anglers commences, and the fish can be caught in dozens from boats, projections and rocks.

Whiffing

Boatmen and fishermen at seaside resorts naturally take advantage of the presence of mackerel to encourage the sporting instincts of visitors, and many hundreds of men and women try their hands at mackerel fishing. The method adopted is known as whiffing, which consists of trailing behind a boat a handline – or a rod line – to which is affixed a streamlined lead of from 1 lb to 2 lb weight. A trace carries a hook or hooks baited with lasts of mackerel skin. Mackerel spinners and white-feather lures are also used. Large numbers of fish are caught in this way both by professionals and amateurs and, since the fish are available in plenty, and the method provides amusement or profit for those who practise it, it need not be decried. Whiffing is the quickest way of getting mackerel for bait when this is required.

The heavy weights used in this method of fishing kill all chance of sport, as must be clear when one thinks of a $\frac{3}{4}$ lb fish and so heavy a weight.

Sporting angling for mackerel is done with float tackle, drift line or spinner. All three can be practised from boats, rocks, projections, and even from the beach later in the season when the mackerel are inshore, but the methods are the same whether from boat or shore; and since the boat season opens earlier and ends later, these three methods of mackerel fishing will be considered from the viewpoint of the boat angler.

Once the boat has put out sufficiently far and there is a reasonable chance of finding mackerel, the professional fisherman's whiffing tackle can be put to good use, and it nearly always saves time if such an outfit is carried in the boat. The whiffer, if I may so call it, indicates at once when a shoal of mackerel is found, and the depth at which they are feeding. When this happens, the boat can be anchored or allowed to drift and real angling can start, but before the lines are let out it is well to lower over the side a previously prepared net or open-work bag of fish scraps, preferably from oily fish such as herrings, pilchards and mackerel, together with any liver, guts, etc, that may be available. This should be let down on a rope to within 2 ft of the depth at which the mackerel are feeding, which will rarely be more than 12 ft. The scraps of fish and oil, drifting down-current, will serve to keep the mackerel in the vicinity.

Drift lining

The principles of drift lining have been explained in the section on bass, and all that is necessary here is to mention modifications in the strength of the tackle. The light rod should be used. As a number of freshwater anglers fish for mackerel for a day or two during their annual holidays, and do no other sea fishing, some amplification of the definition of light rod may be necessary. The expression is covered by the specification given in the tackle section, but that specification can be considerably widened for mackerel fishing. Any rod designed for roach or dace fishing is ideal, while most of the lighter bottom rods will do quite well. Match-fishing rods are too fragile. My own favourite is a light spinning rod.

A line of 2 lb bs is sufficient, but any line up to 5 lb will give good sport. A landing net is essential for use in conjunction with these light lines. A 4 ft monofilament trace with a breaking strain slightly less than that of the reel line is attached to the line by a very fine swivel. At the other end of the trace is a No 5 short-shanked hook. If the mackerel are less than 8 ft down no weight should be necessary unless the current is very strong. If the fish are lower, a small foldover lead can be attached to the trace near the swivel.

A 2 in last of mackerel or other fish skin; a brit; or a white-feather lure are ideal baits. Other baits are often used success-fully, but it is hardly necessary to go beyond these easily procured baits and lures unless one is experimenting.

The bait drifts off with the current, sinking slowly in a natural manner in water which is carrying with it essences from the 'ground' bait bag. It should not be many seconds before a knock is felt and the second after the strike the reel will scream as a pound of hard-fighting miniature tunny does its best to escape. The fish may dash off in a long run, plunge, circle or come at full speed towards the boat: when this happens the only way of keeping a tight line is to recover line with the left hand, neglecting the reel altogether. It may take anything up to five minutes to play a 1 lb mackerel to the landing net, and on this account the string of mackerel which the light-tackle angler takes home is usually smaller than that of the man who goes whiffing – but there is no comparison in the respective sports.

Float fishing

The tackle for float fishing is the same as for drift lining, except that a float and its necessary weights are added.

The line must be treated with a floatant if necessary, for it is essential that the strike should be instantaneous, and this is impossible if the line sinks. For the same reason it is best to recover line when the float has drifted 20 yds or so, for at the strike the rod must pick up the line from the surface, and any distance greater than this will put too great a strain on the rod, and leave a time-lag between strike and hook-setting.

If the depth at which the mackerel are feeding is less than the length of the rod, it is best to use a roach float 5 or 6 in long. The split shots or small foldover lead should be attached to the trace 2 ft above the hook, and should be nearly sufficient to counteract the buoyancy of the float, while still leaving enough of it above water to be clearly visible. This is necessary because a mackerel immediately discards a suspicious mouthful, and if it feels undue resistance exerted by the buoyancy of the float, the strike cannot be made in time.

If the depth is greater than the length of the rod, a sliding float similar to that illustrated in Fig 22 can be used. The same remarks about weighting apply.

Spinning

Spinning can be done from a boat, and from the shore when mackerel are in. A fixed-spool reel is ideal.

The record mackerel weighed 5 lb 6$\frac{1}{2}$ oz. It was caught off Eddystone in 1969.

CHAPTER 8

Tope and Tope Fishing

Tope are small sharks which visit British waters during the spring and summer months, where it is thought that the females give birth to their young. They are common from the Thames estuary to the Dorset coast, but are less frequently found in the waters around the rocky shores of the west of England. They reappear in some numbers off the sandy bays of North Wales and Lancashire. They are less common in the North Sea.

Notch in
tail fin

FIG 51. Tope (*Eugaleus galeus*). Local names: blue dog, miller's dog, penny dog, shark dog, sweet william. *See also* Fig 70(*h*)

It is easy to write 'they are common'. They may be, but that does not mean that they can be easily found. An important point about tope is their unpredictability for they range the seas like the sharks they are. They are sometimes drawn together into chance-met packs when they harry, say, a shoal of whiting, but they cannot be tied down to any particular place of plenty. The nearest approach to a tope mark is some relatively narrow gut they are known to use – the Menai Straits, for example.

The sport of tope fishing is of comparatively recent origin. 'John Bickerdyke,' writing in 1921, said, 'The dogfish is the *bête noire* of the sea fisherman. There are many varieties – tope, piked or spur dog, nursehound, etc, which resemble and are of the shark family. It takes any bait, a piece of fish for preference, but is not often sought after, though tope fishing has become more popular in the Thames estuary in the last few years.' It is still more popular now, and in many places besides the Thames estuary, but it was certainly the Herne Bay anglers who set the fashion. The Thames is still one of the best places for tope fishing, the sandbanks of the estuary providing ideal tope grounds. The Goodwin Sands are exploited by anglers from the east Kent coast, and there are also numerous marks along the south Kent and Sussex coasts. The Solent, Spithead and Southampton Water are deservedly famous. A significant development which gives some idea of the increased popularity of tope fishing is the inauguration of tope festivals by several south-east and south coast towns and the foundation of a Tope Angling Club.

Always ravenously hungry, tope scour the sea-bed in these areas, snapping up anything edible that comes their way, providing it is fresh. They tear the nets of commercial fishermen, and frequently seize baits and swim off with tackle used by anglers for lesser fish. On these accounts they are frequently abused, but the sea angler who fishes specifically for them holds them in great regard, for they are large fish, which on suitably light tackle give very considerable sport. Just as pike are known as the poor man's salmon, so are tope sometimes called the poor man's game fish. With very few additions to an ordinary sea fishing outfit an angler can catch these sporting fish, which almost invariably give a thrilling fight. The one criticism of their fighting quality is that the effort is not long sustained, and that once their spirit is broken they can be hauled in almost inert – but enough happens before that stage is reached to justify the slight trouble and preparation that fishing for them entails. Like all other forms of angling, tope fishing is an unpredictable affair, for experienced tope anglers can spend days without a 'run', or can miss fish after fish, while on other occasions complete amateurs can bring three or four good tope to gaff.

In fishing for tope from a boat, the heavy rod is used with a reel that will hold at least 200 yds of 20 lb bs line. The average tope run from 20 to 30 lb, and the biggest one yet caught on rod weighed less than 80 lb, so a 20 lb bs line is enough, for one is fishing in the open sea where the only snag is the anchor rope. A hooked tope can be allowed its first wild run with only the reel check or tension to slow it.

The reel can be a capacious centre-pin, or a multiplier. I prefer the latter, as it aids quick recovery of line.

An important part of the tackle is the trace. Modern practice in tope angling forsakes the 10 ft wire traces recommended in the past (a tope was supposed to roll itself up) and use a short length of wire next to the hook.

Bait usually consists of whole fish (herring, mackerel, whiting, etc) or halves or strips of fish. Squid are excellent, and the deep-frozen type works well, though fresh squid is better. (Tope gather in packs to attack the dense shoals of squid whenever they are to be found.) Small flatfish are also used as bait, folded along the backbone, and tied to a single hook so that the white sides are outwards. All baits must be quite fresh.

No 6/0, 7/0 and 8/0 hooks are suitable sizes. They should be made up to wire snoods looped at the end. When one hook is used a snood of 6 in is sufficient. The hook can be forced down the throat of the bait and brought out behind the eye (Fig 52). Big tope seem to take baits with a rush which engulfs bait and hook instantaneously. Smaller tope are more cautious, and there

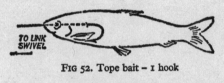

FIG 52. Tope bait – 1 hook

FIG 53. Tope bait – 2 hooks

is often a period of 'knocking' before the bait is really taken. When this happens the angler frequently finds his bait bitten off behind the hook. This can be remedied by using two hooks, and some anglers prefer always to use this tackle.

Two hooks to looped wire, one on a 12 in and one on a 6 in snood are prepared. With a baiting needle the wire of the longer snood is threaded through the eye of the bait and out at the tail (Fig 53).

The wire of the shorter snood is threaded through the flank of the bait on the opposite side from the first hook, and brought out at the tail. A length of string, or piece of spare line, is tied tightly round the tail. The two loops are clipped on to the link swivel and the tackle is complete. It is advisable, when going on a tope fishing expedition, to prepare several baits (with either one or two hooks) before starting, or on the way to the tope grounds. Tope have vicious teeth, and when one is caught it is both safer and quicker to unhook the snood from the link swivel and put on another, leaving the first in the tope's mouth, to be cut out at leisure when the fish is really dead.

This is a useful idea if the fish is to be killed, but an increasing number of anglers regard tope killing as useless destruction. They tail their tope and release them alive. Net

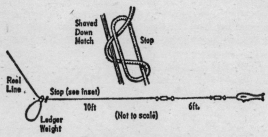

FIG 54. Tope ledger tackle

fishermen regard tope as net-damaging vermin and kill all they catch. Conduct in this matter is up to the individual angler.

With the bait and hook in place below the link swivel, all is ready for lowering. The ledger weight is still in place above the swivel joining trace to reel line. This weight is held until 10 or 12 ft of line have run down. A sliver of match stick is then secured to the line by a hitch below the weight (i.e. on the hook side of it). The weight rests against this and does not slide down the line (Fig 54). The line is released, and the weight sinks to the bottom, where, in order, there is the reel line, the weight, a match stick stop, a swivel, the trace, a link swivel, and the hook and bait. When a tope has been hooked and played, and is being drawn to the boat, the weight, resting against the frail match stop, comes up to the top ring of the rod. Pressure from the reel snaps the match and the weight slides down to the swivel connecting line and trace. In practice, with big tope, the stop often snaps while the fish is being played.

The theory behind this rather elaborate procedure is that if the ledger weight is used in the ordinary way, when it would lie close to the upper swivel, there would only be 6 ft of trace between the tope and the weight, and in its upward movement after seizing the bait the fish would feel the pull of the weight in spite of the fact that line can run through the weight rings. With tackle as described above, the fish has 16 ft of spare line and trace to play with, in addition to whatever line it takes through the rings of the weight.

For a long time I wondered if all this was necessary, but after missing many tope on ordinary ledger tackle because they obviously picked up the bait and then dropped it, I came to the conclusion that those who worked out this principle knew what they were doing, and since adopting it I have had a higher proportion of hooked fish.

On the other hand, I know anglers who fish for tope with a paternoster, casting the lead out from the boat so that the line is at an angle of about 30 degrees from the vertical, and arranging a long snood so that the bait rests on the bottom. They catch good tope in this way, though the fish must feel the weight almost immediately. In recent years a school of anglers has fished for tope with 2/0 or 3/0 hooks, relatively light lines and 2 ft or 18 in wire traces. They catch tope quite successfully and probably have more sporting fishing than those of us who keep to long-established tackle arrangements.

I think it probable that almost any bait and any method will catch tope when they are travelling in a hungry pack, but that for consistent success in tope angling, when lone and suspicious fish can be caught, the more elaborate method may be better.

When the tackle is at the bottom, as in Fig 54, the angler can put his reel on check (or, with a multiplier, increase the tension) and lay the rod down over stern or gunwale to await events. Alternatively, he can hold the rod. There is no hardship in this, since he is sitting down, and it is the method I always adopt. I like to have the rod in my hands and feel that I am in control of anything that happens. One can leave the reel free and hold the the drum, releasing it instantly a preliminary 'knock' is felt. If a big or exceptionally hungry tope takes the bait, line runs out immediately and, after clipping the check down (or increasing tension) a strong strike can be made at once. More often the bait is treated gently and line is drawn off very slowly. Patience is necessary here, for striking too early almost invariably means a missed 'run'. The time to strike is when a tope has really got the bait in its mouth, but correct judgement in this matter can only be learned by experience.

Once the hook is driven home, the tope should be allowed to take its first run against only slight pressure, after which it can be treated more sternly, though the angler must always be prepared to give line if a second or a third run is made.

When a tope gives in it does so completely, and there is rarely any need to fear a second revival. When an angler is alone the fish must be gaffed, and it is best to pass the point of the gaff into the fish below the dorsal fin, roughly at the point of balance. If a tope is gaffed forward or underneath, it discharges quantities of blood which make a mess of the boat. When a second person is present, it is best if he grips the tope by the tail and a pectoral fin and hauls it over the gunwale.

Tope fishing is usually done in deep water from a boat, but an increasing number of tope are caught from the shore yearly, and there are now many anglers who go in for this type of fishing especially on the North Wales, Lancashire and Suffolk coasts.

Tope follow shoals of fish to the breaker line, particularly where the beach shelves rapidly to deep water, and it is in places such as this that tope are caught on tackle and baits similar to those used in boat fishing.

In the accepted forms of tope fishing, both from boats and shore, the bait is on the bottom. The fact that tope take food at varying depths is well known to anglers who fish for whiting, who often lose their catches on the way up. The sharp, smashing bite of a tope taking a moving whiting is quite distinct from the more gentle theft by dogfish. When tope will not take at the bottom, captures may sometimes be effected by slowly reeling up the line. It is useful to know, however, that much time has been spent in experimental fishing for tope with trailed baits, without results. Tope seem to find the unnatural movement of a hooked whiting attractive, but they do not seem to be interested in baits which move horizontally except in special circumstances, when float fishing can be employed.

CHAPTER 9

Other Fish

Bass, cod, flounders, mackerel and tope have been discussed at some length. The pages which follow deal, in alphabetical order, with other fish deliberately sought by anglers or frequently caught by them.

The outline figures are designed only as a general guide and in some cases to show outstanding differences between species which may be confused.

FIG 55. Angler fish

Angler fish (*Lophius piscatorius*)

These hideous creatures are occasionally taken by anglers fishing in waters of medium and sometimes very shallow depth. They grow to a considerable size, the rod record being 74½ lb. The greatest width of an angler fish is the width of its jaws. Behind the head the body tapers away sharply, and it is this shape which has given the fish its alternative name of fishing frog, from its tadpole-like appearance. The first dorsal fin has been modified into a long filament with a flap at the end which hangs over the fish's mouth. It is presumed that small fish are attracted by the movements of this flap and come within range of the jaws.

They have dangerous teeth and enormous mouths and can be uncomfortable companions in a boat until they are stunned or killed.

Considerable numbers are caught annually by trawlers. With their heads removed they are sold as monkfish, a name properly belonging to *Squatina squatina*, a brief mention of which is made under 'Skates and Rays'.

Atherine
See Smelts.

Becker
See Sea Bream.

Black Bream
See Sea Bream.

Bream
See Sea Bream.

Brill (*Scophthalmus rhombus*)
See Fig 57(*f*).

Brill are found in all British waters though they are most plentiful in the south. The majority caught commercially are taken at depths of about 20 fathoms, on both sand and mud bottoms. Individual specimens come into shallower water and are occasionally caught, especially by turbot anglers. Brill feed almost entirely on fish, sand eels being a favourite food.

Bull Huss
See Sharks and Dogfishes.

Coalfish
See Pollack and Coalfish.

Cod family
See Fig 56.

(*a*) Cod. White lateral line
FIG 56. Cod Family

(b) Haddock. Black lateral line. Black blotch on side

(c) Pollack. No barbel, lower jaw projects beyond upper in fish over 12 in long

(d) Coalfish. Very small barbel. Light coloured, thin lateral line

(e) Poor cod. Tail definitely forked. Rarely exceeds 12 in in length

(f) Pouting. Black mark at base of pectoral fins

FIG 56. Cod Family   *continued*

(g) Whiting. Black mark on side. No barbel

FIG 56. Cod Family *continued*

Conger Eels (*Conger conger*)

Conger fishing is a sport which differs in most respects from other forms of fishing except, possibly, fishing for large skate. A conger gives no sporting run, but makes up for this by the tenacity of its resistance.

If really big congers are likely to be encountered, the equipment must consist of a very stout rod, at least 100 yds of 40 to 50 lb bs line, a steel wire trace and a hook $2\frac{1}{2}$ to $3\frac{1}{2}$ in long. Special conger hooks are made with a swivel incorporated in the head, but three additional swivels, of a strength greater than the strength of the line, should be used in the trace.

The bait favoured is squid, herring, pilchard or mackerel. These should be fresh, for though congers have been known to take tainted baits they are generally clean feeders. A conger spends some time mouthing the bait, and it is easy to strike too soon. When one feels the fish at the end of the line for what seems like five minutes but is only probably thirty seconds or so, the inclination to strike is almost irresistible. One must wait until the conger turns and draws off a little line.

The bait must be on the bottom. Some anglers use leads attached above the hook, which are allowed to rest on the bottom. I prefer ledger tackle which enables the conger to move away without feeling the weight.

The strike should be a hard one, and immediately it has been made the rod must be raised as high as possible to get the eel off the bottom before it has a chance to know what is happening. As the rod is lowered to the gunwale, line must be recovered on the reel. The ensuing struggle is likely to be limited to relentless pumping.

Big congers are generally caught at night, for though smaller specimens sometimes feed by day, large ones rarely move until nightfall unless they are at a depth which spells virtual darkness at the sea-bed.

There is an added advantage in night fishing. By day a bait has to be put among the rocks close to the conger's lair. When it feels the hook it has a very good chance of anchoring itself to rocks or weeds, and it is then a case of 'pull devil, pull baker', where the devil, in the shape of a big conger, may often win. Strong hooks can be straightened out in such games of tug-of-war. By night, on the other hand, congers roam the sand or mud near their rocky homes in search of food, and if they take a bait in such circumstances the angler has a better chance of success, for the conger is far less likely to find anything around on which it can get a firm grip.

Once a conger has been hauled on land or into a boat it is essential to stun it, avoiding its jaws and lashing tail while doing so. The 'how' of stunning or killing several feet of writhing eel is a different matter. Any advice given is not easily followed on a dark night in a small boat which seems to be full of eel. Most expert fishermen have their pet methods of killing a conger. Some jab a knife into its head, some give it a blow on the back, and others adopt the method which I favour, that of striking its side with a mallet. Once stunned, its backbone can be severed just behind the head.

The largest conger of which I can find any record weighed 160 lb and measured 9 ft in length. This was pictured in *The Illustrated London News* in 1904. The largest rod-caught conger weighed 92 lb 13 oz. It was caught by Mr P. H. Ascott at Torquay in 1972. Prior to that capture a conger of 84 lb caught by Mr H. A. Kelly off Dungeness had held the record for 39 years.

Smaller congers are, of course, caught in very large numbers both by accident and design, by day or night. Where congers are fished for in daylight in comparatively shallow water, the tackle described above can be toned down to ordinary proportions.

Silver eels, as the freshwater eels (*Aguilla aguilla*) are generally known to sea anglers, are frequently caught in estuarine waters. These are eels which have descended the rivers preparatory to their journey to the Caribbean Sea, where they spawn and die. It is thought that they remain in coastal waters for some time while they undergo bodily changes which enable them to withstand the pressure of the depths in which they spawn.

The silver eel has small scales embedded in the skin. The

conger is scaleless. The eye and gill openings of a conger are much larger than those of the silver eel, the gill opening extending almost to the abdomen.

Dabs (*Limanda limanda*)
See Fig 57(*d*).

Dabs are found in very considerable numbers in shallow water around our coasts, usually on sand. They are much smaller than most of the flatfish, an average weight being about 4 oz, and they give no sport. They are, however, very good eating. By sheer weight of numbers they sometimes add materially to the competition angler's bag.

They can be caught with lugworm and ragworm baits on No 6 or 7 hooks.

Dogfish
See Sharks and Dogfishes.

Dory
See John Dory.

Flatfish (Fig 57)

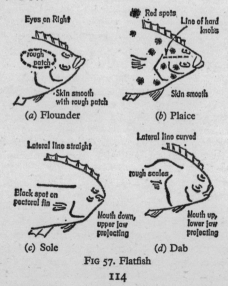

(*a*) Flounder

(*b*) Plaice

(*c*) Sole

(*d*) Dab

FIG 57. Flatfish

114

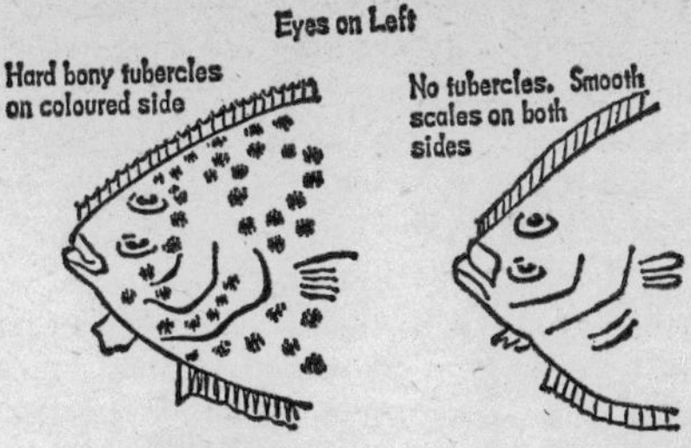

Eyes on Left

Hard bony tubercles
on coloured side

No tubercles. Smooth
scales on both
sides

(e) Turbot   (f) Brill

FIG 57. Flatfish *continued*

Flounders have been discussed earlier in this book, and the
remaining British flatfish appear in this section under their
respective names.

A generalization about flatfish, however, can be inserted here.
Intensive inshore trawling for flatfish, particularly plaice and
soles, has resulted in a serious reduction in their numbers,
so much so that areas once teeming with these fish are now no
no longer worth fishing. The trawls cannot be operated where
rocks are numerous and it may pay the angler to study the coastline or the chart. Flatfish do not care for rocky ground, but there
are many comparatively large patches of sand lying between
rocks which would prevent trawling. Such areas may well prove
profitable to the angler.

Freshwater Eels
See Conger Eels.

Garfish (*Belone belone*)

Local names: garpike, greenbone, longnose, mackerel guide, sea
needle, sea pike, snipe eel, swordfish.

FIG 58. Garfish

Garfish are found in twos and threes among the mackerel shoals, and are occasionally caught by mackerel fishers. If a garfish happens to be hooked on light tackle, sport is out of all proportion to the size of the fish, for it leaps, dives, 'walks on its tail', and performs numerous other acrobatics at such a speed that it is impossible to keep the fish on a tight line.

They cannot be classed as important fish from the angler's point of view, for they average about ¾ lb, and they rarely reach a weight of more than 1 lb. The record is 2 lb 13 oz 14 dm, a remarkably high figure. In spite of their low weight they cause considerable excitement for a few minutes when they are hooked, especially if, as is often the case, they are taken by a mackerel angler using light tackle.

Their bones are green, and most cooks regard them with suspicion. They are edible and superior in flavour to many white fish.

Grey Mullet

Three species of grey mullet are found in British waters, the thick-lipped grey mullet (*Mugil chelo*), the thin-lipped grey mullet (*M. capito*) and the golden mullet (*M. auratus*).* They are abundant in the English Channel and the Irish Sea during the summer and autumn months. The thick-lipped species is the most common, while the golden mullet is described as rare, though in some years there may be a visitation of them.

A 2 lb mullet is a good fish. The record is 10 lb 1 oz.

The thick-lipped can be distinguished from the other two species by the scales which grow in the lower part of the posterior dorsal fin. Thin-lipped and golden mullet do not have these scales, while the golden mullet has a gold spot on the gill cover.

Grey mullet fishing is a specialized sport in which the tactics used are more like those employed by the freshwater fisherman than by the sea angler. The tackle described in this book as suitable for other sea fishes plays no part in grey mullet fishing, and since this form of fishing is one of my favourites, I shall describe my own methods and tackle.

Mullet are very sporting fish if the tackle is light enough for them, but because it must be light, I never fish for mullet from a

* These scientific names are still widely used but the correct up-to-date ones are those shown against the respective species in the British Record Fish List (page 164).

place where I cannot use a long-handled landing net unless I have someone with me who can handle a drop net. Mullet can be, and are, caught from quays and walls where they have to be hauled up from the water, but many fish are lost in their upward journey, and the tackle has to be so strong that, for me, it spoils the sport.

I have found the best time for mullet fishing to be an early morning when the tide is making. Mullet come in with the tide, and as the water surrounds and floats the anchored buoys and boats in a harbour, or rises around the rocks and jetties in an estuary, the mullet nose into the weed-encrusted surfaces sucking off mouthfuls and ejecting what they do not want.

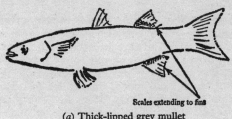

Scales extending to fins

(*a*) Thick-lipped grey mullet

No scales on dorsal
and anal fins

(*b*) Thin-lipped grey mullet

GOLDEN
SPOTS

(*c*) Golden mullet
FIG 59. Mullet

117

I adopt one of two methods for mullet fishing, depending on whether the fish are feeding near the bottom (usually in dense shoals in autumn) or at the surface (usually in small groups in spring and summer). In the first case the fish cannot always be seen, and one must choose a mark and await results. If the shallowness of the water allows (and where one can use a landing net, it often does), I put on a fixed quill float and not a sliding one. The size of float is regulated by the weight of lead necessary to keep the bait down, and this is in turn governed by the force of current or undertow. If there are alternatives, I choose the place where the lightest leads – split shot for choice – are sufficient. Naturally, too, I prefer to fish for mullet in places where there are as few obstacles as possible around which a fish can wind a trace.

Given these conditions, I use a light fibre-glass spinning rod, a fixed-spool reel, a 5 lb bs monofilament line, a 4 lb trace, and a No 10 hook. This tackle is far too light if fishing is being done from, say, a jetty with open piles through which a mullet can manoeuvre.

There are two divisions of grey mullet apart from species. A small proportion of those caught inshore are fish which feed exclusively on natural sea foods. They are usually found far from popular resorts. The majority have become 'domesticated' to the extent that they haunt harbours, piers, estuaries and bays where they have become used to the food discarded by pic-nickers or thrown out from quayside cafés, and from the galleys of anchored ships and yachts. They have become accustomed to fruit, vegetables, and other throw-outs – but above all, bread.

For the 'wild' mullet I in pieces of ragworm, small pieces of crab and fish, and raw shrimps are good baits. For the 'domesticated' fish, bread paste, crust, bits of fruit and vege-table, cooked or uncooked, fish liver, are suitable – as well, of course, as natural baits such as ragworm and shrimp. It is difficult to be dogmatic on the subject of mullet baits, for the fish are the ultimate judges, and it is often possible to see them approach and turn down, apparently with disdain, a wide range of baits offered to them by a line of anglers.

When the fish are visible, I try to keep out of sight. If this is impossible, I keep as still as I can, but I watch the float and not the fish. The float may quiver once or twice or it may be laid flat. When this happens the mullet is mouthing – or, rather, 'lipping' – the bait, and a strike would be premature. When the float goes down I tighten on the fish for an instant to set the hook, and then let go everything except the rod, in order to give the mullet its first wild dash unhindered by anything except the check on the reel. An attempt to hold the fish on its first run with light tackle would lead to a breakage. Once the first run is over, I apply pressure and keep applying it. My experience is that mullet bore down strongly towards the bottom in the second stage of the battle. How long this lasts depends on the size and stamina of the fish, but I always play any fish of a pound or more right out before attempting to bring it to the net.

Mullet cruise around: groundbait helps to keep them within the angler's reach. In summer cloud groundbait may hold near-surface shoals in one spot: in winter a fish's skeleton, with bits of fish still adhering to it, will serve the same purpose if anchored to the bottom with a bit of scrap iron.

In the second type of fishing, when mullet are feeding on or near the surface, I use the same rod with a well-greased silk or braided nylon line, a 4 lb trace and a No 10 hook, un-weighted. If the water is rippled, I use a 3 in roach float a foot from the hook. If there is a mirror-like calm, I use an old tapered fly line, well greased, and cast as in fly fishing.

My favourite bait for this form of fishing is a small piece of breadcrust. In order to gain the confidence of the school, I throw a few crusts on the water. After some preliminary nosing, the fish may elect to sample the crusts, and I then cast the baited hook among them. The bait floats and a bite can be seen.

The tackle described has been used with success, but it was not specially designed for mullet fishing. Most anglers have already among their equipment material which can be adapted to this purpose. Since this is so, mullet fishing is well worth a trial.

Gurnard

Of the six species of gurnard in the British list only three are of interest to anglers. These are the grey gurnard, the yellow gurnard and the red gurnard.

1. The grey gurnard (*Trigla gurnardus*)

   This is, generally speaking, the commonest of British gurnards, though yellow gurnards are more plentiful off the south coast. It rarely grows to a length of more than 15 in.
2. The yellow gurnard (*T. lucerna*)

   This is called also the latchet, tub-fish and tubb. In spite of its name it is pink in colour, and can be distinguished from the red gurnard by the deep blue colour of the pectoral fins.

3. The red gurnard (*T. cuculus*)

This is the smallest and least common of the three species. It is the best gastronomically.

The three species have similar habits and can be dealt with together. They are occasionally caught from projections and

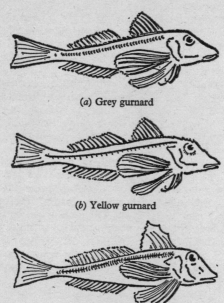

(*a*) Grey gurnard

(*b*) Yellow gurnard

(*c*) Red gurnard

FIG 60. Gurnard. Note differences in lateral lines (exaggerated)

in harbours during the summer months, but are not usually deliberately sought after. In autumn they move out to areas of firm sand, and when anglers are fishing from a boat over such an area it is worth while spending half an hour on gurnard fishing, for though they offer little sport they are extremely good to eat.

Gurnard normally feed on crustacea and other forms of life which they scratch from the sand with the peculiar extensions of their pectoral fins. They will take almost any bait. I attach a

No 6 long-shanked hook to the trace so that it hangs a foot below the weight. I lower the weight to the bottom and raise it about 2 ft. The movement of the boat causes the bait to dance up and down off the sand, and gurnard seem to find the movement attractive. As gurnard do not put up a fight, any tackle will do.

The spines of gurnard are not poisonous, but they can be painful, and it is best to hold these fish in a cloth when extracting the hook.

The record gurnard weighed 11 lb 7 oz 4 dm, but fish of from 1 to 3 lb are more normal.

Haddock (*Gadus aeglifinus*) *See* Fig 56(*b*)

In summer these fish remain in deep water, but their feeding grounds are usually known to commercial fishermen, and if this information can be obtained, it is possible to fish for them with paternoster tackle with a line of the strength dictated by the weight necessary. Haddock take almost any bait, but mussel is one of the best. They fight better than cod, but cannot be described as sporting fish. The average weight caught is about 2 lb, but exceptional specimens grow to more than 20 lb. A haddock of 25 lb 5½ oz was reported from Belfast Lough in 1962 and this appeared in some record lists. It is not accepted by the Record Fish Committee, whose list shows as the record a 10¾ lb haddock caught off Looe in 1972.

In the winter months haddock fishing is at its best, for the fish come nearer the shore and are in good condition. It is usually necessary to fish from a boat, for the fish do not come close in, but many haddock marks are less than half a mile out. They are in some years abundant in the North Sea at this time. Since the water is shallow compared with the depths at which haddock are found in summer, lighter weights and tackle can be used.

Unfortunately there has been such a steady decline in the number of haddock, due to overfishing, that they are now scarcely worth an angler's undivided attention, though this does not apply to waters off the west coast of Scotland and the north of Ireland.

Hake (*Merluccius merluccius*)

Hake are a fairly common fish on the fishmongers' slabs, but are now rarely caught by anglers, though at one time they were plentiful off the south-west coasts. Sixty or seventy years ago they were regarded as inferior fish gastronomically, but fashion changed and the demand for hake became heavy and its price rose. This led to intensive trawling for hake, and it may be due to this that less hake are now found in coastal waters.

They are neither bottom nor surface feeders, and the Spanish trawlers which once concentrated on hake fishing off the Irish coast used to 'trawl' at whatever depth the master thought hake were feeding – usually with considerable success.

There has been a revival in the popularity of hake fishing in Irish waters, where they seem to be staging a come-back. A new record of 25 lb 5½ oz was established in Belfast Lough in 1962.

Halibut (*Hippoglossus hippoglossus*)

Halibut are flatfish which grow to a very great size. They are rightly considered game fish, for they put up a very fine fight.

Few anglers have caught large halibut, for few are prepared to spend the many profitless days which angling for the bigger of these species entails.

Big game tackle, with at least 400 yds of 60 lb bs line and a wire trace with two swivels are recommended. Whole fish are the best bait, and a 2 lb haddock might well prove a winner if fished over one of the haddock grounds off the Scottish coast, which halibut occasionally raid. Pollack and coalfish are also considered good baits. Small halibut are taken in comparatively shallow water in the summer months, but the bigger specimens seem to keep to 30 fathoms or more, while very large halibut are deep water fish.

Most of the big rod-caught halibut have all been taken off the south and west coasts of Ireland, but anglers are now fishing the west and north coasts of Scotland and the waters around the Orkney and Shetland Islands, where most of the commercially caught halibut are found. The 161¾ lb British record was caught in the Orkneys in 1968.

A halibut which weighed 625 lb when gutted was caught off the coast of Massachusetts. Halibut of 588 lb and 504 lb were brought into British ports in 1955 and 1957 respectively.

Herrings (*Clupea harengus*) *See* Fig 61(*a*)

For many years it was thought that herrings fed only on plankton, and that they could not, therefore, be caught on rod and line. This is not the case, and in several places a technique of herring angling has been developed. The tackle consists of a light rod and a line with 4 or more hooks to snoods and a weight at the end of it. The tackle is fished by lowering and raising it under the rod tip.

The 'herring season' for rod and line is from January to March, and the fish are found, like smelts, under quayside lamps at night.

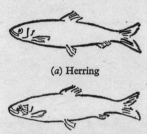

(*a*) Herring

(*b*) Pilchard. Raised lines running back from the eyes

(*c*) Sprat. Serrated belly (much exaggerated)

FIG 61

Angling for herrings was first practised in the Plymouth area, but they have also been caught at Dover, so it seems possible that they can be taken anywhere around our coasts where the water is illuminated by lamps.

Horse Mackerel
See Scad.

John Dory (*Faber Faber*)

These peculiar looking fish are the subject of the legends which attach to several species which bear a black mark on the sides – that of being the fish on which St Peter left his thumb mark when he extracted the tribute money from its mouth.

They are found off the coast from Dorset to North Devon and along the south Irish coast and are not infrequently caught by

FIG 62. John Dory

anglers, though they are of no sporting interest, for they come up like a lump of putty. Their principal food is live fish and prawns, and their mouths open to engulf their prey like extending cameras.

The record is a 10¾-pounder taken at Porthallow in 1963. They are exceptionally good eating.

Lemon Sole (*Pleuronectes microcephalus*)

This flatfish can be distinguished from other species by its very small head, its perfect oval shape, and a marbling of round or irregular spots of lighter or darker shade on the light brown basic colour.

It ranges from Mediterranean latitudes to the sub-Arctic, and is found in water of from 10 to 30 fathoms. This is a species not specifically sought by anglers, but fairly frequently caught by bottom fishers. Lemon soles do not grow to more than 18 in in length.

Ling (*Molva molva*)

Ling are deep water fish, only exceptionally taken in less than 30 fathoms. They are free biters by night and day, and will take any fresh fish bait, dead or alive, but whole fish such as mackerel and herring are to be preferred. They live over rocky ground, and as conger are likely to be caught, particularly at night, it is necessary to use stronger tackle than would be necessary if ling were the only possible capture.

They are likely to be confused only with hake. The ling has one barbel dependent from the lower jaw. The hake has none.

FIG 63. Ling

The record is a 45 lb fish taken at Penzance in 1912, and three others of over 42 lb came from Ballycotton at about the same time.

Megrim (*Lepidorhombus megastoma*)

The megrim is a 'poor relation' flatfish, for it has neither sporting qualities nor gastronomic value. Its greatest claim to fame is its ability to accommodate itself to changing pressure, for Travis Jenkins states that it has been found in depths ranging from 4 to 220 fathoms.

Mullet
See Grey Mullet or Red Mullet.

Nursehound
See Sharks and Dogfishes.

Old Wife
See Sea Bream.

Pandora
See Sea Bream.

Plaice (*Pleuronectes platessa*)
See Fig 57(*b*).

Plaice are usually found on sand, the best of them on sand-banks some distance from the shore. Smaller specimens can be caught on sand or mud bottoms inshore, but they are very rarely found in the vicinity of rocks or prolific weed growth.

Paternostering and ledgering are the two accepted methods of angling for these fish. Beach and pier anglers occasionally catch plaice, but those who fish specifically for these fish find by experience the best off-shore or estuary marks for various states of the tide. The newcomer to a stretch of coast who seeks to catch plaice must be prepared to spend some time in finding their haunts.

Pollack and Coalfish (*Gadus pollachius and G. virens*)
See Figs 56(c) and (d).
Pollack are important fish in the sea angling world for they grow to 20 lb or more, give a sporting run, and are less 'chancy' fish than, for example, bass. They are held in particular regard by the holiday angler, who may have only a week or a fortnight

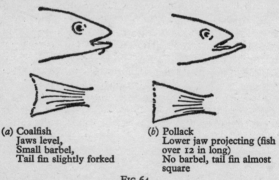

(a) Coalfish
Jaws level,
Small barbel,
Tail fin slightly forked

(b) Pollack
Lower jaw projecting (fish over 12 in long)
No barbel, tail fin almost square

FIG 64

in which to fish; for though pollack fishing cannot be termed a simple pastime, he would be an unfortunate man who failed to land half a dozen in a week's angling on good pollack grounds.

They are found all round the coasts of the British Isles where rock and weed exist together, but they thin out in numbers in northern waters. Conversely their near relatives, coalfish, are abundant in northern waters and found less frequently in the south. As the habits of pollack and coalfish, and the methods of fishing for them, are much the same, they can be discussed under one heading.

Pollack and coalfish have literally dozens of local names, only two of which, widely used in Scotland, need be mentioned. There a pollack is a lythe and a coalfish is a saithe.

There are four distinct methods of pollack fishing:

1. With fly, spinner or float in still water
2. From rocks and jetties
3. From an anchored boat
4. From a moving boat

In each case the tackle and methods differ.

1. In relatively still water. Pollack of from $\frac{1}{2}$ lb to 1 lb, with an occasional heavier fish, enter harbours and still waters (in rock inlets, for example) in shoals, usually at dawn or dusk. Since these are small fish which feed near the surface, very light tackle can be used.

Fly fishing is usually done with a white fly similar to a mackerel fly. The fly should be cast out and then kept on the move by raising and lowering the rod tip, or by recovering line a foot at a time with a pause between each recovery. The expression 'fly fishing' is not altogether apt, for though a fly is used the pollack take it for a small fish. The method is particularly popular in Scotland where, in addition to white feathers, the fly is given a somewhat bulky body of wool or similar material.

Spinning tactics with rubber sand eels (which do not spin), or with any form of spinner or spun dead bait not more than 5 in long, can be employed from rocks, harbour walls or similar places where pollack are known to congregate. A 12 lb bs line is sufficient.

Float tackle can be used in the same way as for bass. A 10 lb line with a No 4 short-shanked hook is recommended. Pollack will take ragworms or lugworms, but the best bait in still water is probably a live prawn or sand eel.

2. From rocks and jetties. Wherever the conditions are rock and weed bottoms, the tactics and tackle described in 3. below may be used, though stronger line is necessary if a fish has to be hauled over rocks.

3. From an anchored boat. The boat should be anchored at a known pollack mark, where the bottom will probably be rock and weed. The depth should be plumbed, and the line marked. Tackle consists of the medium rod, 12 lb bs line, 10 lb bs trace, and a No 1 hook. With this tackle, three methods of fishing can

be practised: (a) float fishing with a sliding float, (b) fishing straight down with a weight sufficient to keep the line roughly vertical, when the hook should hang about 2 ft below the weight, (c) drift lining with a weight sufficient to bring the bait to the bottom at an angle of about 40 degrees from the surface.

Baits can be live or dead sand eels or small fish, rubber sand eels, or lasts cut from a fish, preferably mackerel or herring. These should be from 5 to 6 in long, cut with scissors to a rough approximation of the shape of a fish. They can be a little meatier than the lasts used in mackerel fishing. The hook is put through the broad end of the last, which is then secured to the eye, with thread. When any inanimate bait is used, it must be kept moving by raising and lowering the rod, or by letting out and recovering line. Pollack are not interested in a motionless bait.

When fishing commences, it will not be known at what depth pollack are feeding. It is best to start close to the bottom and reduce depth gradually. When a bite is felt the position of the line should be noted in relation to the depth mark, and the line subsequently marked at what can be called 'fishing depth'.

A pollack does not hesitate with a bait, and one may strike as soon as the bite is felt. Once the fish feels the hook it goes off with an initial burst of speed which provides the thrill in pollack fishing. Pollack usually try to dive for cover and they must be stopped if possible. If the tackle will not stop the rush, the fish must be given its head. With the tackle described above, I have brought fish to the net which have succeeded in reaching the weeds. When an initial rush stops suddenly, it means that the fish has reached what it hopes is a safe place. I ease off line so that there is no strain on the fish, wait for at least a minute, and then take up line with the left hand until contact is felt. Gentle handling in this way will often coax a fish out, and it can then usually be brought to the boat, for its initial run exhausts much of its fighting powers.

4. From a moving boat. The method employed here is to trail a bait (usually a small whole fish) or a large rubber eel behind a boat, so that the bait remains near the bottom or a few feet above the weed level. This method may need a weight of six ounces or more, which in turn calls for the heavy rod and a line of at least 16 lb bs. This reduces the sporting element to some extent, but the biggest pollack are often caught in this way, and a 10-pounder gives plenty of sport even on such comparatively heavy tackle.

Cornwall and south-west Devon are famous for them, and the 25 lb record was caught off the Eddystone in 1972. A 23½-pounder was taken at Newquay in 1957 and a 22⅛-pounder off Looe in 1955. Scotland has produced a pollack of 20½ lb, but it is probable that many notable pollack and coalfish taken in Scottish waters go unrecorded.

Although coalfish are most numerous in Scottish waters, where in some harbours the water is almost solid with them, the 27 lb 12½ oz record came from Land's End.

Recipes for dealing with fish when they are caught belong to the cookery book and not to a book on angling, but a word regarding pollack may not be out of place. Their 'insides' have a powerful and unpleasant smell, and if they are cleaned in a kitchen this may well discourage the cook. It is best to clean them in the sea before taking them home. They are a wet-fleshed fish which do not lend themselves readily to frying, boiling or steaming. They are best when stuffed and baked in an oven.

Poor Cod (*Gadus minutus*)
See Fig 56(*a*).

These fish are of no real interest to the angler, though large numbers of them are caught. They grow to a length of about 7 in.

Pouting (*Gadus luscus*)
See Fig 56(*f*).

(Also known as bib, pout, rock whiting, whiting pout.)

Pouting are prolific fish on which many sea anglers are 'broken in'. Interest in them wanes once more sporting fish have been caught. They prefer rocky bottoms and can be caught most easily on float or paternoster tackle with ragworm or shellfish baits. Most of the specimens caught from projections are small. In deeper water pouting up to 2 lb are met with. They are quite good eating if cooked within a few hours of capture. Record, 5½ lb.

Rays
See Skates and Rays.

Red Bream
See Sea Bream.

Red Mullet (*Mullus surmuletus*)

Red mullet are not anglers' fish, for they are not often caught on rod and line, and when they are they give no sport. I have caught them only in the Mediterranean, where even on the lightest

'Two stiff barbels retracting into slots'

FIG 65. Red mullet. Two stiff barbels retracting into slots

tackle they offered no resistance. They are welcome catches, however, for they rank high for taste. They are summer migrants to our south and south-west coasts, and are occasionally met with in the Irish Sea.

They are bottom feeders, and not fussy in their choice of food.

Red mullet are not likely to be confused with other fish, for their red colour, sometimes marked with yellow bars, is generally sufficient guide. Two barbels, longer and stiffer than in most species, depend from the lower jaw. These fold back into grooves under the jaw.

Saithe
See Pollack and Coalfish.

Sand Smelts
See Smelts.

Saury Pike
See Skipper.

Scad (*Trachurus trachurus*)

(Also known as horse mackerel. Not to be confused with shad.)

These fish are often caught by anglers fishing for mackerel, for they take the same baits and inhabit the same waters. They give a sporting preliminary run, but do not fight to the end like mackerel. They are inferior as food and are often thrown back by professional fishermen.

The scad is distinguished from the mackerel by the presence

FIG 66. Tail of scad   FIG 67. Tail of mackerel

of rigid scales along the lateral line; the spiny nature of the forward dorsal fin, and by two spines on the front of the anal fin. The second dorsal fin is not divided up towards the tail. Scad must be handled with care on account of their spines.

Sea Bream

Sea bream can be identified by (1) rows of teeth in the front of the jaws, (2) long dorsal fins, the forward halves of which are spined, (3) three spines in addition to rays on both anal and ventral fins.

Of the nine species of sea bream in the list of British fishes only three are of interest to the angler. These are:

1. Red break or common sea bream (*Pagellus centrodontus*).
2. Black bream or old wife (*Spondyliosoma cantharus*).
3. Becker or pandora (*P. erythrinus*).

Red bream

Red bream up to 2 lb can be found along the south coast during the summer months, but it is off the Cornish and west coasts that the biggest specimens (5 lb and over) are met with. In addition to their migration from sub-tropical waters to the southern coasts, they have the habit of invading, for one or more seasons, places outside their normal habitat.

They can be best caught on or close to the bottom, at dawn or late evening, in water five fathoms or more in depth. I use a single short-shanked No 3 hook on float or paternoster tackle with an 8 lb bs line. Any of the recognized baits will catch red bream, for they are omnivorous feeders.

The young of red bream are called chad, and they can be a

nuisance to anglers fishing for conger or pollack as they destroy the baits.

Black bream
Black bream have a definite season and are caught in numbers only in clearly defined localities. They reach the waters off the

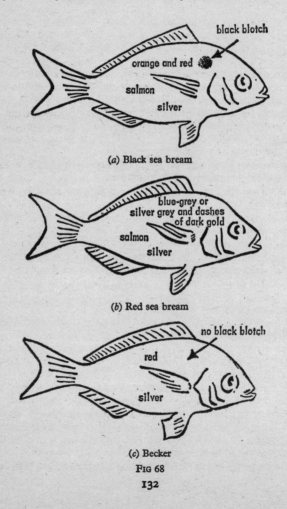

black blotch

orange and red

salmon

silver

(*a*) Black sea bream

blue-grey or
silver grey and dashes
of dark gold

salmon

silver

(*b*) Red sea bream

no black blotch

red

silver

(*c*) Becker

Fig 68

coasts of Sussex, south Kent and Hampshire at the end of April or the beginning of May (dependent on water temperature) and spawn in the vicinity of reefs offshore. The water over these reefs may be no more than 10 fathoms, but the fish do not seem to come into similar areas close to the shores. It is in this period that the heavy bags of black bream are made. By the end of June spawning is over and the fish disperse. Odd fish are then caught in waters north and west of the area mentioned above, but there are then no concentrations of fish that make specific fishing for them worth while.

Bognor Regis and Littlehampton are noted centres for black bream fishing, but before going there it is best to find out if the fish are 'in'. Boats are much in demand during the short season, especially at weekends, and early booking is necessary.

Black bream feed above the weed-covered rocks and it is necessary to find the depth by experiment. If you catch wrasse, which live on the same reefs, you are fishing too low. Raise the bait by degrees until the right depth is found. Drift lining and slider-float tackle will catch black bream, but the standard method is to have a 2 to 4 ft trace attached to a snap swivel which is in turn attached to the reel line. To this same swivel is fixed a weight, which can be quickly varied as the strength of the tide varies. The rod is held all the time, so that the weight is kept at the correct depth.

Bream will take most of the accepted baits: a mussel and lugworm 'cocktail' is a favourite at Littlehampton. The heaviest black bream caught on rod weighed 6 lb 1 oz. Naturally the usual run is much lighter than this, so fine tackle can be used – and is in fact desirable, since these are shy biters.

Shads

1. Allis shad (*Alosa alosa*)
2. Twaite shad (*A. finta*)

Shads are anadromous fish which are becoming progressively rarer in British waters as estuarine pollution reduces the number of rivers which they can ascend to spawn. The allis shad, in fact, is now so scarce as to merit no more than this mention.

Twaite shad still ascend some rivers in the spring, notably the Severn, Wye and Usk, where they offer sport out of all proportion to their size, putting up a sustained and sometimes acrobatic fight. I have caught only four, and those on the same day. I have often been out for them, but one has to hit the right

(*a*) Allis shad. One black spot

(*b*) Twaite shad. Five to seven black spots

FIG 69.

day and the right part of the river with the water at the right level. If you are ever lucky enough to find a shoal of them in a weirpool, you are assured of good sport with a light rod, a 4 lb line and a fly-spoon or small white-feathered lure.

Most of them weigh about $\frac{1}{2}$ lb, though the record is 3 lb 2 oz, caught in the sea off Deal. Shad of either species are caught in the sea only by accident.

The record allis shad weighed 3 lb $4\frac{1}{2}$ oz.

Sharks and Dogfishes

Among the sharks, the porbeagle, the blue shark, the mako shark and the tope are sporting and fairly common fish. They are deliberately sought by anglers and special tactics for their capture have been developed. Odd sharks of other species, and dogfishes, are caught by anglers seeking other quarry, though there may be some deliberate fishing for the latter in competitions where they are allowed to count. Dogfishes can be a nuisance to anglers and commercial fishermen, for not only do they take bait intended for better fish but when present in large shoals they scare all other fish from the vicinity.

Blue Sharks (Carcharinus glaucus)

These are the commonest species of true sharks found in British waters. They usually arrive from southern waters towards the end of May and leave again in early October, the actual time at either end being to some extent dependent on water temperature.

The largest concentrations of blue sharks are found off the south and west coasts of Ireland and the coasts of Devon and Cornwall. The fish are not rigidly confined to these areas and a proportion of them move up the Channel and the Irish Sea.

Very little attention was paid to these sharks by anglers until 1952. They are usually found eight to twelve miles off shore and few anglers fished for them specially. Some were caught by anglers using strong gear (notably at Ballycotton) but usually by accident rather than design.

In 1952 a group of enthusiasts at Looe, in Cornwall, ex-

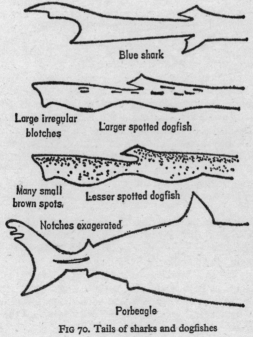

Blue shark

Large irregular blotches Larger spotted dogfish

Many small brown spots Lesser spotted dogfish

Notches exagerated

Porbeagle

FIG 70. Tails of sharks and dogfishes

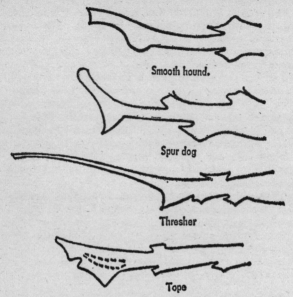

Smooth hound.

Spur dog

Thresher

Tope

FIG. 70. Tails of sharks and dogfishes *continued*

perimented with shark fishing. 'Rubby-dubby' was used to
attract the fish and this improved the somewhat hopeless chance
of a shark's finding a bait in a limitless sea.

Rubby-dubby consists of chopped or mashed fish fragments,
the oilier the better. They are sometimes laced with pilchard
oil. This is lowered from the fishing boat and the boat so
manoeuvred (taking current and wind into consideration) that a
scent-lane leads up to the baits. Sharks encountering this scent
follow it to its source.

Success was immediate. The Shark Angling Club of Great
Britain was founded by Brigadier J. A. L. Caunter, CBE, MC,
and the sport has become very popular with visiting anglers as
well as the local experts.

In 1953, 350 sharks were caught at Looe; 600 in 1954; 1,200
in 1955; 1,650 in 1956; and 4,171 in 1957. Since then the figure
for this port has varied between 4,000 and 7,000. Other fishing
ports now have shark boats that cater for anglers, and the sport
is widespread.

Tackle is hired out by the boatmen or local tackle dealers, because few visiting anglers possess the strong rods and large capacity reels necessary for shark fishing.

Bait is usually whole pilchard or mackerel – though other fish of similar size or fillets of larger ones will do.

The rod record (218 lb) was set up in 1959 by Mr N. Sutcliffe, who was on holiday at Looe.

Larger spotted dogfish – bull huss (Scyliorhinus stellaris)
(Also known as greater spotted dogfish, huss and nurse hound.)

These dogfish have some sporting qualities and they occupy a place in sea angling records – 21 lb 3 oz.

Lesser spotted dogfish (S. caniculus)
(Also known as smaller spotted dogfish, huss, rough hound.)

These are the commonest of the British dogfish. They are found on sandy bottoms and are frequently – all too frequently, in fact – caught by anglers using bottom tackle. They give no sport, but as food they are by far the best of the sharks and dog-fishes. They should be unhooked with care. If held by the tail they can twist round and bite the hand or wrist. Record, 4½ lb.

Monk fish (Squatina squatina)
Scientifically the monk fish, or fiddle fish, is grouped with sharks, though it is more like a ray in appearance.

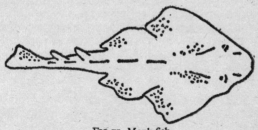

FIG 71. Monk fish

It is common all round our coasts and is not infrequently caught by anglers.

Commercial fishermen apply the name 'monk fish' to the angler fish. Record, 66 lb.

Mako shark (Isurus oxyrinchus)

It is not often that anglers have the chance to prove that an un-expected species of fish live in British waters. This is what happened with mako sharks, however. For many years porbeagle sharks have been caught by anglers. In 1955 Mrs H. Eathorne caught a fish presumed to be a porbeagle which weighed 352 lb. The Shark Angling Club of Great Britain claimed this fish as a world record and sent particulars to the headquarters of the International Game Fish Association. Experts there decided from the photographs submitted that the fish was a mako shark. A new species was added to the angler's list.

Mako sharks are not very common, but they are caught occasionally by anglers fishing for blue sharks. As can be imagined, they look very much like porbeagle sharks. In the mako sharks a vertical dropped from the forward root of the dorsal fin falls behind the pectoral fin. In a porbeagle shark the line bisects the pectoral fin. A more definite identification can be obtained from the teeth. A mako's teeth are plain at the base and irregularly arranged in the mouth. A porbeagle's teeth are set regularly and have small 'cups' in the base. The record is 500 lb.

Porbeagle shark (Lamna nasus)

Porbeagle sharks are widely distributed throughout the waters of the world including those around the British Isles. They are not as numerous as blue sharks, but at least a score of sizeable specimens are caught yearly. Many of them are taken off the south coasts of Ireland and England and it is probable that they can be taken almost anywhere, with luck and patience, if anglers go after them. It seems that whenever a group of anglers decides to concentrate on porbeagle fishing, they succeed.

Record, 430 lb: off Jersey, 1969.

(See 'Mako shark'.)

Smooth hound (Mustelus mustelus)

The smooth hound is similar in appearance to the tope, and grows to approximately the same size. It is a common species around our coasts, but is not caught so frequently as tope since its food consists in the main of crustaceans and molluscs. It has not the sporting qualities of tope. Record, 28 lb.

Spur dogfish or Spurdog (Squalus acanthias)

(Also spiny dogfish [USA], piked dogfish, common dogfish.)

Easily identified by the sharp spike which precedes each of the dorsal fins (Fig 70), this most prolific species of dogfish is found on both sides of the North Atlantic in the temperate and cool temperate belts. An American writer* says: 'Like a seething carpet flung by some nemesis of fishermen, gigantic schools of spiny dogfish descend upon fishing grounds, where they devour or mutilate netted fish, eat both bait and captives on hand-lines, tear nets to shreds, and raid lobster pots.' They swim in packs, in British waters the packs usually running from a dozen to a couple of hundred, though packs of more than 20,000 have been reported.

It is most unlikely that any angler survives a seaon's boat fishing without catching some specimens of spur dog. They should be handled with care, the fish being stunned and the spiked fins held down before a hook is extracted. They are not often eaten in the home, but their food is quite palatable and the large commercial catch finds its way to the fish-and-chip shops. Record, 20 lb 3 oz.

Thresher shark (Alopias vulpes)
Thresher sharks are found throughout the seas of the world, and in areas where they are plentiful they are sought by game fishermen. The world record is 922 lb (Bay of Islands, New Zealand); the British record is 280 lb, taken off Dungeness in 1933.

Tope
See Chapter 8.

Skates and Rays

Skates and rays are cartilaginous fishes closely allied to sharks. They have a flattened appearance due to the disproportionate enlargement of the pectoral fins, which are popularly known as 'wings'. They lie on and feed near the sea-bed.

They belong to the *Raiidae*, and scientifically there is no distinction between skates and rays. For convenience, the sting ray, which is one of the *Trygonidae*, is included under this heading.

All the British species of rays lay their eggs in leathery capsules,

* H. W. McCormick, *Shadows in the Sea.*

roughly rectangular in shape. The eggs are fertilized while still in the body of the female. Empty capsules can often be picked up on the beach. The largest of them are those of the bottle-nose ray, and measure 6½ in by 4¼ in. There is a long incubation period, varying from five months in the thornback ray to fourteen months in the bottle-nose ray.

In spite of their apparently unwieldy shape, skates and rays must be able to move with considerable speed, for their principal food consists of small fishes – herring, mackerel, etc – which they engulf in their 'wings' before swallowing them.

Excluding the sting ray, there are thirteen rays on the British list. It is difficult to lay down rules for the easy identification of

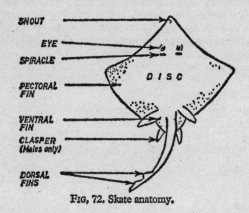

FIG, 72. Skate anatomy.

rays, for in many cases they are closely alike in structure. Colouration is normally a poor guide to the identification of fishes, but in rays it is sufficient to distinguish several species. The flapper skate, the long-nosed ray, the painted ray, the shagreen ray and the undulate ray are too rare to deserve more than this mention. If an angler catches a ray not identifiable in the following descriptions, it will probably be one of these five, and he is advised to get it examined by an expert.

Of the remaining rays the species most often caught by anglers are the common skate, the sting ray and the thornback skate (or thornback ray), and these three will be discussed first. The remainder will follow in alphabetical order.

Common skate (Raja batis)

The common skate varies in colour between grey, purple and brown on the upper surface. The under surface has a light purple tinge, and it is by this light but definitely tinted under-surface that common skate can be usually identified.

Large numbers of common skate are caught inshore, from projections and beaches, and from boats in comparatively shallow water. They are often taken with paternoster and ledger tackle by anglers fishing for flatfish. They vary in size from two to 20 lb.

Large skate are found in deeper waters. The record is 226½ lb (Duny Voe, Shetland, 1970). A 221-lb fish was taken at Bally-cotton in 1913, and the south and west coasts of Ireland have seen the capture of others of more than 200 lb. Several skate of over 100 lb have been taken in English waters, and skate fishing for big specimens is now an established and particularized sport.

Experiences differ regarding the sporting qualities of skate. The small inshore specimens often put up a good fight, but with big skate the general opinion is that they provide little sport; and many anglers agree with Mr C. O. Minchin's statement that catching a skate is like 'fishing for a large tombstone'. In many cases skate appear to grip the bottom by suction, and 'pumping' them up is a slow and laborious process. On the other hand, some captors of skates of more than 100 lb have described their struggles in thrilling terms. I have not caught a skate of more than 40 lb, so I cannot add any personal opinion on the fighting qualities of big fish of this species.

A stout rod must be used for big skate fishing – something heavier than the 'heavy' rod referred to in the section on tackle, 300 yds of 50 lb bs line is required, together with a 6 ft trace of steel wire, fitted with two swivels.

Skate have formidable sets of crushing teeth, and it is essential that the one large hook (6/0 to 8/0) should be of the finest quality obtainable. Skate will take any small whole fish providing they are fresh. The hook can be baited as in single-hook tope fishing (Fig 52). The swivel nearest the hook should be a link swivel, so that baits can be easily changed. This tackle can be arranged with a lead of the necessary weight on the ledger principle.

The strike should be delayed until the fish definitely moves off with the bait.

Sting ray (Trygon pastinaca)
Sting rays can be identified by the long serrated sting rising from the tail. They come into shallow water around the British Isles in autumn and are most numerous in the south. They are often caught by anglers, though few people fish for them deliberately. The spine can inflict a nasty wound, which may become poisoned, for though there is no poison gland the mucus with which the sting is covered can have poisonous qualities.

The record rod-caught sting ray weighed 59 lb. It was caught at Clacton in 1952.

Thornback ray (Raja clavata)
Of all the skates and rays found in British waters, thornback rays are the most common. Anglers catch thousands of them every year, and most of these are below 10 lb in weight. The record weighed 38 lb. Thornbacks can be easily identified by the numerous thorn-like spines on tail, disc and snout.

Investigations into the habits of the younger fish of this species have proved not only that they are non-migratory, but that individual specimens remain in one very limited area for months at a time. The same investigation proved that they feed extensively on small fish, particularly sprats and herrings.

For thornback rays I use the medium rod, 12 lb line, ledger weight, and a single 2/0 or 1/0 hook baited with a small whole fresh fish, half a fish or a thick fillet. With a whole fish force the hook down the throat and bring it out behind the eye.

Blonde ray and spotted ray (Raja brachyura and R. maculata)
Blonde rays and spotted rays are liable to be confused since they are similar in shape and occupy the same grounds. The blonde ray is a light brown or fawn on the upper surface, and the spotted ray a chocolate brown, but it is often difficult to decide which is which unless both species are present for comparison. The blonde ray is decorated with small black spots, roughly circular, and the spotted ray with large irregular black spots, but again it is difficult to judge unless both species are available. The best clue to identification lies in the distribution of the spots; those of the blonde ray go right to the edge of the wings; but in the spotted ray there is a clear margin between the end of the spots and the edge of the wing. The records are respectively 35 lb 9 oz, and 16 lb 3 oz.

Bottle-nose ray (Raja marginata)

This ray is a dirty grey on the upper surface, without markings. A feature which helps in identification is the dead, chalky whiteness of the under surface, which accounts for the alternative names of *Raja alba* and white skate.

It is much thicker than most rays, and though not long-nosed, its snout is very pointed. There are spines on the snout and tail, and at the extremity of the disc. It is possible that small bottle-nose rays are mistaken for thornbacks.

This is the largest of the British rays and specimens of more than 500 lb have been taken commercially. The 76 lb rod-caught record was taken off the Needles, Isle of Wight, in 1970.

If an angler catches a big bottle-nosed ray, he will be well advised to get expert identification if the fish is to be registered as a record or a notable fish.

Cuckoo ray (Raja naevus)

This species is common in the deeper waters of the North and Irish Seas. It can be distinguished from other rays by the presence of a large round spot on each 'wing' near the spine. These spots are black, with yellow lines at their centres and, in some specimens, rings of yellow dots around their edges.

It grows to a length of about 3 ft. Record: 5 lb.

Sandy ray (Raja circularis)

The sandy ray is found in specialized localities, but is fairly common off south Devon. The upper surface is a uniform dark khaki decorated with symmetrically arranged yellow blotches ringed with dark brown. It grows to a length of about 3 ft. Record: 5 lb 10½ oz.

Spotted ray
See Blonde ray.

Skipper (*Scomberesox saurus*)

The skipper, or saury pike, is similar to a garfish in appearance and habits, from which it can be distinguished by the dorsal fin (Fig 73(*a*) and (*b*)).

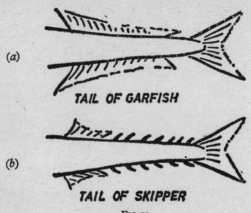

(a)

TAIL OF GARFISH

(b)

TAIL OF SKIPPER

FIG 73

Smelts

Two species of fish of different orders are called smelts. These are the sand smelt (*Atherina presbyter*) and the true smelt (*Osmerus eperlanus*).

Sand smelt or atherine (Fig 74).
These little fish rarely attain a size of more than 7 in, so they cannot be considered sporting quarry. Nevertheless, they provide good fun and an excellent breakfast. As far as the angler is concerned, they are winter fish, invading our harbours in packed

NORMAL
DORSAL FIN

FIG 74. Sand smelt or atherine

shoals from November to February. They are attracted by lights, and are best caught at night, when the tide is making, under quayside lamps.

Any rod can be used, providing it is at least 10 ft long. The lighter it is the better, but it is an advantage if the top is not too whippy. Any line of 5 lb bs or so will do, with any sort of reel. Six or seven hooks-to-gut are attached to the line. Size 8 freshwater hooks are suitable.

The hooks are baited with small scraps of worm, bits of fish, crab, etc, but no loose ends should be left dangling.

The tackle must be lowered into the water gently, and without splashing. If a shoal of sand smelts is present, the soft, dragging bites will be felt. Each bite should be struck, but not with sufficient force to raise the tackle from the water. I strike by pulling the line with the left hand. It is usual to wait until two or three bites have been felt before recovering the tackle.

A method of smelt fishing I have seen but not tried is done with line and hooks similar to those mentioned above, tied direct to the top of a long bamboo. This is practicable only when the tide is nearly full and there is no great drop between quay and water.

FIG 75 True Smelt

True smelt (Fig 75).
The true smelt, or sparling, differs from the sand smelt in several important ways, but it is necessary only to note the second dorsal fins in both species. In the sand smelt the second dorsal fin is a normal rayed one. In the true smelt it is an adipose fin, a rayless, lumpy piece of fat similar to that of the Salmonidae.

True smelts are more common in northern than in southern waters, and in the spawning season, from March to May, they crowd into estuarine waters. They are taken commercially, but are of little interest to anglers.

Smooth Hound
See Sharks and Dogfishes.

Soles

There are four species of British soles, the common sole (*Solea solea*); the French sole, or sand sole (*S. lascaris*); the thickback sole (*S. variegata*); and the solenette (*S. lutea*).

The French sole only occasionally comes the way of the

angler. It is covered with black blotches and dots. The thick-back sole is common off the south-west coasts. It can be distinguished by its reddish colour, and by a number of dark bands across the body, which become black where they meet the fins. The solenette is plentiful, but grows only to a length of 4 in. It is often mistaken for the young of common soles, from which it can be distinguished by the fact that every sixth or seventh fin-ray is black.

Common soles (see Fig 57(c)) are the ones most frequently caught by anglers. They are primarily night feeders, and are not, therefore, caught so often as plaice and flounders. The best condition for daylight fishing is when the water is cloudy.

Paternoster or ledger tackle with ragworm, lugworm or shrimp bait on a No 6 long-shanked hook is a good combination.

Soles should be kept for 24 hours or more before being eaten.

Spur Dog
See Sharks and Dogfishes.

Tunny (*Thunnus thynnus*)

The bluefin tuna. In the 1930s and 1950s numbers of tunny accompanied the herring drifters in the North Sea, and anglers set out to catch them from bases at Scarborough and Whitby. A British Tunny Club was formed. The fish no longer appear. A British record of 851 lb was established in 1933.

Turbot (*Scophthalmus maximus*)

See Fig 57(e).

Turbot are found all round our coasts, though they are most numerous on the east and south. A particularly good area is the Skerries Bank. They prefer sand to other bottoms. They are caught on paternoster and ledger tackle from boats and occasionally from the shore. I have caught them using ledger tackle from a boat, particularly when the bait has been a live sand eel. They will take other live fish baits, and dead baits providing they are fresh. Turbot have also been caught on ragworm and lugworm.

They are a sporting fish, but they are rarely caught in conditions where light tackle can be used.

A suitable tackle for boat fishing is a No 3 long-shanked hook, a 10 lb bs trace, 12 lb line, and ledger weight. Record, 31¼ lb.

Whiting (*Gadus merlangus*)

Whiting are found off all coasts of the British Isles. They spawn between March and June, and are at that time to be found in water from 10 to 30 fathoms deep. In the late summer and autumn they come into shallower water, and with the arrival of sprats in October or November they come closer in-shore. They prefer a sandy bottom.

Whiting fishing is not an exciting sport, for it consists of dropping a 2-hook or 3-hook paternoster to the bottom, waiting for one or more bites, and then reeling up the fish. Since they give no sporting run there is no object in fishing with particularly light tackle, though the snoods should be of fine monofilament, for big whiting are suspicious fish. No 4 or 5 short-shanked hooks, with small pieces of bait are advisable, for these will attract the bigger fish, but at the same time catch the usual run of $\frac{1}{2}$ to 1 lb whiting. A big reel or a multiplier saves time when reeling in. Whiting travel in shoals, and one must fish quickly when a shoal is passing below. Almost any bait will catch whiting; and pieces of mackerel or other fish are used successfully. When the sprats are in, whiting will rarely take baits other than sprat.

Off the south-west coast, whiting often keep to deep water, and tackle should be strong enough to deal with bigger fish which may be encountered. Record, 6 lb 3 oz 3 dm.

Witch (*Glyptocephalus cynoglossus*)

Long narrow flat fish which are fairly common trawler catches, but they are not of much interest to anglers as they live beyond the 20-fathom line. They rarely exceed 18 in in length.

Wrasse

Six species of wrasse are common in British waters. Three of them only interest the angler, for the others are too small to give sport.

Ballan wrasse (Labrus bergylta)
Colour varies considerably, being green, brown, red, or mixtures of these colours. Skin of sides is sometimes marbled. Record, 7 lb 10 oz 15 dm.

Corkwing wrasse (L. melops)

Highly coloured in green, brown, orange and red. The pre-opercular bone (Fig 76) is serrated. In other wrasse it is smooth. Record, 7¼ oz.

FIG 76. Corkwing Wrasse

Cuckoo wrasse (L. mixtus)

Both sexes basically red in colour. Males have vivid blue patches on head, and blue horizontal lines across gill covers and sides. Females have black blotches. Record, 1 lb 12½ oz.

Wrasse are not fish normally sought by keen sea anglers, but they are sporting fish on the right tackle, and afford a good deal of amusement on hot, calm days when other forms of light shore fishing are unlikely to succeed.

They are to be found in fissures and crevices of rocky coasts, and are most often caught on a rising tide.

Almost any tackle will catch wrasse – I have even seen wire traces used – but for sport it is necessary to use light tackle, even if one loses a hook or two to wrasse who reach their holes in the rocks. I use a long light rod, with a 7 lb line, 5 lb trace and 2 dram lead, with a roach float just buoyant enough to carry the weight. Wrasse make determined attempts to reach the rock crevices in which they live, but it is often possible to prevent this, and if a hooked wrasse is not too heavily handled at the beginning, it may not even try to escape until it has used up much of its energy.

If wrasse have to be hauled up several feet from the surface of the water stronger tackle must be used.

Wrasse are edible, but they are well down the list of tasty fish, and unless they are required for food, they should be returned to the water alive. They are quite harmless and it is senseless to kill them needlessly.

For many years the ballan wrasse record stood at 12¾ lb. There are doubts about this fish and the official record is 7 lb 10 oz 15 dm.

CHAPTER 10

Sea Anglers' Encyclopedia

Abyss The deeps beyond the Continental Shelf.

Algae Collective term for seaweeds and other marine plants.

Anadromous fish Fish which migrate from salt to freshwater to spawn, e.g. salmon.

Antenna A sensatory organ appearing in pairs on the heads of some crustaceans, e.g. prawns, lobsters.

Anterior In relation to fish, towards the head. Thus the anterior dorsal fin of a fish is that nearest the head.

Armed Bullhead (*Agonus cataphractus*) A small fish common on all coasts of the British Isles in the summer months. It migrates to deeper water in winter. (Fig 77.)

FIG 77. Armed Bullhead

Backing Old, or less expensive line, wound on a reel before the main reel line is attached. It serves to increase the diameter of the drum for recovery purposes, and is useful if an unexpectedly big fish is hooked. Unless it is absolutely necessary, on account of expense, to use backing, it is better in sea fishing to use thoroughly trustworthy line throughout. Backing should be spliced to the main line, not knotted.

Backlash See *Over-run.*

Balsa wood A wood with great buoyancy, suitable for making floats. Scrap pieces sufficient for this purpose can often be bought in the shops which cater for amateur model makers.

Barbel (1) Barbels are the sensitive feelers which grow from the heads of certain fish (eg cod). Their functions are not yet fully known, but some barbels are equipped with taste buds. (2) A freshwater fish.

Basking shark Basking sharks are not uncommon around the coasts. They are plankton feeders, and quite harmless. As they attain a length of more than 20 ft it is not always easy to believe they are harmless when one of them approaches a small open boat.

Billet A Scottish and north-country name for young coalfish. In other areas it is applied to coalfish of any size, and in others it may include pollack.

Bird's nest A slang name given to the often inextricable tangle which arises from over-runs (which see).

Bivalve A creature with two hinged shells, e.g. oyster, mussel, razor-fish.

Blenny Several species of these small fish are found in our coastal waters. They can be distinguished as a group by the position of the ventral fins, which are well forward, almost under the jaw. (Fig 78.)

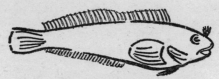

FIG 78. Typical Blenny
Note small tail fin and flattened 'forehead'

Blind hook An eyeless hook.

Blockan Coalfish (Northern Ireland).

Boar Fish (*Capros aper*) Known also as the cuckoo fish or 'Zulu'. Common in deep water off the south-west coasts. Similar to the John Dory (Fig 62) but lacking the black spot and the extended filaments of the dorsal fin.

Brake An arrangement on a reel to govern the speed at which line can be taken off. In some reels the brake is built into the mechanism. In others it is a device by which pressure is put on the rim of the reel or on the line itself.

Brit The young of herrings, sprats and pilchards. So many fish live on brit that the knowledge of where brit shoals swim is an important part of the sea angler's aids to success.

British Conger Club A club whose aims are to foster and develop interest in conger fishing throughout the country and to improve the techniques used in conger fishing. It is an active body with a considerable membership. There are several regional officers. Particulars can be obtained from the Hon Secretary, Mr R. Quest, 5 Hill Crest, Mannamead, Plymouth, Devon.

British Record (rod-caught) Fish Committee The body responsible for deciding on the validity of the claims for record fish, both marine and freshwater. Its address is 12 Queen St, Peterborough, PET 1PJ, England. Tel Peterborough 4084. (*See* Records, British *and* Records, Claiming, British.)

BSAS The British Sea Anglers' Society was founded in 1893 to promote the interests of sea anglers and all that remotely concerned them. In this it was successful, and the work carried out by the society is beyond all praise. Its members were interested in both the practical and scientific aspects of fishing and fish, and many world-renowned anglers and famous scientists spoke at its periodic meetings. Its journal, *The British Sea Anglers' Society Quarterly*, contained a wealth of information and material, some of which could with advantage to all be collated and published today. Its headquarters were in Fetter Lane, in the City, and the records of the society were kept there. The building, which also housed the society's museum, was completely destroyed by enemy action during the war and the society, to the regret of all sea anglers who knew it before the war, has faded out of existence.

Bulter A long line, armed at intervals with baited hooks on snoods. It can be set on shore at low tide or, weighted and buoyed, lowered from a boat.

Buoys Navigational buoys are useful aids to finding fishing marks, but they can also give other useful information. Deep water channels used by shipping are marked by Starboard Hand Buoys on the starboard, or right-hand side of a ship approaching the harbour. These are conical and black or black and white chequered.

Port Hand Buoys are moored on the opposite side of the channel. They are can-shaped and flat-topped, and are red and usually chequered.

Middle Ground Buoys mark shallow water in an otherwise navigable channel. They are spherical, and are usually painted in horizontal stripes, white alternating with some other colour.

Wreck buoys have the word 'wreck' on them. Fishing is nearly always profitable over old wrecks, and is well worth trying over new ones.

Burglar alarms Slang term applied to the bells which bottom anglers sometimes fix to their rods to indicate bites.

Butcher A heavy lead implement, armed with two or more hooks, used by commercial fishermen to foul-hook cod.

Carapace A hard shield covering the back of certain crustaceans, eg crabs.

Cartilaginous fish Fish in which cartilage takes the place of bones. Sharks, dogfishes, skates and rays are among the cartilaginous fish.

Catadromous fish Fish which migrate from freshwater to saltwater to spawn, e.g. eels.

Catfish See *Wolf fish.*

Charts Admiralty charts of the areas around the coast can be of the greatest interest and value to sea anglers, for they provide a vast amount of information about factors which affect fishing, the two most important of these being the nature of the sea-bed and the depth of the water.

The nature of the sea-bed is given by recognized abbreviations: cl = clay, fs = fine sand, g = gravel, gy s = grey sand, h = hard, m = mud, r = rock, s = sand, sh = shell, shin = shingle, sm (as a prefix) = small, st = stones, wd = weed, etc.

Depths are shown in fathoms and in exceptional (and indicated) conditions, in feet. On most charts they are in fathoms, depths close inshore being shown in fathoms and feet. Thus, the figures 2_4 indicate a depth of 2 fathoms 4 ft, or 16 ft. Since the tide affects the depth from hour to hour and from day to day, the depths shown are based on the level of mean low water springs.

Charts are prepared on many different scales, and it is possible to buy charts of estuaries and harbours much used by shipping on as large a scale as 27 in to one mile (Cowes harbour, for example). There are no standard scales for charts as there are for maps: all depends on the importance of the waters to seamen, their navigational dangers, and the area to be covered.

Charts are made for seamen and not for anglers, which is in some cases a little unfortunate for the latter. The most useful large-scale charts are prepared for well-used estuaries and harbours which are also well-used by anglers, where the best fishing marks have been known for generations. It is on the lonely and little-fished coasts that an angler may most need a chart, and it is here that charts are on a smaller and less useful scale – 1 in or $\frac{1}{2}$ in to a mile, for example, where there are no navigable inlets and the coast is of little interest to seamen. Nevertheless, charts on even these scales are helpful to anglers. On long stretches of monotonous coastline they show just where the water deepens by that trifle which might attract fish. They still show the nature of the bottom with great accuracy, so that an angler can elect to fish over sand, mud or rocks at his discretion.

These factors affect the shore angler as well as the boat fisherman, and both are equally interested in the speed (given in knots) and the direction (shown by arrows) of tidal currents, which enable them to choose millraces or sluggish streams according to their requirements.

Tidal races or rips are shown by wavy lines, and these are places carefully to be avoided by small boats.

The boat angler can find marks – either deeps or shoals – by aligning his position with some of the objects on shore. The land area of a chart shows few details, but whatever is marked is clearly to be seen and identified from the sea. He can fix his position with even greater accuracy if he has a compass, though it must be borne in mind that bearings taken with a compass are magnetic, while those on the chart are 'true', but the chart gives information necessary for converting one to the other. (See *Marks*, page 159.)

The standard price of charts, irrespective of size, is 83p. Charts for instructional purposes are also available for some districts at 5p each. They are reproductions of Admiralty Charts printed in black only on tough paper, are not corrected, and are sold only on the understanding that they are not to be used for navigation. They can often give an angler most of the information he needs. They are not fully listed in the catalogue and it will be necessary to find out if the area required is covered by this type of chart. A catalogue of Admiralty charts is available at 20p.

They can be obtained from agents in the principal ports and towns, or direct from the Superintendent of Issues, Admiralty Hydrographic Supplies Establishment, Creechbarrow House, Taunton, Somerset.

Check (1) The arrangement on a reel which enables the angler to put pressure on a fish. The check is usually actuated by a knob which, when pushed down, engages a springed tooth in a cog-wheel. (2) 'To check a fish.' This is an expression used to indicate that a fish has been stopped on its run, either by application of pressure through the check, brake or tension, or by refusing line.

Checkers School bass.

Clubs Sea angling clubs, societies and associations have been formed at many ports and resorts around the coasts, and in some inland towns, and many freshwater angling clubs have sea angling sections. These clubs have been adversely criticized on the grounds that they are interested only in promoting competitions. This may be true in a few cases, but most clubs exist for the promotion of sporting fishing, for the exchange of ideas, and for the mutual assistance of members. In places where the competition element is supreme, the remedy lies in the hands of those who dislike competition fishing. If they joined a club they would exercise some measure of control over its functions: if they remain aloof, the competition element may grow stronger.

There can be no doubt that membership of a fishing club encourages discussion, and newcomers can benefit by the experience of members who have fished the area for many years. Practical considerations also make club membership advantageous, for arrangements are usually made for boats and bait.

Cod murderer See *Butcher*.

Continental shelf The high submarine plateau on which the British Isles stand.

Copepods See *Plankton*.

Courge An elliptical shaped wicker-basket for live bait, particularly sand eels and prawns.

Crabs See also *Hermit Crabs*.

There are at least a dozen species of crabs found in British waters. Of these only the common shore crab, the edible crab and the spider crab have any interest for anglers. Common shore crabs have been dealt with under 'Baits'. They are useful as bait but they, and other species, are a considerable nuisance to anglers fishing with bottom baits.

Edible crabs are caught by anglers from time to time, but such captures are accidental.

Spider crabs are found off the south and south-west coasts, but they occasionally invade other areas. In 1951, all fishing, commercial and sporting, was made impossible in parts of the Bristol Channel by immense numbers of spider crabs.

Cuddy fly A lure similar to a mackerel fly, with white wings, but with a 'fuzzy' woollen body. It is used extensively for coalfish in Scottish waters.

Demersal That which sinks to the bottom or inhabits the lowest levels of water; e.g. demersal eggs are eggs which sink.

Depth recorder An instrument which records the depth immediately below the craft on which it is fitted. This can be read visually, and better models record the depth on a moving roll of paper marked off in fathoms. It is invaluable in finding banks, reefs, wrecks, etc, avoiding the time-wasting method of fixing marks by prominent objects on shore (see *Marks*).

Drag An adjustable device fitted to some reels, especially multiplying reels, to increase or decrease the strength of the pull necessary to draw off line. Used when playing a heavy fish.

Dragonet A common fish on all coasts and estuaries from February to August. It is rarely more than 6 in in length and has no food or sporting value, but should be handled with care on account of its spines. (Fig 79.)

Brown and yellow body with blue camouflage markings

FIG 79. Dragonet

Drop net A drop net is a useful item for anyone who fishes from piers or jetties. The normal rigid type is an awkward thing to carry about. Mrs D. Brace, of Deal, has designed a thoroughly practical drop net that, when collapsed, can be carried in a flat shopping bag only 14 in by 14 in.

The requirements are 70 in of plastic garden hose, $\frac{3}{4}$ in external diameter; about 80 in of pliant garden cane; four stout cords, of equal length (about 3 ft); a large piece of cork; lead weight; netting (with large attachment loops); and the main rope.

To assemble, thread the cane through the hose. Then thread the hose through the loops of the net and fit the spare length of cane into the hose, seeing that it fits tightly. Attach the four cords to the circumference, knot them to the main line (on which the cork has already been threaded), and secure the cork with a peg or some other stop to prevent its running up the line.

The two lengths of cane in the hose at the join should fit tightly: if they do not, a bicycle handle bar grip can be used to make a tight fit (inset to Fig 80). If this is necessary, the cane should be the same length as the hose.

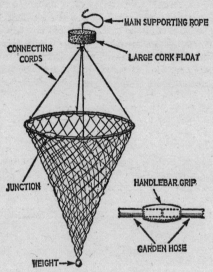

FIG 80. Collapsible drop net

Wide mesh netting can be used. If this is temporarily lined with shrimp netting the whole apparatus can be lowered to the bottom as a trap for prawns, hermit crabs and other useful baits. If this is done, attach a small plastic net bag to the knot below the cork, filled with scraps of fish offal.

Eel-grass Masses of long thin weed occurring near the low tide mark. Haunt of eels, prawns and weevers.

Father Lasher See *Sea Scorpion*.

Fathom   Six feet.

Festivals   Sea angling (or sea fishing) festivals were held in a few coastal resorts before the war, but their revival or inauguration in a long list of towns is a feature of post-war sea angling.

In some places festivals are organized by the local angling club; in others by the town councils; and in many cases by the two bodies working in conjunction. A very wide range of competition fishing is arranged, for beach, pier and boat fishermen. There are usually classes for different species of fish, biggest fish caught, aggregate weight caught, etc, and many cups, medals and prizes are offered. Festivals may last only over a weekend or for a week or more. In many places shore and boat festivals are held at different times.

Fish breeding   Experiments in the artificial hatching of sea fish have been carried on for many years, but in this country it has not attained measurable proportions. In the United States a large number of hatchery-bred fish and lobsters are released annually.

Foul ground   Ground on which an anchor, a net or a fisherman's tackle is likely to be caught up.

Foul hooked   A fish is said to be foul hooked when the hook is lodged in some part of it other than the mouth or jaws.

Gobies   Several species of gobies are found in British waters, but as the largest of them do not exceed 5 in in length they are of no interest to anglers. (Fig 81.)

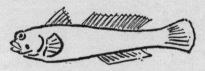

FIG 81. Typical Goby
Note protruding eye and thick upper lip

Ground fishing   Bottom fishing.

Gut   (1) Natural silkworm gut was at one time used for traces. It has now been generally superseded by monofilament in sea angling, though in freshwater angling some fishermen still prefer gut. (2) A narrow channel between rocks or sandbanks through which the tide races.

Hermit crabs   Hermit crabs inhabit the discarded shells of other creatures, particularly whelks. They are good bait. A species of ragworm (*Nereis furcata*) is sometimes found in the top of a hermit crab's shell. This is also good bait.

Hybrids Natural crosses between different species of fresh-water fish are not uncommon. Travis Jenkins states that 'sea-fish rarely or never form hybrids'.

Insurance Several insurance companies issue policies specially designed for anglers, for premiums of about £1 a year. They insure an angler's rods and tackle against loss and damage, and the angler himself against personal injury or death, but their most valuable feature is their third-party risk coverage.

Minor accidents are of frequent occurrence in sea angling, and comparatively serious ones occur from time to time. Substantial damages are awarded in the Courts for injury, and if an angler were unfortunate enough to disfigure or blind someone when casting, the damages awarded the injured person might be financially crippling, unless covered by insurance.

International Game Fish Association The IGFA adjudicates on claims for world record marine game fish. Periodically it issues lists of game fish records under the schedules 'all tackle', 130 lb, 80 lb, 50 lb, 30 lb, 20 lb and 12 lb lines. Separate record lists are maintained under each head for women.

Address: IGFA, 2190 SE 17th Street, Fort Lauderdale, Florida 33316, USA.

Claims should be accompanied by supporting evidence, clear photographs and, in the case of sharks, by some of the teeth. Claims for sharks should be made through the Shark Angling Club of Great Britain and for other species through the British Record (rod caught) Fish Committee.

Species of fish on the IGFA's list likely to be caught in British waters are:

Species	All tackle record	Place and date of capture	
Coalfish*	43 lb	New Jersey	1964
Cod	78¼ lb	Massachusetts Bay	1966
Blue shark	410 lb	„ „	1960
Mako shark	1,000 lb	Mayor Island, New Zealand	1943
Porbeagle shark	400½ lb	Fire Island, New York	1965
Thresher shark	922 lb	Bay of Islands, New Zealand	1937

* Known as pollack in USA. (*Gadus virens* Linn: USA. *Pollachius virens*).

Jardine leads See Spiral leads, under *Tackle*.

Joey West country name for small mackerel.

Killick Technically, a small anchor, but the name is often applied to a stone used as an anchor.

Kirby bend Term applied to hooks with a particular bend. (See Figs 12 and 14.)

Knock The name given to the tap or jolt which an angler feels through the rod when a fish takes or strikes the bait.

Lampern, Lamprey The smaller of these eel-like creatures are good baits for whiffing, and for spinning for bass and mackerel. They can also be used in the same ways as sand eels. They are found under stones in brackish and fresh water, but are now scarce. Tons of lampreys were exported to Holland annually in the eighteenth and nineteenth centuries, where they were used by fishermen as bait for turbot. Their increasing scarcity later raised their price to a level too high for this trade.

Last, Lask Strips of skin cut from shiny fish (e.g. mackerel) and used as lures on spinning, trailing or drift-line tackle. (See page 73.)

Laternal line A line, visible on most species of fishes, running along the sides of the body from head to tail fin. The scales along the lateral line cover sensory organs, the functions of which are not yet fully understood.

Launce Greater sand eel.

Leader An American term used by both freshwater and sea anglers for the cast or trace connecting hook to line. It is being used increasingly in this country.

Lee tide A tide running in the same direction as the wind.

Limerick bend Term applied to hooks with a particular bend.

Lobsters Three species of lobster are occasionally caught by fortunate anglers. These are the common lobster; the squat lobster and the spiny lobster. The squat lobster is similar in general appearance to the common lobster, but it has a short tail. The spiny lobster is known popularly as the crawfish (sometimes pronounced 'crayfish'). Its general shape is that of the common lobster, but it has very small, weak claws, and its antennae are very long.

Lobworm A term applied by some commercial fishermen to lugworms. It is not to be confused, in this sense, with the earthworm of that name, used by freshwater anglers, and occasionally by sea anglers for wrasse and flounders.

Marks Fishing marks are positions where fish are known to

congregate or pass. In inshore waters and in estuaries their position can often be fixed by some nearby object – e.g. 20 yds south of a particular buoy. Where, in the open sea, no such aids exist, a mark can be fixed by taking two lines on prominent objects ashore. (Fig 82.)

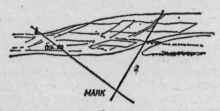

FIG 82. 1. House and spire (308 degrees true). 2. End of bridge and corner of field (33 degrees true)

In actual practice it is not often that such clear-cut natural objects present themselves, and it is necessary to be content with rather indefinite points like the corner of a field or a patch of gorse.

On this account, it is better to use a compass, and to take bearings on two prominent objects. These are taken from the boat when over the mark, and jotted down. If it is desired to find a place at sea which has been noted from the chart, the true bearings of the chart readings must be converted to magnetic bearings before they can be used with the compass. The local variation is shown on the chart.

Monofilament A nylon product which looks like gut. It can be obtained in lengths up to 500 yds and in breaking strains from 1 lb to 100 lb.

Mudworm Ragworm.

National Anglers' Council A Council made up of groups, associations and individual members with angling interests. It represents all aspects of sport fishing, game, coarse and sea and actively seeks to promote in every possible way the welfare of the sport. It is a truly national body and is thus in a position to make representations to the Minister of Sport and the Minister of Agriculture, Food and Fisheries. There is a sea-angling sub-committee.

Address: National Anglers' Council, 12 Queen St, Peterborough, PET 1PJ, England. Tel Peterborough 4084.

NEFSA The North-Eastern Federation of Sea Anglers was

founded in 1950. It is devoted to the interests of sea angling clubs on the north-east and east coasts. Its headquarters is at South Shields.

Nekton   Free swimming forms of very small aquatic creatures, as distinct from plankton which is incapable of willed direction.

NFSA   The National Federation of Sea Anglers stands at the head of the sea fishing organizations in this country. A large number of clubs and societies are affiliated to it. Unattached anglers may join as personal members. The NFSA promotes the interests of sea anglers, and has standardized rules for competition fishing.

Nylon   Monofilament lines are often referred to as nylon lines. Braided nylon lines have the appearance of silk lines.

Oil pollution of the sea   The National Anglers' Council, through its Sea Angling Sub-Committee, asks sea anglers to assist in observing oil pollution at sea.

The Board of Trade have informed the Council that they would welcome the help of sea anglers who observe a discharge of oil from a vessel or a substantial patch of floating oil, in reporting the facts as soon as possible to the nearest station of HM Coastguard. The recommended procedure for sea anglers is to advise the nearest Coastguard of the following details:

1. The date and time the pollution was observed.
2. The position, nature and extent of the oil slick.
3. The direction and speed of the wind and the state of the sea.
4. Where a vessel is seen to be discharging oil, the name and nationality of the vessel should be taken or, failing this, any distinctive or descriptive markings that would help to identify the vessel.
5. The vessel's estimated course and speed.

If possible, photographs of ships' discharges should show the vessel's name or markings, that oil was in the wake of the vessel and that there was no oil lying directly ahead of the vessel.

Photographs alone are not sufficient evidence that oil and not some other substance was discharged. Witnesses should therefore be ready to give evidence to show why they were convinced that the pollution was caused by oil. The most conclusive evidence would be a sample of the pollution taken from the surface of the sea and sealed in a container about the size of a jam jar or rather larger.

Every report is investigated and the offender is prosecuted if there is sufficient evidence and the ship is British or the offence occurred within UK territorial waters. Foreign ships, if the offence occurs outside UK territorial waters, are reported to their governments who, if they are members of the International Convention, have agreed to take similar action.

The Board of Trade are responsible for enforcing the Oil in Navigable Waters Acts in areas outside harbour limits. Reports of ships seen to be discharging oil within harbour waters should be sent to the harbour authority, which has the primary responsibility for enforcing the Acts within harbour limits.

Otoliths Otoliths are hard, bone-like, flat discs, found in the heads of bony fishes. They are formed by a concretion of carbonate of lime, and they are not attached to the structure of the skull. Their interest to anglers lies in the fact that the age of a fish can be determined by its otoliths more accurately than by scale reading.

Overfall A turbulent area of water with short breaking waves caused by a strong current or tide passing over a ridge, bar or shoal, or by the meeting of tides. A race.

Overhead cast A cast in which the rod tip comes from behind the back vertically over the head. It is more accurate than the side cast, and is essential when one is fishing from a crowded pier.

Over-run When a cast is made, the reel is 'free', and as the weight flies out, line is taken off the reel at high speed. The speed of the weight slows down but, unless there is an automatic drag, the speed of the reel does not. It must be slowed at the right time with the thumb or fingertips. If this is not done, the reel casts off line which is not being taken up by the weight, and at the same time reels some of it back on the drum in the wrong direction. The result is a tangle which usually takes some time to sort out. If one is fishing from a beach, a simple over-run may sometimes be cured by walking back up the beach, leaving the reel free.

Peelers or peeler crabs Shore crabs about to shed their shells.

Pelagic That which floats or inhabits the surface levels of the water, e.g. pelagic eggs are floating eggs.

Phytoplankton   See *Plankton*.

Plankton   Plankton is the name given to myriads of tiny particles, vegetable or animal, which float in the sea. Vegetable
plankton (phytoplankton) consists of extremely minute plants
which subsist on salts contained in the water. Animal plankton
(zooplankton) contains hundreds of species of minute animal
life, including, in spring and summer, larval forms of many
creatures of the tide flats, e.g. mussels. Zooplankton feeds on
salts, phytoplankton, and other zooplankton. Copepods con-
stitute a large proportion of zooplankton, and each contains a
minute quantity of oil.

Plankton plays an important part in the life of all sea
creatures, for directly or indirectly their continued existence
depends on it. Some fish, such as herrings and pilchards, feed
in the main directly on plankton, particularly copepods, which
accounts for the rich oily nature of these fish. Other fish, such
as cod and halibut, feed on small fish which have fed on
plankton, and the oil is then concentrated in the livers of the
fish and not in the flesh.

Plankton cannot achieve direction of its own volition, but
must drift with the currents, and its vertical movements are
governed by light. On bright days plankton sinks out of the
direct light, but on dull days it can be found at or near the
surface.

Pogge   See *Armed bullhead*.

Pollack worm   Ragworm.

Posterior   In relation to fish, towards the tail. The posterior
dorsal fin of a fish is that nearest the tail fin.

Predatory   The term 'predatory fish' is applied to those which
eat other fish. There are very few species of sea fish which
are not wholly or partially predatory.

Priest   A blunt instrument for killing fish.

Pumping   'Pumping a fish' describes the action taken by an
angler to get a heavy, slow swimming fish (skate, ray, conger,
etc) to the surface. The rod is held horizontally over the gunwale of the boat and, without giving line, raised to an angle of
about 45 degrees. It is then lowered quickly to the horizontal
position, while the line gained is wound on the reel. This
process is repeated until the fish comes to the surface.

Race   An area of disturbed water, usually caused by meeting
tides or currents. See also *Overfall*.

Railing   Trailing a bait or lure behind a sailing boat, as distinct

from whiffing, where the bait is towed behind a rowing boat.
Rays (1) A group of fishes. (2) The bone-like framework on which fins are built. These are soft and can be bent. Where they are hard they are called spines.

Records (British) The British Record (rod-caught) Fish Committee is the body responsible for investigating records. It admits for consideration only fish caught off Great Britain and Northern Ireland, (including the Isle of Man, the Scilly Islands and the Channel Islands) within the 12-mile limit so the official list of records shown below does not include fish caught in waters off the Republic of Ireland. (See *Records (Irish)*.)

BRITISH RECORD FISH LIST

Recognized as at January 1973

Species	Weight lb	oz	dm	Date	Captor and Location
Allis shad	3	4	8	1964	B. H. Sloane, Torquay
Angler fish	74	8	—	1972	J. J. McVicar, SW Eddystone
Argentine	—	4	1	1972	T. G. Allan, Firth of Clyde
Bass	18	2	—	1943	F. C. Borley, Felixstowe
Blenny, tompot	—	2	6	1972	M. S. Marriott, off Elizabeth Castle Breakwater, Jersey
Blenny, viviparous	—	6	10	1971	W. Atkins, Rhu (Garetoch), Scotland
Bluemouth	—	11	12	1970	A. J. Williamson, Lunning Head, Scotland
Bogues	1	9	14	1968	Mrs S. O'Brien, Sorel Point, Jersey
Bream, black (old wife)	6	1	—	1969	F. W. Richards, off the Skerries
gilthead	1	8	—	1970	A. J. Pratt, Hayle Basin, Cornwall
Ray's	7	15	12	1967	G. Walker, Hartlepool
red	7	8	—	1925	A. F. Bell, Fowey
Brill	16	—	—	1950	A. H. Fisher, Isle of Man
Bull huss	21	3	—	1955	J. Holmes, Looe
Catfish	9	12	—	1971	A. Miller, off Stonehaven, Scotland
Coalfish (saithe, coley)	27	12	8	1972	J. J. McVicar, off Eddystone Light
Cod	53	—	—	1972	G. Martin, Start Point, Devon
Comber	1	—	8	1972	D. J. McClary, off Wolf Rock Lighthouse area
Common skate	226	8	—	1970	R. S. Macpherson, Duny Voe, Shetland
Common topknot	—	11	2	1972	P. Andrews, St Catherine, Jersey

Species	Weight lb	oz	dm	Date	Captor and Location
Conger	92	13	—	1970	P. H. Ascott, Torquay, Devon
Dab	2	10	12	1968	A. B. Hare, The Skerries
Dogfish, lesser spotted	4	8	—	1969	J. Beattie, off Ayr Pier
spur	20	3	—	1972	J. Newman, South of Needles Lighthouse
Dragonet	—	3	6	1972	K. Pedder, off McInroy's Point, Gourock, Scotland
File fish	2	—	1	1970	J. H. Rault, St Aubins Bay, Jersey
Flounder	5	11	8	1956	A. G. L. Cobbledick, Fowey
Forkboard, greater	4	11	4	1969	Miss M. Woodgate, Falmouth Bay
lesser	—	14	4	1968	G. E. Severs, Seaham Harbour
Garfish	2	13	14	1971	Master Stephen Claeskens, off Newton Ferrers, Devon
Greater weever	2	4	—	1927	P. Ainslie, Brighton
Gurnard, grey	1	10	—	1971	D. Cameron-McIntosh, Brodick Bay, Isle of Arran
red	3	2	—	1970	W. S. Blunn, off Stoke, Nr Plymouth
streaked	1	6	8	1971	H. Livingstone Smith, Loch Goil, Firth of Clyde
Gurnard (tubfish, yellow)	11	7	4	1952	C. W. King, Wallasey
Haddock	10	12	—	1972	A. H. Hill, off Looe, Cornwall
Haddock, Norway	—	14	12	1972	M. J. Flaws, off Bressay, Scotland
Hake	25	5	8	1962	H. W. Steele, Belfast Lough
Halibut	161	12	—	1968	W. E. Knight, Orkney
Herring	—	13	—	1971	W. Strachan, Millport Bay, Scotland
John Dory (St Peter's fish)	10	12	—	1963	B. L. Perry, Porthallow
Ling	45	—	—	1912	H. C. Nicholl, Penzance
Lumpsucker (sea hen)	14	3	—	1970	W. J. Burgess, off Felixstowe Beach
Mackerel	5	6	8	1969	S. Beasley, north of Eddystone Light
Megrim (sail, fluke, whiff)	3	10	—	1966	D. Diccicco, Ullapool
Monk fish (angel ray)	66	—	—	1965	G. C. Chalk, Shoreham
Mullet, golden grey	1	11	8	1969	H. C. L. Pike, Braye Bay, Alderney
red	3	10	—	1967	J. E. Martel, Guernsey
thick lipped grey	10	1	—	1952	P. C. Libby, Portland
thin lipped	1	13	8	1971	D. A. Morgan, off Lancing Beach
Pelamid (bonito)	8	13	4	1969	J. Parnell, Torbay
Plaice	7	15	—	1964	I. B. Brodie, Salcombe
Pollack	25	—	—	1972	R. J. Hosking, off Eddystone Light
Poor cod	—	10	—	1970	D. E. Clark, off Gourock, Scotland
Poutassou	—	9	8	1972	N. Hunt, off Falmouth
Pouting (bib, pout)	5	8	—	1969	R. S. Armstrong, off Berry Head

Species	Weight lb oz dm	Date	Captor and Location
Ray, blonde	35 9 —	1970	A. J. Pearce, The Shambles
bottle nosed	76 — —	1970	R. Bulpitt, off the Needles, Isle of Wight
cuckoo	5 — —	1968	N. C. McLean, Isle of Arran
eagle	52 8 —	1972	R. J. Smith, off Nab Tower, Isle of Wight
electric	61 12 —	1972	R. Moate, off Skerries Bank
sandy	5 10 8	1969	J. Boyd, Gourock, Scotland
small-eyed	13 11 8	1971	H. T. Pout, Bolt Tail, Devon
spotted	16 3 —	1970	E.Lockwood,Lerwick, Shetland
sting	59 — —	1952	J. M. Buckley, Clacton
thornback	38 — —	1935	J. Patterson, Rustington
undulate	19 6 13	1970	L. R. LePage, Amfrocque, Bank, Herm CI
Red band fish	— 2 10	1972	D. R. Allard, Portland Harbour
Rockling, three bearded	2 14 4	1972	S. F. Bealing, Poole Bay, Dorset
five bearded	— 9 4	1968	P. R. Windsor, Lancing Beach
Scad (horse mackerel)	3 4 8	1971	D. O. Cooke, off Mewstone, Plymouth, Devon
Scorpion, short spined			
sea	2 — —	1971	A. Holt, Gourock, Scotland
Shark, blue	218 — —	1959	N. Sutcliffe, Looe
mako	500 — —	1971	Mrs J. M. Yallop, off Eddystone Light
porbeagle	430 — —	1969	D. Bougourd, Jersey
thresher	280 — —	1933	H. A. Kelly, Dungeness
Smooth hound,			
(mustelus)	28 — —	1969	A. T. Chilvers, Heacham
(asterias)	16 6 —	1972	B. E. Hurdle, Herne Bay, Kent
Sole	4 1 14	1967	R. A. Austin, Guernsey
Sole, lemon	2 2 15	1971	D. R. Duke, Victoria Pier, Douglas, Isle of Man
Spanish mackerel	1 — 6	1972	P. Jones, off Guernsey
Sunfish	60 — —	1969	K. Parsons, off Porthcawl
Tope	74 11 —	1964	A. B. Harries, Caldy Island
Torsk	12 1 —	1968	D. Pottinger, Shetland
Tunny	851 — —	1933	L. Mitchell Henry, Whitby
Turbot	31 4 —	1972	Master Paul Hutchings, off Eddystone Light
Twaite shad	{ 3 2 —	1949	T. Hayward, Deal
	3 2 —	1954	S. Jenkins, Torbay
Witch	1 2 13	1967	T. J. Barathy, Colwyn Bay
Whiting	6 3 3	1971	Mrs R. Barrett, off Rame Head, Cornwall
Wrasse, ballan	7 10 15	1970	B. K. Lawrence, off Trevose Head, Cornwall
corkwing	— 7 4	1972	B. R. Steerment, Chesil Beach, Portland
cuckoo	1 12 8	1972	L. C. LeCras, off Guernsey

Records, *claiming British*

1. Claims must be made in writing to the Secretary, British
Record (rod-caught) Fish Committee, 12 Queen St, Peterborough, PET 1PJ, England. Tel Peterborough 4084 stating:
   (i) the species of fish and the weight;

(ii) the date and place of capture, and the tackle used; and

(iii) the names and addresses of reliable witnesses both as to the capture by the claimant and the weight.

If there are no witnesses to the capture available, the claimant must verify his claim by affidavit.

2. No claim can be accepted unless the Committee is satisfied as to species, method of capture and weight. The Committee reserves the right to reject any claim if not satisfied on any matter which the Committee may think in the particular circumstances to be material.

3. *Identification of Species* (*a*) To ensure correct identification, it is essential that claimants should retain the fish and immediately contact the Secretary of the Committee who will advise as to production of the fish for inspection on behalf of the Committee.

(*b*) All carriage costs incurred in production of the fish for inspection by the Committee (if this is required) must be borne by the claimant.

4. *Method of Capture* Claims can only be accepted in respect of fish which are caught by fair angling.

5. *Weight* (*a*) The fish must be weighed as soon as possible on scales or steelyards which can be tested on behalf of the Committee.

(*b*) The weight must be verified by two independent witnesses who should not be relations of the claimant or a member of his club or party.

6. Claims can be made for species not included in the Committee's Record Fish List.

7. The Committee will issue at least once a year its list of British Record (rod-caught) Fish for the guidance of freshwater and salt-water anglers.

8. No fish caught out of season, that is caught at any time other than during a statutory open season or that laid down by byelaw, shall be accepted as a new record.

9. A fish for which a record is claimed must be normal and not suffering from any disease by which its weight would be enhanced.

10. *Photographs* If permission has been granted to submit photographs these must be large and in focus, taken against a plain background with fins erect so that they can be counted.

The picture should include a rule or some object (e.g. a cigarette packet) of known size.

11. *Preserving* Medium-sized fish can be preserved for considerable periods by refrigeration or by immersion in formalin. If a large refrigerator is available the fish should be deep frozen but if it is to be sent by post or rail it is best immersed in a solution of one tablespoon of formalin (40 per cent solution of formaldehyde) to a pint of water. For dispatch the fish should be wrapped in cloth soaked in this solution and placed in a plastic bag.

The fish should be weighed as soon as possible after capture and before being placed in preserving liquids.

The claimant should contact the Committee Secretary by telephone, telegram or letter as soon as possible after the capture of the fish. Advice will then be given concerning preservation and identification.

Records (Irish) Irish records are maintained by the Irish Specimen Fish Committee, Bolnagowan, Mobhi Boreen, Glasnevin, Dublin 9, to whom claims should be submitted. The records shown below are those recognized by that Committee at December 1972.

IRISH RECORD FISH LIST

December 1972

Species	Weight lb oz dm	Date	Captor and Locality
Angler fish	71 8 —	1964	M. Fitzgerald, Cork Harbour
Bass	16 6 —	1972	J. McClelland, Causeway Coast
Coalfish	24 7 —	1967	J. E. Hornibrook, Kinsale
Cod	42 — —	1921	I. L. Stewart, Ballycotton
Conger	72 — —	1914	J. Green, Valentia
Dab	1 12 8	1963	I. V. Kerr, Kinsale
Dogfish, greater spotted	19 12 —	1969	M. Courage, Bray
lesser spotted	open		
spur	16 4 —	1969	C. McIvor, Strangford Lough
Flounder	4 3 —	1963	J. L. McMonagle, Killala Bay
Garfish	3 10 4	1967	E. G. Bazzard, Kinsale
Gurnard, grey	3 1 —	1967	B. Walsh, Rosslare Bay
red	3 9 8	1969	J. Prescott, Belmullet
tub	10 8 —	1970	C. Gammon, Belmullet
Haddock	10 13 8	1964	F. A. E. Bull, Kinsale
Hake	25 5 8	1962	H. W. Steele, Belfast Lough
Halibut	156 — —	1972	F. Brogan, Belmullet
John Dory	7 1 —	1970	S. Morrow, Tory Island, Co Donegal
Ling	46 8 —	1965	A. J. C. Bull, Kinsale

Species	Weight lb oz dm	Date	Captor and Locality
Mackerel	3 8 —	1972	R. Ryan, Clogherhead Pier, Co Louth
Monkfish	69 — —	1958	M. Fuchs, Clew Bay, Westport
Mullet, grey	7 10 —	1972	K. Boyle, Killybegs Pier
Plaice	7 — —	1964	E. Yemen, Portrush
Pollack	19 3 —	1904	J. N. Hearne, Ballycotton
Pouting	4 10 —	1937	W. G. Pales, Ballycotton
Ray, blonde	36 8 —	1964	D. Minchin, Cork Harbour
cuckoo	5 6 —	1971	K. Derbyshire, Causeway Coast
homelyn	6 15 —	1972	J. S. Mullan, Causeway Coast
sting	46 8 —	1961	P. Charlton, Rosslare Strand
thornback	37 — —	1961	M. J. Fitzgerald, Ling Rock, Kinsale
undulate	16 8 8	1972	I. Kestle, Tralee Bay
Red sea bream	9 6 —	1963	P. Maguire, Valentia
Shark, blue	206 — —	1959	J. McMonagle, Achill Head
porbeagle	365 — —	1932	Dr O'D. Browne, Keem Bay, Achill
Skate, common	221 — —	1913	T. Tucker, Ballycotton
white	165 — —	1966	J. Stack, Inniscannon, Clew Bay
Tope	60 12 —	1968	C. McIvor, Strangford Lough
Turbot	26 8 —	1915	J. F. Eldridge, Valentia
Whiting	4 8 8	1969	E. Boyle, Kinsale

The Committee is prepared to consider claims for species of fish other than those listed above.

Reel line   The line on the reel. Also called the running line.

Rip   A rip or tide-rip is an area of fast flowing water, usually caused when an ebb or flood tide is restricted in its passage by rocks or shoals. See also *Race* and *Overfall*. Races, rips and overfalls are marked on charts, and should be avoided. Small ones are not marked, and it is wise to avoid broken water even if there is no indication of a race, etc, on the chart.

Rod socket   A socket in which the butt end of the rod is placed when an angler is fishing for big fish – tunny, halibut and so on. It can be contained in a belt worn by the angler (with a quick release attachment), or fitted to the seat of the boat or fishing chair.

Running line   The main line wound on the reel. It is referred to throughout this book as the reel line.

Sandworm   Lugworm.

School bass   Bass up to 1 lb or 1½ lb in weight. These usually remain inshore during the winter months.

Scutes   Hard bony plates which take the place of scales on some fishes, e.g. sturgeons, sticklebacks.

Sea angling festivals   See *Festivals*.

Sea scorpion The short spined sea scorpion (*Cottus scorpius*) is occasionally caught among rocks on the west coast. It is generally brown and white in colour. Though not actively poisonous, it is a mass of spines and sharp plates, and should not be handled. (Fig 83.)

Fig 83. Sea scorpion

Sea fishing festivals See *Festivals*.

Sea trout Sea trout are occasionally encountered by anglers in estuaries, where they may be caught on fly, spinner or bait. They are considered freshwater fish as far as angling is concerned, and a score of books are devoted entirely to methods of catching them.

Seaweed The angler's interests in seaweed are threefold. It can be a trap for his end tackle. After a gale heavy masses of it may float around and catch up on his line. On the credit side is the fact that it provides a home and food for countless small creatures and many fish which attract predators such as pollack.

   The various species of seaweed (called 'wrack') have definite zones. The highest level holds channelled wrack, with deeply grooved fronds. Then, in order, come flat wrack, bladder wrack and knotted wrack, all with self-explanatory names. At the extreme edge of the tidal zone serrated wrack can be seen at low spring tides. Other species grow beyond the tide line and are seen only when torn adrift and cast up on shore by a gale. Oarweed is a common example, whose long, broad, crinkly brown fronds often litter a beach for miles.

Shoal bass School bass.

Side cast A cast in which the rod tip moves in a nearly horizontal plane from the back of the body to the front.

Sile Brit.

Size limits On 1 August 1948, the Sea Fishing Industry (Immature Sea Fish) Order came into force. This lays down that the landing and sale of fish of less than the following sizes is prohibited:

	Length in inches		Length in inches
Brill	12	Megrims	10
Cod	12	Plaice	10
Dabs	8	Soles	9½
Haddock	11	Turbot	12
Hake	12	Whitings	10
Lemon Soles	10	Witches	11½

'Any person landing, selling, exposing or offering for sale, or having in his possession for the purpose of selling, any fish of the above descriptions of a smaller size than is stated above is liable to a fine not exceeding £50.'

At the time of the appearance of the Order and for some time after it, it was generally considered that its provisions did not apply to anglers. It has since been ruled in a Court of Law that the Order *does* apply to anyone fishing by any means for sport.

In addition to this Ministerial Order, local Sea Fisheries Committees have by-laws covering species of fish not mentioned in the Order, and anglers are advised to find out whether any such by-laws govern angling in their own areas.

The National Anglers' Council has petitioned the Ministry with a view to getting bass and mullet added to the list.

Slub Masses of drifting weed. These sometimes make any form of fishing impossible. (See *Weed.*)

Snood The length of line to which a hook is directly attached. In angling with a paternoster, hooks are attached by their snoods to the trace, or to the reel line where a trace is not used. Hundreds of hooks on snoods are tied to bulters, a mile or more long, used by professional fishermen.

Soft backs A term applied to shore crabs after they have shed their shells and before the new shell hardens.

Spiller See *Bulter.*

Spines Bony, pointed projections, found in the fins of some fish (e.g. the first dorsal fin of bass) in place of rays.

Spoon A spoon-shaped lure.

Steep-to A beach is said to be steep-to when it slopes quickly to deep water.

Sting fish See *Weever.*

Stop Any object on a line, such as a split shot or rubber loop, which prevents an object from passing beyond it, e.g. a stop above a sliding float to prevent its moving farther up the line; or a stop below a ledger weight to prevent its running down to the hook.

Storm signals When a gale is expected, storm signals are hoisted at most harbours. A triangular signal or a cone pointing downwards indicate a southerly gale, i.e. one blowing anywhere from SE through S to NW. The same signals with points uppermost indicates a northerly gale, i.e. one blowing anywhere from NW through N to SE.

On the appearance of these signals, anglers at sea should get back to harbour as quickly as possible.

Sturgeon Sturgeon are becoming increasingly scarce, but odd ones still ascend rivers to spawn. They are of little interest to anglers for they rarely take baits. They can grow to 6 ft and more.

Sun fish (Mola mola) A few of these large fish, weighing anything from 2 to 8 cwt, usually drift into British waters in the summer months. They are of little interest to anglers.

Tailer An instrument designed to grip fish by the tail, used instead of a gaff. A cord or wire loop tightens round the tail.

Tension Multiplying and fixed-spool reels are fitted with a control by which the tension (i.e. the weight of pull required to take off line) can be adjusted.

Tides An incoming tide is a flood tide, and is said to be 'making'. An outgoing tide is an ebb tide, or falling tide.

Tides are affected by the attraction of the moon and sun. At the period of new moon and full moon, both moon and sun pull in the same direction, with the result that tides ascend higher and recede farther than at other times. These are called tides or, simply, springs. They last for about $14\frac{1}{2}$ days in every lunar period, divided into two halves, each of about $3\frac{1}{2}$ days each side of new moon and full moon. A spring tide has no connection with spring, the season.

At the time of the first and third quarters of the moon, the sun exerts an attraction in a direction opposite to that of the moon, and tides do not rise so high or recede so far as at other times. They occur in the $3\frac{1}{2}$ days each side of the first quarter and third quarter moons, and are known as neap tides or neaps.

The highest and lowest springs coincide with the spring and autumn equinoxes (the third weeks of March and September respectively).

Flood and ebb tides last for roughly 6 hours 10 minutes. They do not increase or decrease steadily during this time. If the total rise or fall of tide is 12 ft it will rise or fall, in rough figures.

1 foot in the first hour	3 feet in the fourth hour
2 feet in the second hour	2 feet in the fifth hour
3 feet in the third hour	1 foot in the sixth hour

In addition to the differences in levels between spring and neap tides, both the time and height of a tide can be affected by a high wind, not necessarily blowing in the area affected. In extreme cases a wind can make a difference of an hour in time and as much as 2 ft increase or decrease in height.

Flood tides set very strongly into large bays into which no rivers run.

The times of high and low tide are displayed in some public place at most coastal towns, and published in the local papers. Extracts from tide tables to cover one area can be bought for a few pence. These usually show Greenwich Mean Time.

Tide tables Many newspapers and periodicals, notably those dealing with sea angling and yachting, publish in advance for the week or month the time of high tide at London Bridge. The conversion table which follows covers a representative selection of places in the British Isles. Before making the conversion note whether the London Bridge time is given in Greenwich Mean Time or Summer Time.

Tope Angling Club of Great Britain A club formed to promote the interests of tope anglers. Headquarters in Llandudno. (*See* page 210.)

Trace A length of gut, monofilament or wire connecting the reel line and the hook; or, in the case of paternoster tackle, the weight.

Trolling In sea angling, trolling describes a method of fishing by towing a bait or lure behind a moving boat. It is sometimes wrongly used in this sense in freshwater angling where, correctly, trolling consists of fishing a dead fish on the 'sink and draw' method.

Trot See *Bulter*.

Tubercle A wart-like growth, usually hard, found on some species of fish.

Univalve A creature with a single shell, e.g. a limpet.

TIDAL DIFFERENCES FROM LONDON BRIDGE

Add or subtract the following times to or from the London Bridge times.

Aberdeen	−0200	Largs	−0142
Aberystwyth	−0612	Leith	+0056
Arbroath	+0026	Littlehampton	−0238
Arran (Lamlash)	−0158	Llandudno	−0319
Ayr	−0512	Londonderry	−0541
Ballycotton	+0343	Looe	+0350
Banff	−0145	Lossiemouth	−0202
Bangor (North Wales)	−0305	Lowestoft	−0426
Barmouth	−0547	Lyme Regis	+0450
Barrow-in-Furness	−0233	Mablethorpe	+0418
Belfast	−0248	Margate	−0204
Berwick-on-Tweed	+0055	Menai Bridge	−0303
Bideford	+0400	Milford Haven	+0435
Blackpool	−0242	Montrose	+0040
Bognor Regis	−0238	Morecambe	−0237
Bo'ness (Firth of Forth)	+0110	Newlyn	+0308
Boston	+0448	Newquay	+0325
*Bournemouth	−0345	Oban	+0413
Bridlington	+0300	Orford Ness	−0251
Brighton	−0252	Paignton	+0435
Bude Haven	+0350	Penzance	+0308
Caernarvon	−0402	Peterhead	−0100
Cape Wrath	+0554	Plymouth	+0354
Cardiff	+0517	Porthcawl	+0435
Castletown	+0318	Portland	+0505
Clacton	−0211	Phwllheli Road	−0556
Cleethorpes	+0407	Ramsgate	−0222
*Cowes	−0228	Redcar	+0207
Cromer	+0510	Rhyl	−0307
Dartmouth	+0427	Rosslaire Harbour	+0418
Deal	−0232	Salcombe	+0405
Dornoch	−0150	Scarborough	+0245
Dover	−0242	Sidmouth	+0450
Dundee	+0110	Skegness	+0430
Dungeness	−0256	Southend	−0129
Dun Laoghaire	−0212	Southport	−0250
Eastbourne	−0252	Southsea	−0226
Exmouth	+0450	South Shields	+0148
Falmouth	+0330	Southwold	−0351
Felixstowe	−0218	Spurn Head	+0359
Filey Bay	+0247	Start Point	+0412
Fishguard	+0538	Sunderland	+0148
Folkestone	−0254	*Swanage	−0359
Fowey	+0348	Swansea	+0441
Gairloch	+0509	Teignmouth	+0432
Girvan	−0152	Tenby	+0421
Gorleston (Gt Yarmouth)	−0501	Torquay	+0435
Hartlepool	+0155	Valentia Harbour	+0250
Harwich	−0218	Ventnor	−0256
Hastings	−0247	Weston-super-Mare	+0459
Herne Bay	−0139	Weymouth	+0505
Holyhead	−0332	Whitby	+0219
Ilfracombe	+0415	Whitehaven	−0236
Inverness	−0140	Wigtown Bay	−0218
Irvine	−0152	Wick	−0230
King's Lynn	+0451	Worthing	−0238
Kyle of Lochalsh	+0509	Yarmouth (IOW)	−0233
Lamlash	−0158	Youghal	+0354

* — a stand of tide occurs for approximately two hours around high water.

Viviparous fish   Fish which give birth to living young, e.g. tope.
Weather tide   A tide running in a direction opposite to that of the wind.
Weed   On occasions, masses of seaweed, torn from their hold, drift with the tidal currents and make any form of fishing impossible. If paternoster or ledger lines are put down and left unattended for a few minutes when drifting weed is about, so much may collect on the line that a breakage occurs when an attempt is made to recover it. Even drift lining and float fishing are impossible in these circumstances. These drifting weed masses are sometimes called slub.
Weevers   The weever is a fish which every angler should learn to recognize at sight. The Lesser Weever (Fig 84) has poison glands at the bases of the grooved spines of the dorsal fin and the strong spines on the operculum. It is not likely to be more than 8 in long. A sting from a weever is an extremely painful business, though its effects can be much reduced if treatment from a doctor or at a chemist's can be quickly arranged. Failing this, some relief can be obtained by placing a tourniquet above the affected part, opening the wound, and squeez-

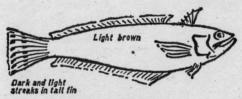

FIG 84. Lesser weever

ing out as much blood and venom as possible. The tourniquet should not be allowed to remain in place for more than fifteen minutes.

Weevers half bury themselves in the sand, and are sometimes trodden on by bathers. They are occasionally hooked, particularly by anglers fishing close to jetties and piers. They are often swept up in shrimp nets. The bather who steps on one is unlucky; the angler who gets stung can only be called careless, for nothing which comes out of the sea should be touched with bare hands until it has been identified. Do not pull a mass of weed off the hook before ensuring that it does not conceal a hooked weever.

The Greater Weever is not so common as the Lesser, and lives in deeper water. It, too, has poison glands. It is similar in structure to the Lesser Weever, but its body is mainly yellow.

Whiffing   Trailing a bait behind a boat, usually for mackerel.

Whitebait   Brit.

White cat   White worm.

White worm   A worm with a silver sheen, sometimes found in sand when lugworms are being sought. It grows to a length of 4 in and can be used as bait.

Wolf fish (*Anarhichas lupus*)   Also known as catfish and sea-cat. It is an ugly fish equipped with powerful teeth. It grows to a length of 4 ft and is common in the North Sea and English Channel. It is marketed, without the head and skin, as rock salmon. Very few have been taken by anglers. The British Museum guide to the fish gallery states that it has been known to attack bathers.

The skin makes a fine leather known in the trade as 'sea-leopard'. (Fig 85.)

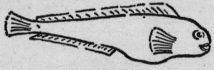

FIG 85. Wolf fish

Zooplankton   See *Plankton*.

CHAPTER 11

Where and When to Fish

This section shows the sea angling picture at various places on the coast, arranged in order from north-east to north-west, with diversions to the Channel Islands, the Isles of Scilly and the Isle of Man.

The information has been provided for this section by the courtesy of the secretaries of angling associations and by officers of town and other councils. It is diverse in form but two points common to all entries are that they are the latest known and have been compiled by people with personal knowledge of the localities. My indebtedness to them is acknowledged on pages 7 and 8.

Notes on the sea angling of Scotland, Northern Ireland and the Republic of Ireland are dealt with on a different basis: they follow the entries for English fishing.

The details of seasons and baits for different species make an interesting study for sea anglers, since they indicate something of the diversity of the fishing to be found around the English coast and the wide differences in locally favoured baits even in places not geographically far apart. They also prove that local knowledge is of the utmost importance to an angler fishing an area new to him.

FISHING IN ENGLAND AND WALES

Sunderland Area

The area stretches from beaches south of South Shields pier to the beaches north of Seaham north pier. The area constitutes the boundaries of the Sunderland SAA (Mr W. Samuelson, Harbour View, Roker, Sunderland, Co Durham. Tel: Sunderland 56797).

Beaches from South Shields to Marsden Point
This comprises approximately three miles of sand with

occasional rock outcrops. Good fishing for flatfish although very few specimens landed. Also codling, coalfish, whiting and very rarely, a skate.

Marsden Point to Whitburn Bay

About one mile of very heavy bottom with large rocks and extensive weed beds. Cod up to 20 lb in winter, also all fish previously mentioned, plus mackerel and other summer fish. A very good area in winter.

Whitburn Bay to Roker Pier

Two miles of sand with the unusual geological feature of the Cannonball Rocks in the middle of this section. Good fishing for medium-sized codling with some good fish from the rocks. Beaches should be fished with low water but the Cannonball Rocks, which form the base of Seaburn Promenade, are only fishable roughly two hours before and two hours after high water.

Roker Pier

Undoubtedly the finest pier on the north-east coast for all local species but out-of-bounds except for competitions.

River Wear

As a result of action taken by the Town Council and the River Wear Commissioners to reduce the amount of pollution in the river, catches of flatfish have been very good for almost the whole of the tidal stretch which extends for about five to six miles. Cod, coalfish, whiting and mackerel are also caught in the harbour entrance.

South Docks Estate

This is under the management of the River Wear Commissioners and is out-of-bounds except to a limited number of permit holders. Together with Roker Pier this constitutes one of the best fishing grounds on the north-east coast for all fish caught in this region.

Grangetown, Ryhope and Seaham beaches

Roughly four miles of good all-the-year-round fishing with a mixture of rocks, shingle and sand. Very good bags of most fish have been taken from these beaches with the best cod over 24 lb and occasional skate up to 12 lb.

Baits: There are no good digging sites for worms but lugworm can be dug at Whitburn. Lugworm and ragworm can be bought at three local tackle dealers and mussels when in season from several fishmongers. Peeler crab is the best bait for codling and these can be gathered locally. Most fish will readily take worm baits and mussel fishes well in winter.

There are about fifteen clubs in the area, the biggest being the Seaham SAC, Sunderland SAC, Ryhope AC, and South Shields SAC.

Seaham (Co Durham)

Very good winter fishing for cod and whiting and for mackerel in July and August. Many other species taken including coalfish, dabs, flounders, plaice, pouting and skate. Ling are occasionally caught. February and March are usually poor months.

There is ample beach fishing, and much is done from the pier and the promenade.

Seaham Sea Angling Club is an energetic organization with which the visitor is advised to get in touch. Sec: Mr K. B. Fox, 27 Normanby Close, Seaham.

Boats used for off-shore angling are owned by individual part-time fishermen. Bait is sold in several shops in the town.

Some further points are covered in the Sunderland Area entry.

Whitby

West Pier

Fishing allowed only from the lower deck of the extension. A mainly sandy bottom, some rocks and weed towards and at the seaward end, but this area particularly suitable for float fishing for mackerel and billet, mid-July to end of September. Bottom fishing may yield billet, flatfish, codling and whiting.

East Pier

The fishing seawards from the stone pier is on fairly weed-free rock; from the extension seawards it is among 'tangle' weed; this seaward side of both the stone pier and the extension often provides the better codling. The seaward end of the extension is often suitable for mackerel fishing. The harbour side of this pier is mainly free from obstructions. Anglers should make sure their lines do not obstruct harbour traffic. Bottom fishing as for West Pier, but with more and better codling.

The Council reserve a safe corner for fishing by children only.

Beach

Sand from Happy Valley (below Bathing Pool) westwards to and including Sandsend Railway Station. Sea wall yields flatfish, billet, whiting, mackerel, codling and very occasional bass.

Saltwick

Rocks and sand – about three-quarters of a mile on the cliffs from the Abbey; yielding codling, flatfish (including plaice), billet, whiting and mackerel.

Mussel is a good bait for bottom fishing. It is obtainable in containers ready for fishing (not cooked or preserved) from sellers on the quayside and other points. Peeler and softback crabs are considered the best baits locally for bottom fishing: they can be gathered in the usual way at low tide. Lugworm (not usually on sale) can sometimes be dug in the east side of the harbour. Herring strips and mackerel skin are used successfully in the usual way.

Boats are available for fishing, bait provided, charges advertised on the quay. Private hire boats available from Mr V. Boocock, 7 Broomfield Terrace; Mr G. Clarkson, 3 Cliff Street; and Mr J. Whale, 2 Larpool Crescent – all of Whitby.

The Hon Secretary of Whitby Sea Anglers' Association is Mr J. Swalee, 5 Rose Avenue, Whitby. The Association organize a one-day festival in late October or early November, particulars of which can be obtained from the Hon Secretary.

Scarborough (Yorks.)

Rock angling

The north-east coast provides some of the best English fishing of this type. The most plentiful fish at all times of the year is the codling. They generally run between 1½ and 3 lb, but many larger ones are caught each year, some up to 12 lb. Whiting, coalfish, mackerel and dabs are plentiful in their season, and other species such as wrasse and pouting are taken at times. The usual baits are mussels or lugworm, both obtainable from local tackle shops.

Boat angling

The main local boat activity is that of the Scarborough Boat

Angling Club. Up to a dozen club boats put to sea each Sunday. It is not unusual for a 3-rod boat to return with 30 to 50 lb of fish, mainly codling, after a 3 hour to 4 hour fishing trip. Whiting and mackerel are plentiful during the summer. Boats can be hired at the harbour and the skippers usually know the best fishing marks.

A useful map of the fishing points on the coast for six miles north and south of Scarborough has been prepared by Messrs Pritchard, tackle manufacturers of 56 Eastborough, Scarborough, copies of which can be obtained at the premises free of charge.

Filey (Yorks)

Nearly all the fishing here is done from the famous Filey Brigg, a long stretch of flat rocks from which casts can be made into deep water.

The principal fish caught, according to the season, are cod, whiting, billet, pollack and mackerel. Dabs and plaice are reasonably plentiful, and brill and turbot are occasional catches. Interesting and rewarding sport can be had with sliding float tackle during the summer, notably for mackerel, billet and gurnard. This enables light tackle to be used: stout tackle is needed for bottom fishing because of weed.

Fishing parties are taken out from the Coble Landing during the season. Private parties can make arrangements with the boatmen.

Lug and razor fish can be dug on the beach. Bait can be bought from R. Dale, Tackle Dealers, 12 Hope Street, Filey.

A nine-day fishing festival, usually about the first week of September, is organized by the Filey Brigg AS (Hon Sec: J. T. Spivey, Esq, 7 Cooper Road, Filey).

Bridlington (Yorks)

There is good fishing in Bridlington Bay for cod, haddock, plaice, dabs, coalfish, whiting, mackerel, thornback rays. Ling and catfish are occasionally caught from boats.

The North and South Piers are open for fishing throughout the winter season, but in summer fishing is allowed only from the South Pier.

Local boat owners take out fishing parties for periods of not less than 2 hours, and for set periods of 2 hours; 3½ hours or 7 hours. Season: Easter to 31 October. These are mainly for holiday makers, the boatman supplying tackle and bait. Private parties of anglers can make their own arrangements with these boatmen. Small rowing boats can be hired, with an extra charge if a boatman is required. A list of boatmen (9 of whom own craft licensed to carry 12 passengers, and who operate throughout the year) can be obtained from the publicity department at the information centre.

Bait can be bought from Linford's Fishing Tackle Shop, Hilderthorpe Road; Wren's Fishing Tackle, Crane Wharf; Mrs Genton, The Warehouse, Harbour Slipway; Buckley's Angling Supplies, Harbour Road.

Bridlington AA organizes a popular and well-attended festival every September.

Grimsby and Cleethorpes (Lincs)

There is excellent fishing to be had from the land, and those who can get out in boats do well, but the boat situation is difficult. Some boat owners take out parties of a dozen or more anglers, but as they are all professional fishermen they prefer to go fishing themselves whenever fish are present in numbers.

The two local clubs (Humber SAC and Cromwell SAC) have rights for fishing from the sea wall, which gives a good depth of water and, therefore, fine winter cod fishing. Another good winter point is the West Pier at the mouth of Grimsby Fish Docks. This runs out into really deep water.

On the coast, Killinholme Haven provides about 3 miles of beach fishing. One part is rocks, where a single hook and trace is advisable to avoid getting snagged. The other area is mud and long casting is necessary to attain depth. Flounders and occasional soles are caught here. In addition to the fish already mentioned seasonal catches account for coalfish, dabs, eels, plaice and whiting.

Mussels, whelks, cockles, squid and herring are all used at times, but the bait most used from land is lugworm. These can be dug at low tide. An even more valued bait is king ragworm, but these are scarce. They are found in the mussel beds, which are uncovered for only about an hour, so much depends on luck. They grow here to an exceptionally large size.

The secretary of the Humber SAC is F. A. Allenby, Esq, 134 Daubney Street, Cleethorpes, Lincs. The Club has its headquarters on the North Wall, No 3 Fish Dock, Grimsby.

Skegness (Lincs)

The gradient of the sandy coast is very gentle and it is difficult to gain any depth of water. Pier fishing is considered the best, from about half to full to half tide. It is an open coast and small-boat fishing can be dangerous in moderate and stronger winds and at spring tides (owing to tide rips).

Lugworm is the local bait, though herring is used extensively and successfully. Lug can be dug almost anywhere below the tide mark.

Winter fish are cod, whiting and dabs. Summer fish are soles, thornback rays, silver eels, tope and – usually July and August – mackerel. Flounders are caught throughout the year.

Boats may be chartered.

There are two clubs – the Skegness Pier A C and the Skegness S A C.

Cromer (Norfolk)

The beach is generally rocky, with small areas of sand here and there; at the eastern end there are flat stretches of sand. Few fish are caught from the beach during the summer by day, but night fishing is profitable, and good catches can be made at any time during the winter. The pier is a popular fishing place: it is open day and night.

Boat fishing is limited, and little is known about its possibilities. From boats there is excellent tope fishing (June to September) and skate and thornbacks are caught in the same period. There is good shore and breakwater fishing for plaice, soles, silver eels, dogfish and occasional bass in summer: and for cod and whiting in winter. Dabs, flounders and coalfish have been caught throughout the year. Tope (*see above*) can also be caught in their season from the pier.

Lugworm and mussels are the locally favoured baits. The former can be dug on the beach and the latter gathered from the pier piles. Fresh and frozen baits can be bought from Randalls (Gifts) Ltd and from F. Pearce, Church Street. Both shops sell tackle.

Club: Cromer and District S A C. Hon Sec: Mr Tim Riches, 17 Lynewood Road, Cromer.

Great Yarmouth (Norfolk)

There are many miles of unobstructed sandy beaches north of

the harbour, and to the south there is another mile or more around Gorleston. Beach fishing is good at night and in the winter, but there are too many holiday makers about in summer to make daylight fishing worth while.

The Harbour provides about two miles of wharves and quays from which fishing is free. Fishing from the jetty is free. The Britannia Pier is open from 8 AM to dusk daily: the Wellington Pier is open throughout the year at all times with some summer limitations on special occasions.

Cod are plentiful from September to early April. The better-sized fish come inshore in late December and remain until March. Whiting are caught from September to March, best months being September and October. Some soles and plaice are taken in summer and, from the boats, occasional tope and skate. Smelts ascend the river in the summer months. Dabs and flounders are taken throughout the year, the winter months providing better and more numerous fish. Flounder fishing from the wharves is a local sport of some importance in winter. Coalfish are caught in the winter but their visits are sporadic and unpredictable. When they do come in they come in considerable numbers.

Most of the boat fishing is done within a quarter-mile of the shore. In summer boatmen are more interested in the holiday traffic than in anglers. If boats are required for parties it is well to contact Mr F. Moore, 9 Nelson Road South, Great Yarmouth (Tel: 3804), secretary of the Inshore Fisherman's Association.

Apart from mussels, bait cannot be gathered locally, but supplies are available from several tackle shops in the town.

Several clubs are affiliated to the Great Yarmouth and District AAA (Hon Sec: Mr W. Platten, 1 Audley Street, Great Yarmouth).

Southwold (Suffolk)

Angling is mainly carried out from the beach, but fishing is also done from the north pier of the harbour (free) and from the Pleasure Pier (normal small charge for entry).

Cod and whiting are caught from mid-September to March and dabs up to December. Silver eels and some sole and bass in summer.

Bait is available from Mr H. C. Land, 13 East Street, Southwold (Tel: 3478). Boats: Mr P. Pile, 33a Station Road, Southworld (Tel: 3161).

Felixstowe (Suffolk)

Beach fishing is difficult and unproductive by day in summer, but good at night and in winter both day and night.

Fishing from the Town Pier is possible throughout the year during daylight hours. Local clubs have arrangements whereby night fishing is possible.

The main winter fish are cod and whiting. Summer offers tope (from boats), conger, plaice, thornback rays and occasional soles. Bass are caught from the pier and from boats in the estuary of the Stour, but estuary fishing is dangerous from boats unless a professional boatman is in charge. Flounders throughout the year, though the late spring months are poor ones.

There are no natural bait supplies. Bait (and tackle) can be obtained from Mr L. T. Bobby, 57 Undercliffe Road, Felixstowe (Tel: 2709) and from Mr M. Brien, 2a Bent Hill, Felixstowe (Tel: 5318). Advance ordering necessary in winter months.

Several owners have dinghies and boats for hire.

Felixstowe SAC (Hon Sec: Mr P. Thain, 61 Langer Road, Felixstowe) admits temporary members. It organizes two festivals with open events in the October–November period.

Note: The British record bass was caught at Felixstowe in 1943 (Weight: 18 lb 2 oz).

Walton-on-the-Naze (Essex)

Fishing from pier, beach and boats may in summer be expected to produce bass, skate, dogfish and flatfish. Cod, whiting and flatfish are caught in winter.

Bait (to order) and tackle, from Mr W. Farrence, 15 Newgate Street. Boats may be booked from Mr J. Oxley, 18 Newgate Street; Mr F. Bloom, The Brents, Butcher's Lane; and Mr R. Hipkin, Norfolk House, Kirby Road.

Membership of the Walton-on-the-Naze AC is limited: inquiries to the Hon Sec: Mr L. T. Crofts, MBE, 5 The Parade.

Southend-on-Sea (Essex)

Situated only forty miles from London on the Thames Estuary, with the longest pier in the world, Southend is a magnet to tens of thousands of London anglers. The authorities encourage them and fishing of all types is available with the exception of surf casting. Fortunately the fish are there to be caught. From boats in the estuary and around the islands and sandbanks a wide variety of species is to be caught. Near the mouth of the river, in the Maplin Sands area, big skate and the best of the tope are found, but a professional boatman is necessary as tides and currents are dangerous. Nearer Southend there is safe dinghy fishing, and anglers take, in their season, bass, cod, dogfish, mackerel, garfish, thornback rays and tope, with the constant likelihood of dabs, flounders and pouting.

It is not a popular area for beach fishing: in the summer the beaches are too crowded with visitors to make casting possible, and in winter there is the pier, which enables everyone to fish in relatively deep water without heavy casting.

In spite of the many boats available for hire, with or without boatmen, the pier is *the* angling attraction. A booklet, obtainable on the spot or through the Publicity Officer (add postage), gives a diagram of the pier and the places, roughly, where different species are to be caught.

There are several sea angling clubs in and around Southend. The one of most interest to visiting anglers, possibly, is the Pier Head Amateur Angling Society, which has its headquarters halfway along the pier, opposite the Lifeboat Station. The pier closes at dusk and only holders of special tickets can fish during the night.

Lugworm and ragworm can be dug at many points along the shores, but it is necessary to buy a licence for this purpose. This can be got from the Pier Foreshore Officer, Pier Hill. Fresh bait can be ordered, and frozen and other baits bought, from the following tackle shops: Going Bro, 8 High Street (Tel: SOS 66439); C. Hoy, 8 Market Place (Tel: SOS 43163); F. Page, 11 Sidmouth Road (Tel: SOS 47235).

There are many boats for hire, with or without skippers. Anglers' boats leave the pier head daily during the season at 9 AM.

East Kent

Before dealing with individual places it may be useful to consider East Kent as a whole. Herne Bay and Margate face north on the seaward end of the Thames Estuary: they command the excellent fishing of that area and are sheltered from southerly winds.

The twenty miles of coast between the North and South Forelands (roughly Broadstairs to St Margaret's Bay) face east, opposite the Goodwin Sands and The Downs.

From the South Foreland the coast bears away south-west (Dover, Folkestone) and is well protected from the north.

None of the area is more than 80 miles from London, and many thousands of anglers in that huge complex pick their venues according to the prevailing winds.

Herne Bay (Kent)

With a combination of sand, mud, shingle and rocky sea bed many species of fish are available, and the deeper water of the estuary mouth provides, in the appropriate seasons, good cod, skate and tope. Inshore, from April to September with a little give and take at each end, the standard species are bass, thornback rays, mullet, soles, dogfish, silver eels and garfish. Cod and whiting are the winter fish, and dabs, flounders and pouting can be caught throughout the year.

The water is relatively shallow and there are many areas sheltered from the main stream of tidal currents, so the light tackle enthusiast can fish very light indeed.

There is rocky ground off Reculver that holds bass in summer and cod in winter; Swalecliff Beach has occasional good bass in autumn. The Pier provides the best of shore fishing.

Lugworm are plentiful on most parts of the shore; ragworm and mussels on the banks around the Clock Tower jetty. Fresh and frozen baits from the following tackle dealers: R. Edwards, 50 High Street (Tel: 2517); F. Whitehead, 29 William Street (Tel: 2503); Jacks, Broadway Bdg, Sea Street (Tel: 3692).

Margate (Kent)

Like all places in the East Kent area, Margate is noted for its mixed catches of fish. Many good and countless average bass are taken from the beach and rocks at low water. The stretch of sand outside the Newfoundland Rocks is noted for its flatfish. Tope fishing is good and well-catered for by local boats and skippers. Winter cod fishing always produces a run of twenty-pounders and over.

Bait and tackle can be obtained from Jebbs, 34 King Street (Tel: Thanet 23866) and tackle from Anchor Boats, 18 King Street (Tel: Thanet 22467).

Arrangements for boats can be made with T. Rooke, 4 Edinburgh Walk, Garlings, Margate (Tel: Thanet 31381).

Ramsgate (Kent)

Summer catches include tope, skate, bass, mackerel, dogfish, conger, plaice, flounders, dabs and pouting. In late autumn and winter heavy catches of cod are made, some of them exceeding 30 lb for individual fish. Catches totalling 200 lb are not unusual.

About 50 licensed fishing boats, manned by licensed and experienced skippers, are available seven days a week. Local lugworm and most of the standard baits are readily available.

Anglers and club secretaries can get further information from the secretary of the Royal Ramsgate Invicta Angling Association (Mr R. Hall, 71 Kennedy House, Ramsgate). The club organizes many competitions, some of which are open to the public, while the annual 3-day boat and beach festivals are very popular.

Tackle dealers are: Mr L. Dent, 'Bunny's', 30 Harbour Street; Decca Sports, 36 King Street; Success Stores, 6 Turner Street; Woodwards, 7 Westcliffe Arcade.

Motor boats can be hired and bait bought at the Harbour from local boatmen or through Mr L. Dent, 'Bunny's', 30 Harbour Street.

Deal (Kent)

All the usual Channel species of fish can be caught from boats and from the pier, which gives access to deep water. Angling is strongly encouraged here, and boatmen, tackle dealers, bait merchants, the Corportion itself and, perhaps even more important, the two angling clubs set out to help them. These are The Deal and Walmer Angling Association (Mr A. Gregory, HQ, Deal Pier) and the Deal Angling Club (Mrs H. Green, c/o Royal Navy Association, The Marina, Deal). Each of these societies has a cabin on the pier.

Eleven boat owners are listed in a pamphlet which can be obtained on application to the Entertainments and Publicity Manager, Dept A B, Time Ball Tower, Deal.

Tackle and bait merchants are J. Bingham, 11 Market Street; D. Finn, 67 Beach Street; T. Franks, 98a Middle Street; The Foc'sle, opposite Deal Pier; W. & F. Willis, 3 Brewer Street; and the Angler's Shop, King Street.

Dover

Dover is noted for its bass during the summer months from external piers, boats and beaches. All the usual remaining species can be caught (including unlimited pouting) and good skate, tope and huss. In winter excellent cod and whiting are available, the latter averaging $1\frac{1}{2}$ lb, with the local record standing at 4 lb 8 oz. Main flatfish are dabs and plaice.

One of the main fishing attractions of Dover is its Breakwater. This stands about a mile offshore and is 1,400 yards long. Except when the weather is really tempestuous, boats leave the Prince of Wales's Pier at 8 AM to take anglers to the Breakwater, returning at 4 PM.

For those who are less ambitious or who have limited time, fishing can be done from the Admiralty Pier, which forms the southern arm of the harbour. Mackerel are caught here by thousands in July and August, but at all times it offers fish of many species on the seaward side.

The Prince of Wales's Pier is entirely within the harbour. Big specimens are rarely caught, but it provides fishing when the Breakwater cannot be reached and when waves are breaking over the Admiralty Pier. Permits to fish this pier and the Breakwater can be obtained at the Pier Gate Office.

Tides run strongly in the Straits of Dover and heavy leads are necessary to hold the bottom when fishing from boats or the Breakwater.

Lugworm is the favoured bait and this can be bought from the bait shops listed below, all of which sell tackle. It is well to order in advance during the summer season. Other fresh baits are often available, and supplies of frozen bait and fresh fish are unlimited. D. J. Brazil, 162 Snargate Street (Tel: Dover 1457); J. C. Kinson, 3 Snargate Street (Tel: Dover 20); D. Finn, 43 High Street (Tel: Dover 1059).

The Dover SAA is open to all. Hon Sec: Mr D. Edwards, 12 East Cliff, Dover.

Folkestone (Kent)

Bass, cod, conger, plaice, whiting, mackerel, mullet, pollack and sole are the main species. The heaviest fish are usually the cod (October to February) though conger of more than 30 lb are caught in the summer.

The harbour pier is a popular fishing venue. The current is always strong here and, according to the state of the tide, weights of from 4 oz to 8 oz are necessary.

Light fishing for pollack and mullet can be done with float tackle on the sheltered side of the harbour wall. Many mackerel and pollack are caught on feathered lures.

Beach fishing in the area is popular, though in the summer it is done usually at night, since crowds on the beaches by day make fishing impossible. The beach should be studied at low tide. There are many ridges of rock offshore within casting distance, and it is on these that fish are to be found.

The Warren (between Folkestone and Dover) is a good beach fishing area with several concrete stands from which spinning and float fishing are possible. Bass are taken by these methods, but cod and plaice particularly, and a mixture of fish generally, can be taken by bottom anglers in the same vicinity.

Boat fishermen are well catered for, and some idea of the quantity of fish available in the vicinity can be gathered from the results of the annual Boat and Pier Festivals, where between 2½ and 3 tons of fish are regularly weighed in. Light tackle fishing from boats off the Warren yields great numbers of plaice.

It is advisable to book boats well in advance. Boat owners: F. Taylor, 95 Joyes Road (Tel: Folkestone 52446); J. Coker, 21 St Anns Road, Dymchurch (Tel: Dymchurch 2329); Milton & Smith, 12 Tontine Road (Tel: Folkestone 53881). Bait: Milton & Smith; J. B. Walker & Sons, 14 Dover Road (Tel: Folkestone 56161); J. Blackman, 27 Sandgate High Street (Tel: Folkestone 38712).

The Folkestone Sea Angling Association welcomes new members. (Hon Sec: Mr A. Collcott, 105 Cheriton Road, Folkestone.)

Dungeness (Kent)

A long pebble ridge extending into the sea to make Dungeness Point. Noted for mixed boat and beach fishing, but particularly famous for its beach cod fishing. Nearest town: Lydd.

Hastings and St Leonards (Sussex)

The main winter fish are cod, dabs, whiting – and plaice (up to December). In summer cod and pollack can be caught around the many wrecks offshore, and other fish are black bream, mackerel, conger, tope, bass, dogfish, thornback rays and plaice.

There is good winter fishing from the beaches but in summer night fishing is advised, as bathers are too numerous to make angling possible. The pier is open by day all the year round.

Boats are available for hire, and the three local clubs also have boats available on hire to members. Temporary membership is available in all of them.

Clubs: East Hastings SAA, Mr K. G. Bailey, 140 Queen's Road (Tel: 7200); Hastings & St Leonards AA, Mr E. Banks, 128 Fairlight Road (Tel: 5322); St Leonards SAA, Mr G. E. Dawson, The Hall, Market Passage.

Tackle can be hired and bait obtained at the Pier Kiosk. Tackle and bait also from: Redfearns, Castle Street; Amber Dolphin Ltd, 5 Marine Parade; The Modern Angler, 65 Eversfield Place, St Leonards; Wisden's Sport Shop, 1 Trinity Street.

Eastbourne (Sussex)

Boat fishing provides the best sport, with tope, spurdog, dogfish, conger, skate, black bream, pouting, cod, bass, whiting, dabs, a few turbot, and plaice, soles and flounders. Local club members and boatmen have a good knowledge of the feeding grounds of the various species.

Beach fishing around Beachy Head gives good summer sport with bass. Bass and other fish can be caught from the beaches generally. The landing stage of the pier is open for fishing in the summer, and the whole pier in the winter. Bottom fishing for mixed species is normal, but float fishing for mullet and bass can be profitable in summer.

The two clubs are Eastbourne AA (Mr E. O. Brown, The Clubhouse, Royal Parade, Eastbourne); and Nomads AC (Mr W. A. Winchester, 4 Woodgate Road, Eastbourne). Tackle and bait can be obtained from The Compleat Angler, 22 Pevensey Road, Eastbourne, and through local boatmen.

Newhaven (Sussex)

Summer fish from May to the end of September, with peak periods in July and August, are black bream, mackerel, conger, bull huss and pollack. Over a more extended period (roughly April into November) come the bass, skate and rays, plaice, and dabs, the last named being caught as late as December. Turbot can be caught as early as May and as late as the end of November, but their peak months are July, August and September. The winter fish are cod and whiting, with odd dabs up to the end of December.

The best of these fish are, with the exception of bass, normally taken from boats, though winter beach and pier fishing produce excellent cod and whiting.

Much of the Sussex coast is open to the sea, making boat angling difficult, but Newhaven Harbour provides moorings for hundreds of craft, many of them available for charter. You can take a chance and go there with the hope of picking up a place in a boat or you can book in advance. There are so many boat owners that it is impossible to list them here. Many of them advertise in the angling periodicals.

There is good beach fishing by night in the summer and throughout the winter. The East Pier and the Breakwater are popular venues, both being particularly good in the winter months for cod and whiting.

Clubs: Newhaven Deep Sea Anglers (Mr D. F. Wood, 56 Slindon Avenue, Peacehaven, Sussex); Hand in Hand A C (Mr J. Baldwin, 42 Hill Crest Road, Newhaven); Seaford A C (Mrs I. Hopkins, 28 Cinque Ports Way, Seaford, Sussex).

Tackle and bait (the latter if ordered in advance) can be obtained from Dennis's Tackle Shop, 107 Fort Road; and Books 'n Baccy, Bridge Street, both in Newhaven.

Brighton (Sussex)

All the normal sea fish of the Channel put in an appearance in their seasons. Bass fishing from piers and beach is excellent; black bream from boats; cod to 25 lb from boats and to 20 lb from beach regularly caught in autumn and winter. Also good winter flounder fishing. That mentions only a few noteworthy items, but every south-coast species from tope to pouting are caught, many of specimen size and in large numbers, at the right time and place.

There are several sea angling clubs, some of which can supply boats to members. The chairman of the Angling Section of the Brighton Cruising Club is Mr J. Kelly, 178 King's Road Arches, Brighton. The Brighton Palace Pier A A is helpful to visiting anglers: there is bait and tackle shop on the pier.

The Palace Pier is open to fishermen from about 8.45 AM to 6 PM. It is possible to fish from the top deck of the West Pier during the winter months, approximately October to Easter.

Of the many tackle dealers and bait suppliers, Butler's Fishing Tackle Ltd, 80b St James's Street, specialize in the hire of shark tackle. Another useful establishment for tackle, bait and information is The Brighton Angler, 24 Duke Street.

Information about boats for hire can be obtained from Mr G. Wheeler, Secretary of the Brighton Fishermen and Boatmen Protection Society, 200 King's Road Arches.

Worthing (Sussex)

Boat, beach and pier fishing brings in most of the usual species. Bass and flatfish are caught in numbers from beach and pier, and from June to September there is good pier mullet fishing. Worthing is in the black bream area and these fish are caught in numbers from boats in the limited season of this species. The River Adur, east of Worthing, is noted for mullet and silver eels.

The Worthing Sea AA has its headquarters on the pier. Tackle, bait and detailed information about Worthing's fishing can be obtained from Mr K. Dunman, 2 Marine Place.

Littlehampton (Sussex)

All the common species are caught here, with black bream a speciality off the Kingsmere Rocks, and a good supply of mixed skate, rays and dogfish, together with heavy turbot and monk-fish. The beaches and the offshore waters offer a thoroughly mixed bag.

Fishing from the beaches is as good as is to be found any-where along the south coast, especially for bass, and the West Works – a very long wooden structure extending well into deep water – provides mixed fishing from an unusual stance. The estuary of the Arun, confined between concrete quays, is popular for float and baited spoon fishing.

Except when weed growth is at its height in July and August, there is good fishing in the tidal reaches of the river for bass, flounders, silver eels and mullet.

The keynote of Littlehampton's sea angling is boat fishing, however. The River Arun enables scores of anglers' charter boats to find moorings, whereas along many featureless miles of the South Coast boats have to be hauled on to the beach. Boatmen have responded to the anglers' demands and a high safety standard is demanded. Most boats are also equipped with radio/telephone and echo-sounding equipment.

Boats have heavy bookings, some being engaged a year ahead. There is little hope of hiring a boat in the peak summer months, or at weekends over a longer period, but if you want to look ahead, you should contact the Littlehampton Skippers' Association, c/o Harbour View Café, Pier Road.

For general information and talk about local fishing you can visit the Arun View Hotel, HQ of the Littlehampton and District A C.

Bognor Regis (Sussex)

This is another important centre for black bream fishing, and in their season it is necessary to book boats well in advance. At other times, for general boat fishing, the situation is easier.

Miles of sandy beaches are available to surf casters, and fishing is allowed from the pier, which houses a tackle and bait shop.

The local club is the Bognor Regis Amateur AS (Mr F. Waldron, 9 May Close, Bognor Regis).

HAMPSHIRE

Selsey Bill, a dozen seagull's miles from Littlehampton, marks the beginning of an area with a complete change in fishing outlook from that of the Sussex and south Kent coasts. It marks the approaches to Spithead, Chichester Harbour, Hayling Island, Portsmouth and Southsea, Southampton Water, the Solent – and, interposed between them and the open Channel, the Isle of Wight. On the seaward side of the island the fishing is much the same as elsewhere along the coasts, but anglers in other parts of the area have peculiar tides to combat, and vast parts of it are mud flats which are the home of countless flatfish.

Portsmouth and Southsea

Bass are caught in the Solent from mid-March to September. Spring to autumn fishing also noted for thornback rays, plaice and tope. Black bream are caught at marks in the eastern approaches in June and July; large mackerel shoals arrive in June. Turbot are found at offshore marks from August to September. Dabs and flounders are plentiful and are taken throughout the year. Cod and whiting are the late autumn and winter fish most in evidence.

Sharks – certainly porbeagle and thresher – follow the mackerel to the eastern end of the Solent (but see 'Isle of Wight').

Beach fishing is good at night in summer, and at all times in winter (the latter mainly cod and 'flats'). The South Parade Pier is open for fishing only from October to March.

There are many boats available, with or without boatmen, and there are extensive sheltered reaches where boat fishing is safe without a skilled skipper. Boats taking forty or so anglers leave Gosport, Portsmouth and Langstone harbours regularly. Information about these can be found in the angling Press or by local inquiry.

Fresh bait must be ordered in advance. Frozen bait is usually available at any of the following tackle dealers. At Portsmouth: R. Huggett, 222 Arundel Street; North End Tackle Shop, 59a Chichester Road; Nick's Bait and Tackle Shop, 90 Tangier Road. The following at Southsea: L. J. Bloxham & Son, 14 Highland Road; R. W. Wakeley, 65 Highland Road.

Two of several clubs in the area accept temporary members and it may be possible for these to use club boats. They are: Southsea SAC (Mr H. Kennedy, 42 Granada Road, Southsea (Tel: Ports 25508) and Langstone Harbour Fishermen's Association, Milton Locks, Portsmouth (Tel: Ports 25083) (Hon Sec: Mr A. E. Halliwell).

Isle of Wight

Beach fishing of every sort can be had: distances on the Island are short, and it is easy to move to sandy bays, rocky inlets or shingle reefs. Roughly speaking the north-east, the south-east and east of the Island have the big tourist resorts – Cowes, Ryde, Sandown, Shanklin, Ventnor – and at these beach fishing in summer is limited by bathers and pleasure boats. There is good pier fishing, and fishing at night proves profitable when the bathers have gone home.

Except at a few smaller but still popular places the south-west and south coasts are far less populated. The latter opens directly to the Channel; the former to the Solent, including the Needles passage and the narrow gap between the Island and Hurst Point. Yarmouth, an important yachting town, is the largest of the towns on this coast.

All the southern species of fish can be caught, and cod of considerable size are now regular winter visitors. A small group of Isle of Wight anglers believed that sharks were to be caught offshore, and they justified their belief by catching many and – in 1968 – a record porbeagle (324 lb).

It is impossible here to list all the fishing stations, and a choice would be invidious. Anyone thinking of fishing from the Isle of Wight should send for a booklet – *Angling in the Isle of Wight* – published by the Isle of Wight Angling Society, The Sir John Barleycorn, Trafalgar Road, Newport, IOW. Every coast town, village, bay and promontory is listed – 45 entries – giving details of species, baits and methods.

Christchurch, Boscombe, Bournemouth

There is good beach fishing for all the usual Channel species along this stretch of coast. Boats are available for hire, and a good deal of fishing is done from rowing boats in the bay when weather is quiet. Much of the sea-bed is sand and there are normally good catches of plaice and dabs with occasional soles. Bournemouth Pier is noted for its grey mullet in addition to bass, flatfish, etc.

The principal clubs are: Boscombe and Southbourne SFC (Mr J. J. Elliott, 35 Exton Road, Boscombe, E. Bournemouth. Tel: Christchurch 5581). Bournemouth and District SAA (Mr F. J. Seear, York Lodge, Cliff Cottage Road, Bournemouth. Tel: Bournemouth 22872).

Poole (Dorset)

It is said that Poole Harbour, counting all the inlets and islands, has 100 miles of coastline. Certainly the harbour is big enough to provide varied and sheltered fishing in any weather.

The normal species caught, in their season, are bass, flounders, plaice, pollack, dabs, silver eels, pouting, conger and tope. Experiments carried out by the local angling club resulted in the capture of several sharks, including a 120 lb porbeagle and a 114 lb blue shark. This opened up a new sport. An early drawback was that the fishing grounds were 12 miles out and much time was spent going to and from the area. Fast motor boats specially designed for shark fishing are now available. During the season several shark boats now leave the Quay daily.

Bait is plentiful around the shores of the harbour, and frozen bait (and fresh on order) can be bought from Poole Sports Depot, 160 High Street (Tel: 3157).

The local club is the Poole Dolphin SAC.

Swanage (Dorset)

A fine angling centre for all the normal Channel species. Excellent catches are obtained from many shore and boat marks. The Swanage and District AC (Hon Sec: Mr D. L. Maxwell, 'Bonnie Braes', Durnford Drove, Langstone Maltravers, Swanage. Tel: 3862) organizes weekly boat or shore competitions from April to December. Visitors are accepted as temporary members for 14 days. This entitles them to enter all the competitions, though they cannot be awarded club trophies. Apart from competitions, membership is of value to visitors in many ways.

Weymouth (Dorset)

The famous Chesil Beach is the overriding angling feature of this area. From it are regularly caught, in winter, cod, whiting and pouting; and in summer, thornback ray, common skate, various dogfishes, mackerel, black bream and pouting. It is especially noted for very good conger. Tope can be caught from the shore, and on occasions a shark is hooked.

Weymouth's two piers fish well (at the right times and seasons) for mackerel, pollack, pouting, conger, wrasse and flatfish.

Bass are caught from the sea front.

Boats are available throughout the year from the harbour, and good catches are made of many species of fish, notably skate, tope, conger, black bream and turbot. When it is too rough 'outside', sheltered fishing can be had by the Portland Breakwater for conger, bass, bream, pouting and pollack.

Tackle, live and frozen bait, and tide tables can be bought from: The Anglers' Tackle Stores, Park Street; and Gilbert Sports, 4 St Alban Street.

CHANNEL ISLANDS

Guernsey

Rock fishing and inshore boat fishing provide bass, red and black bream, conger, flatfish, horse mackerel, mackerel, grey and red mullet, pollack, pouting and whiting.

Many boats are available, and the Hon Secretary of the Guernsey SAC may be prepared to arrange fishing trips.

Bait can be dug or collected on the beaches, and fresh bait (to order) and frozen bait can be obtained from two tackle dealers in St Peter Port – Leale Ltd, Bordage; and Marquand Bros, North Esplanade.

Jersey

There is excellent fishing in the warmer months, but fishing of some sort can be obtained throughout the year. Congers are all the year round possibilities. January is the leanest month, but for those who can face a January night there is atherine smelt fishing at the Town harbours, St Aubin's and Bouley Bay. In February the smelts are still available, and pollack come into Bouley Bay, Bonne Nuit and the Town harbours. March brings a general run of pollack, and bass are caught from many beaches. The Jersey record (11 lb 2 oz) was caught from the beach at Grave d'Azette.

April and May bring in the garfish and the larger bass and pollack, and spinning with spoons and rubber eels (the latter especially for bass) is practised. The boats are brought into use in late May and June, and this increases the average size of pollack and other fish available. Porbeagle sharks can now be taken, as can, on a lighter but equally sporting scale, the black bream. Wrasse are now plentiful around the rocks. July intensifies all the fishing for species so far mentioned and is also the best mullet month.

August and September continue the general fishing, and many of the bigger fish come closer in. In addition plaice, soles, various skate and rays, and monkfish are caught in numbers. Red gurnard are a September speciality and red mullet and John Dories appear in the catches. It is the best month for anyone who likes a really mixed bag; anything may turn up.

October can still be a good month, especially for bass, but as the temperature falls and the atherine smelts again make their

appearance, the general fishing dies off. The principal fishing in
November and December is for the 2 lb to 3 lb pollack, especially
at St Catherine's and from the Town Pierheads.

The Jersey SFC does all it can to help visiting anglers. The
Caesarean AC is a boat-only club with a strictly limited membership. The island has its own Specimen and Records Committee.

Portland Bill to Start Point

These two points mark the extremities of a deep, semi-circular
cutting-back of the Dorset and Devon coastlines to form Lyme
Bay. The Chesil Bank lies along the eastern side. Bridport,
Lyme Regis, Seaton and Sidmouth are on the central curve, and
all have excellent beach and boat fishing for the Channel fish.
Beach fishing for bass is excellent. The same large indentation
includes on the west Exmouth, Teignmouth, Torquay,
Paignton and Brixham. Exmouth, at the end of the estuary of the
largest river in the west, has some special angling features.

Exmouth (Devon)

Exmouth, from boats and beaches, provides excellent general
fishing, especially for bass. The best bait is the sand eel (for bass,
turbot and every other sort of predatory fish), and in the whole
of this western area live sand eels can be bought, providing
orders are given well in advance. All the other standard baits
are naturally accepted by fish.

There is a small-boat harbour, so that boats are plentiful. In
addition to the 'open sea' fishing, which is common to every
resort around this coast, Exmouth has the estuary of the Exe,
and this provides first-class bass fishing – as well as many 'flats',
particularly flounders. The Banjo Pier is also good for bass and
the other species, and the Exmouth SAA has a club room on the
pier. The Association is most helpful to visiting anglers.

Torbay (Devon)

Torbay includes, among many other places, Torquay, Paignton
and Brixham. All are important angling centres from which
boats, tackle and bait can be readily obtained. With Teignmouth
(midway between Exmouth and Torquay) all these places are
within comfortable reach of the Skerries Bank, from which top-
weight turbot and brill are taken every year.

Every species of fish common to the south-west can be caught in the bay or 'outside', and there are now boats equipped for shark fishing. Around the bay there are many piers, breakwaters and jetties from which fishing is permissible and profitable.

The fishing is so varied in scope that the visitor is advised to get in touch with one of the following: Tuckerman's Fish Tackle, Victoria Parade, Torquay; Fletcher's Fishing Tackle 9 Fleet Street, Torquay; Cove Clerk Sports, 45 Torbay Road, Torquay; George Dyer, Scylla, Windmill Road, Brixham.

Boats may be hired on the spot (off season) and advance bookings may be made for shark, The Skerries bank and general fishing from Tuckerman's Tackle Shop (as above) (Tel: Torquay 23261); and for Skerries and general fishing from Russ Evans, 67 Newton Road, Torquay (Tel: Torquay 63981).

Clubs: Torbay Association of Sea Anglers (J. C. Stevenson, 48 Padacre Road, Torquay. Tel: Torquay 39984); Babbacombe SAA (Mr W. J. Hern, 29 Westhill Road, Torquay); Torquay SAA; Brixham SAS.

Salcombe (Devon)

Excellent sheltered shore and boat fishing can be had within the long harbour, and the Wolf, Blackstone and Poundstone Rocks are noted for bass. Plaice, soles and dabs can be had along the many miles of sandy bottom just outside the harbour. The muddy creeks which join the harbour, and much of the harbour itself, provide all-the-year-round fishing for flounders and dabs. Pollack are found around the rocks at the estuary mouth at all times, large fish coming inshore in the early autumn.

Turbot are important fish for the boat fisherman, on the sandy stretches. Other boats' marks are the numerous wrecks, around which can be found conger, bream (red and black), dogfish and rays.

Visitors can join the Salcombe and District SAA, Shipwrights Arms, Fore Street (Tel: Salcombe 2205).

Lugworm, prawns, shrimps, crabs, mussels and cockles can be gathered from appropriate sites along the beaches. Live and preserved baits can be bought from Roy's Tackle Shop, Clifton Place, Salcombe.

Private boats can be hired from L. Stone, Island Street (Tel: Salcombe 2877). Boats with boatmen (live sand eel bait supplied) from H. Cook, White Strand. Shark and general deep sea fishing trips arranged by J. French, Lowick, Main Road (Tel: Salcombe 2584) and B. Martin, Customs Quay.

Plymouth (Devon)

Angling to suit all tastes is available, from boats inshore or at deep sea marks, notably the Eddystone; from beaches; and, particularly, from Millbay Docks and from the many piers and landing stages. Much of the fishing from these is done by night.

Fish of almost every species found in the English Channel can be caught at or from Plymouth. The Plymouth SAC has produced an excellent and detailed brochure on the sea fishing of the neighbourhood. This can be obtained from Messrs Jeffries Ltd, Old Town Street, who also supply frozen baits and tackle of all descriptions.

Membership of Plymouth SAC is open to visiting anglers. Hon Sec: Mr J. A. Higginson, 34 Western Drive, Laira, Plymouth.

The British Conger Club (see Chapter 9) has its headquarters here.

Looe (Cornwall)

Shark fishing in British waters was developed at Looe, and although other ports now have properly equipped shark boats, Looe is pre-eminent in this respect. It is the headquarters of the Shark Angling Club of Great Britain. Well over 20 shark boats put out daily, the agents for these being J. Bray & Son, Lower Quay, East Looe; and Frank Hoskin, The Tackle Shop, East Looe.

Shark fishing became the rage, and for a time it overshadowed the excellent general fishing available. Many people are now using Looe as a base for shore and rock fishing, especially for bass and pollack, and for inshore boat fishing.

A good guide to the general fishing and to shark fishing can be obtained from the Looe and District SAC, The Ship Hotel, East Looe, Cornwall. Visiting anglers are invited to join the club.

Falmouth (Cornwall)

Shore and inshore boat fishing in the extensive harbour and from piers. Good deep sea fishing, that in the Manacle Rocks area being famous.

In their seasons the following species are regularly caught at and from Falmouth: bass, cod, conger, dogfish, flatfish (all kinds), gurnard, hake, ling, pollack, pouting, whiting and wrasse.

The Falmouth and Penryn AA organizes an autumn festival. The Falmouth Shark and Big Game AC covers the type of fishing its name implies.

Shark and deep sea boats can be booked through Messrs Harveys, Tackle Dealers, 2 Market Strand; or Mr Frank Vinnicombe, West Winds, Mylor Bridge, Falmouth.

Mount's Bay Area (Cornwall)

Although the Mount's Bay area is perhaps not so well known to anglers as some other south and south-west locations, the quantity and quality of fish brought to the scales, per rod, compares favourably with any other area.

Boat parties are catered for and boats can be hired at Penzance, Melwyn and Mousehole. Tides and weather can be extremely tricky for the inexperienced and foolhardy. Enjoy the fishing this rugged coast has to offer, but take care.

Boat Marks
St Anthony (*Manaccan*)
Mouth of Helford River. Wide variety of marks, including Manacle Rocks, provides pollack, conger, bream, bass, spurdogs, whiting, mackerel and garfish.

Coverack
On the Lizard peninsula. A few boats for hire. Fishing same as St Anthony with addition of fine turbot on nearby ground, best caught at slack water on a neap tide.

Porthleven
Between Helston and Praa Sands. Caters for fishing parties daily. Main catches; spurdogs, bream, whiting, conger and mackerel.

Penzance
Excellent inshore marks between the Mount, Newlyn and Mousehole for all types of fish over mud and rocky bottoms. Runnelstone Rocks teem with fish, but only experienced boatmen can safely fish this area owing to fierce tides.

Shore Stations

Penzance

Lighthouse Pier. Mud, rock, weed and sandy patches can be fished. All the usual species including good conger and flounders. Fishing into the harbour from the Albert Pier yields flounders and mullet. Also pollack and wrasse from the end of the pier and conger after dark. On the seaward side, bass and larger mullet, wrasse and flounders can be caught. They have to be hauled up the pier wall so stout lines are necessary. There is the usual beach fishing from the promenade. Larrigan Beach, between the Promenade and Newlyn, gives good bass and flounder fishing.

Newlyn

The North and South Piers and the Old Harbour Pier provide a very wide variety of species and fish of some sort are to be caught throughout the year. From Newlyn to Mousehole the bottom is rocky with small sand patches. General fishing over the rocks for deep-water species, and good turbot and plaice in the sandy areas.

Mousehole

From Mousehole around the coast to St Ives (on the north Cornish coast) are high cliffs broken into significantly at Porthcurno and Sennen (the two most south-westerly fishing stations in England) and with several small coves, best known of which are Lamorna and Penberth. Excellent beach fishing from all coves.

Porthcurno

A popular fishing station from which all species of fish so far mentioned can be caught. A special feature is mackerel fishing. Shoals come right into the rocks under the Minack Theatre in summer and autumn and are caught in thousands by all means. Sea trout are sometimes caught – as are weevers!

Sennen

Main sport is surf fishing for bass.

Penzance and Marazion

Eastwards from Penzance there is a three-mile beach of shingle dropping into sand. Good bass and flounder fishing.

Praa Sands

Between Marazion and Porthleven the coast is rocky except for Perran Sands and Praa Sands. Where fishing is possible in the rocky areas (and most parts are accessible) there is really good fishing for pollack, wrasse, mackerel, garfish, mullet and bass. At Perran and Praa Sands the beach is of fine sand and the home of good-sized flatfish. Bass fishing is good when there is surf. The fishing on both beaches is best after dark. Here, and on other sandy beaches mentioned, sand eels are plentiful, and are a favourite bait for predators. Lugworm and ragworm for the flats.

Porthleven

There is good fishing for many species in this quiet village, from the beach or projections with bottom tackle, and with float, drift line or spinning tackle for pollack and mackerel from the piers and jetties.

Loe Bar Sands

Noted for above-average bass. Heavy weights are needed to keep the bait beyond the breakers on the steep-to shingle bank.

Lizard Peninsula

From Mullion on the west to Cadwith on the east there are many small coves where fishing for bass proves profitable. Flatfish can be taken at all times. From various rock stations at the extreme end of the peninsula float fishing and spinning for mackerel and pollack is popular.

Newquay (Cornwall)

The following is an extract from *Newquay Angling Guide*, published by the Newquay Angling Association.

The possibilities of sea fishing in the Newquay area have never been fully explored.

From the shore innumerable school bass and several bass from 7 lb to 12 lb are taken annually. With these are taken flounders, turbot, skate and dabs. From the rocks droves of mackerel are found, and pollack and wrasse haunt the weed-covered bottoms.

Boats can be hired from the Harbour to take parties to fish

the deep marks, and they return loaded with large pollack, pouting, coalfish, conger, dogfish and even tope and shark.

Mullet shoals appear in late June and do not leave till September, and during the winter catches of flounder, whiting, bass and codling are made.

Newquay has a broken coastline where rough, unfishable ground, sand and deeply submerged weed-beds may be found within twenty yards of each other. This Guide sets out to give the visiting angler sufficient marks and a few tips to ensure good fishing, subject to his own skill and the perversity of the fish.

This it does, and a map on which numbers indicate the marks and their relation to the text helps this aim.

The Isles of Scilly

In spite of their apparently favourable position the Isles of Scilly have been little exploited by sea anglers. Fish of many species can be caught from all the beaches of all the islands, but boat fishing is no job for the amateur boatman. Boats can be hired for fishing, but it is essential that they be skippered by experienced local boatmen, for the intricacies of the tidal currents and many concealed hazards make the whole area dangerous. Obviously shark fishing is a good bet off the islands, and some efforts have been made to test it, but it needs anglers with the right tackle and some experience to show what the possibilities are.

Anyone thinking of doing some sea fishing in the Isles of Scilly is advised to write or talk to Mr C. J. Mumford, Hugh Street, St Mary's, Isles of Scilly.

Ilfracombe (Devon)

Although the coastline is mainly rocky there are several small bays with sand or shingle beaches. In the harbour itself, fishing is allowed from the pier, which has plenty of room since it is a 'working' one providing berths for the passenger and pleasure boats that ply in the Bristol Channel. There is an average rise and fall of about 25 ft in the tide, so that beach and rock anglers are advised to study the sea-bed at low tide and pick out the gullies and weedy ridges likely to give sport when the tide rises.

Fish taken from the shore and pier are mullet, mackerel, pollack, coalfish, conger, dogfish, bass, wrasse, pouting, and a few plaice, turbot, soles and dabs.

Boats are available but they cannot be taken out except in charge of a local boatman, owing to the dangerous tides. All the species mentioned can be caught in the Bristol Channel, with the addition of tope, codling and whiting. Dogfish are plentiful – bull huss, lesser spotted and smooth hound – and good-sized skate and rays are taken.

Ragworm and mackerel are the principal baits, the latter brought in by fishermen during the season. When no mackerel is available herring is used.

The Ilfracombe and District AA (sea only) welcomes visitors. The Hon Secretary, Mr J. V. Cope, 16 Greenclose Road (Tel: Ilf 2383) is always ready to advise visitors, though he prefers a a personal talk to letters.

Porlock Weir, Minehead, Watchet (Somerset)

Porlock
Beach fishing at a few spots, mostly over rough bottom. Red Sands, Bossington and Greenaleigh (between Hurtstone Point and Minehead).

Boat fishing brings in mackerel, conger, pollack, dogfish, cod, bass and skate, with occasional tope. Boats from A. Ley or P. Ley, Porlock Weir.

Minehead
Boats from S. Rawle, or through the Harbourmaster, 7 Quay Street. Species as for Porlock.

There is a stretch of sand to the west of the Lifeboat House from which bass are caught. Codling, whiting and bass are caught from the harbour wall. Bass, whiting and a few flatfish are taken from Minehead beach. There is an easily fished, long beach from Dunster Beach to Blue Anchor: bass, flatfish, thornback, skate.

Watchet
From the beaches at West Beach, Mellwell Bay, Doniford and St Audries all the local species are caught. Fishing from the harbour walls. The Watchet and District SAS organizes monthly competitions.

The main species caught offshore are bass, cod, skate, dogfish and whiting. For boat, bait or tackle contact H. Wilkes at the Tackle Shop.

In all these places lugworms, ragworms and fish strips are the main baits. The worms can be dug on most of the beaches.

Weston-super-Mare (Somerset)

There are three sea angling clubs in the area. The largest, the Weston-super-Mare Sea Angling Association offers a temporary membership of one month to all anglers. Details may be obtained from the Hon Secretary, matches are staged each year in May and September.

Due to the strong currents in the Bay, boat anglers bringing their own craft are advised to obtain full local information before attempting to fish the Bay. There are no vessels for private hire due to the dangerous waters but professional boatmen are available to take out parties of anglers in their well-equipped and large craft.

Many different species inhabit the area and include bass, soles, conger, thornback skate, dogfish, flounders, pout, mullet and silver eels during the warmer months and whiting and cod from autumn onwards.

Vast beds of lugworm are to be found along the sand-mud mark of the town beach and also just off the Kewstoke Rocks. The locally obtained bait is well favoured. Soft crab and ragworm may also be had on occasions.

Three tackle shops will cater for all the anglers' needs. They are: Bill Evans, Weston Model Aero & Fishing Tackle Supplies, 1 Oxford Street, Weston-super-Mare (Tackle and Live Bait); Maroli, 19 Orchard Street, Weston-super-Mare (Tackle and Live Bait); Weston Decorators, 22 Boulevard, Weston-super-Mare.

There are numerous shore marks to try for sport with estuary fishing from the banks of the River Axe, beach work from Weston Sands, Brean Sands and Sand Bay. Rock-fishing from Brean Down and Sand Point, also from the cliffs bordering the toll road at Kewstoke. No fishing is permitted from the central Grand Pier, but the main bridge of the Old Pier is available to anglers during the period when the cross-channel boats are in operation.

A comprehensive survey of all known marks, baits, tackle,

etc, is given in a 24-page booklet, written by international sea angler, Mr Don Metcalfe, who lives at Weston. Available from all tacklists.

Tenby (Pembrokeshire)

Around the coast the sea angler will find some of the best fishing in Britain. For the expert and novice alike there is a wide variety of methods that can be employed. Spinning for mackerel, bass and pollack from the rocks, using light tackle with lines down to 4 lb bs is very popular.

Large beaches like Newgale, Marloes and Freshwater West which are continually churned by the Atlantic swells are ideal for the beachcasting expert who can expect large bags of bass and other varieties of fish.

The increasingly popular sport of tope fishing is catered for mainly at Saundersfoot. Here, in 1964 the world record tope of 74 lb 11 oz was taken and a record of 39 tope each over 33 lb was set up. Tope are also caught from the beaches and rocks. If fishing from the latter one should inquire locally regarding tides and, if any, the danger of cliff falls.

Boats may be hired at various resorts such as Saundersfoot, Tenby, Pembroke, Little Haven, Solva and Fishguard.

Saundersfoot is the main centre for tope fishing, and there are many boats available for hire. Inquiries at these resorts and with tackle dealers will give information.

For organized beach fishing, and competitions, details may be obtained from the Secretary of the Pembroke and District Angling Club, Mr T. Cavenay, 1 School Houses, Bush Hill, Pembroke.

Milford Haven (Pembrokeshire)

This long narrow estuary of several Welsh rivers offers, together with nearby 'outside' marks, fishing for all the south-western species. Bass fishing from the shore is noteworthy. Herring shoals penetrate as far as Llangwym on the Daugleddyf, a good dozen miles from the sea. Bass and mullet can be caught at Haverfordwest, many miles farther inland. A famous shore mark is the hulk of HMS *Warrior*, the first of the ironclads, which is now used as an oiling quay at Milford Haven itself. Noted marks for boat fishing within the haven are the Haven

Rock, Thorn Island and, just outside to the south, Sheep Island.
   Boats, tackle and bait can be obtained in Milford Haven.
   Club: Milford Haven SAC (Mr B. Mills, Competition Secretary, 227 Haven Drive, Hakin, Milford Haven).

St David's (Pembroke) to Aberdaron (Caernarvon)

There is excellent shore and boat fishing along most of this stretch of coast for all the western species of fish according to season and, in the case of shore fishing, the nature of the coast. The main stations are St David's, Newport, Aberystwyth, Aberdovey, Pwllheli and Aberdaron. Boats are available, and the estuary towns have bridges, groynes, piers, etc, at which fishing is possible.

Llandudno (Caernarvon)

   Beach fishing: Although fishing is not permitted from Llandudno Pier during the summer months (May to September) excellent fishing can be enjoyed from Llandudno's beaches at any time.
   Little Orme opposite Villa Marina: Fishing for bass at low water. Bait – soft crab, ragworm, prawns, also caught spinning. Prawns may be found among the rocks; bottom rather rough, with odd patches of sand.
   Little Orme to Arcadia Theatre: From three hours before high water for bass, flounder, plaice, dabs, codling and whiting, evening tides best. Bait – ragworm or lugworm; bottom sand and shingle.
   Long Jetty near Pier: After the motor boats have ceased operating for the day, usually after 6 PM fishing from the long jetty at low water and casting out towards the pier, anglers may be rewarded with plaice, dabs, and flounders. Bait – ragworm, lugworm or mussels.
   Rocky Shore beyond Pier: At the south side of the slips leading down to the rocky shore below Happy Valley, fishing for dabs, codling and whiting is possible at high water from the rock ledge; the bottom is very rough. Baits as above.
   West Shore: Opposite the Gogarth Abbey Hotel, fish the channel in from low water for bass and flat fish.
   Black Rocks towards Deganwy is a well-known spot for bass: fish the tide in on rag, lug or soft crab; also spinning.

Anglers fishing the West Shore should carefully watch the incoming tide as they may get cut off by the water creeping in behind them.

Rock fishing: Fishing from some of the rock ledges around the Marine Drive for the following variety of fish is possible: cod, conger, pollack, mackerel, whiting, wrasse and skate, but apart from Pigeon's Cove should only be visited accompanied by a local angler as access to them can be dangerous and the rocks themselves are sometimes swept by waves during rough weather.

Boat fishing: A variety of fish can be caught in Llandudno Bay including cod, conger, tope, skate, whiting, pollack, dabs, bream, mackerel and gurnard. Tides run fast and heavy lead is needed to hold bottom, particularly during spring tides. Local boatmen run trips to some of the fishing grounds, about two miles out.

Bait – Mussel of medium size is plentiful under the Pier at low water, also ragworm. Lugworm can be dug at West Shore and soft crab can be found among the rocks towards the Old Gogarth Abbey. (Compiled by E. B. Quiney.)

Clubs: Llandudno and District SAC (Miss C. C. Jones, 7 Gogarth Avenue, Penmaenmawr. Tel: Penmaenmawr 2352). The Tope Angling Club of Great Britain has its headquarters here (J. D. Williams, 24 Church Walk, Llandudno. Tel: Llandudno 75105).

Rhyl (Flint)

Beach fishing almost anywhere along the coast. Main species: dabs, flounders, plaice and whiting. Two favourite stations are Splash Point (fished at low tide: see that the gullies do not fill up behind you when the tide makes); and the estuary, fishable at all states of tide.

Much fishing is done from boats, and fish of all Irish Sea species are caught, including many tope, a speciality of all this area. Pamphlets describing the fishing available, the boats and their cost, can be had on application to: Marina Sea Fishing Trips, Harbour End, Wellington Road, Rhyl (Tel: Rhyl 2547); and Rhyl Boat Fishing Centre, Wm. Roberts, 131 High Street, Rhyl (Tel: Rhyl 3031).

Club: Rhyl SAA.

Anglesey

The coast of Anglesey is claimed to have some of the richest inshore fishing grounds in Britain. Bass and tope fishing are noteworthy, and wrasse, mullet, pollack, thornback rays, cod, flatfish, whiting, dogfish and conger are plentiful from the rock and beach marks all round the island.

The best shore fishing for bass is found along the sandy surf beaches on the south side of the island. The creeks, inlets and estuaries of the west side are the home of very large grey mullet, and bass and sea trout are caught on spinning tackle.

Pier fishing is done from the two-mile-long breakwater at Holyhead and the stone jetty at Amlwch.

Inshore and deep sea fishing brings catches of every species available in the Irish Sea. The best places for boats are at Menai Bridge, Rhosneigr and Holyhead, but small boats are available for hire at most coastal villages.

The best area for a variety of natural baits is the Menai Strait, but lugworms are plentiful and easily dug at Llanddwyn, Malltraeth, Aberffraw, Cymyran Straits, Traeth Dulas, Benllech and Red Wharfe Bay. Fish such as bass and flatfish come into all these beaches.

Bait can be bought from tacklists, and from a number of fishermen's houses which display 'Bait for Sale' notices.

Blackpool (Lancashire)

The piers at Blackpool probably offer the best of the shore fishing, but it is poor in summer anywhere. In autumn the dabs come in in thousands and remain until well into the winter. Codling are present in autumn until the end of December.

Central Pier: Depending on the tide, fishing is allowed from 8.30 AM to dusk.

North Pier: Summer: fishing from 8 AM to dusk. Autumn, winter and spring: 8 AM to 5 PM and from 6 PM to 8 AM.

Sea Wall: Fishable at high water.

In addition to dabs and codling, catches of bass, plaice, flounders and silver eels are made from piers and from small boats just offshore. Sea-going boats add tope and several other species to the list of possibles.

In summer the boatmen are all too busy with pleasure trips to worry about anglers, but small boats without boatmen can be hired, and inshore fishing can be done from these. Deep sea boats may be hired at Fleetwood.

Popular baits are lugworm, ragworm and crab, but crabs are so plentiful in the area that they rob the hooks of worm before other fish can reach them. Unless in one of the few crab-free areas, crab – either peeler or softback – is the best bait.

These baits and others can be bought from three tackle dealers: D. J. Nicholson, 41 Warley Road (Tel: Blackpool 22557); Brian Ogden, 254 Church Street (Tel: Blackpool 21087); S. Waterhouse, 38 Cookson Street.

Of several clubs in Blackpool the two largest are Blackpool and Layton AS (Mr E. Wadeson, 24 Elgin Place) and Blackpool Central AS (Mr P. French, 6 Ipswich Place, Cleveleys).

ISLE OF MAN

Manx fishing provides a wide variety of sport: the gullies and crevices of the rock-bound coastline with the sand and gravel layers beyond form the natural feeding grounds of the fish.

The stock of fish round the island, virtually undisturbed by the heavy trawl-scraping so common on more populous coasts, consists mainly of cod, pollack, coalfish, whiting, wrasse, and flatfish of all types. In their season fantastic catches of mackerel are taken from the piers of Peel.

Douglas

From boats off Douglas Head, using feather streamers and lugworm, excellent cod and mackerel and pollack can be obtained. Closer inshore, off the rocks behind the Lighthouse, spinning with artificial eels, feathers and spinners gives fine sport for pollack, and from the rocks itself pollack and congers can be caught in large numbers. Off the various piers flatfish, coalfish, pollack, dogfish, conger, gurnard, cod and grey mullet can be obtained, but it must be remembered that during the height of the season Douglas is a very busy passenger port and it is sometimes difficult to obtain access to piers other than the Breakwater. Boats can be hired at reasonable rates.

Peel

Regarded as one of the best centres for fishing, particularly for mackerel which congregate in large numbers at the entrance to the harbour feeding on the offal which is discharged from the

kipper houses in Peel district. A 4 lb 8 dr mackerel held the
British record from 1952 to 1963. Mackerel of from 3 lb to 4 lb
are regularly caught. This fish was caught from the breakwater,
and from this point are also taken cod, flatfish, pollack, coalfish,
gurnard, mullet, dogfish, skate and conger. Boats from Peel
bring in excellent catches.

The Peel and District AC organizes a series of sea angling
competitions during the season.

Port Erin

There is good fishing in Port Erin from the pier and breakwater
where spinning with artificial eels for pollack and mackerel can
be very successful, as also is float fishing for pollack, wrasse and
conger. Exceptionally good fishing is available in Port Erin Bay
for mackerel, pollack, flatfish, conger, cod and wrasse.

A must is a visit to the Sea Fish Hatchery and Aquarium
where large numbers of lobsters and plaice are hatched and
liberated round the coast at suitable intervals.

Port St Mary

The centre for boat fishing expeditions to the Whorts, Carrick
Rocks and Langness Bank. Off there the British record brill
(16 lb) was caught.

Expeditions are arranged from Port St Mary for shark and
tope fishing off the Chicken Rock and boats can be hired for this
purpose.

The Port St Mary Angling Club and the Isle of Man Yacht
Club have their headquarters here.

Castletown

Castletown makes a good centre for the angler. Sea fishing is
good all along the nearby coast, especially on Scarlett and
Langness.

Laxey

Fishing from boats in Laxey Bay can give good sport, and very
large catches of whiting can be obtained. Closer inshore flatfish
are plentiful. Bass can be caught with lug bait from the beach.

Sea angling in Scotland has undergone a revolution in recent years. The fish were always there but only really enterprising anglers were able to get at them. Ten years ago only a few centres understood the requirements of anglers: twenty years ago, with two or three areas excepted, sea anglers had to find their own way about, and if they hired a boat they had to explain exactly what they wanted.

All that has changed. Mr J. A. Kerr Hunter, MBE, Honorary Secretary of the Scottish Federation of Sea Anglers and an early promoter of the sea angling side of the Scottish Council of Physical Recreation, has had much to do with the changes, though naturally many other people and factors have been at work.

There are now scores of centres in Scotland where boats may be hired, bait bought, marks located and expert information obtained. About fifty sea angling clubs in all parts of Scotland, including the larger islands, are now affiliated to the Scottish FSA.

Many festivals and competitions are held, and it is interesting to note that in a three-day event out of Stornoway, Isle of Lewis, 17,773 lb of fish were landed, mostly pollack and coalfish with some sizeable skate. The one-day British Skate Championship brought 10,773 lb of fish to 140 rods. The two most spectacular individual fish were both taken in Orkney waters, each establishing a new British record. Provost W. E. Knight of Stromness caught a 161¾ lb halibut, and Mr Jan Olssen of Sweden a skate weighing 214 lb (this record has since been bettered).

The best advice for an angler thinking of sea fishing in Scotland is to send for a booklet – *Scotland for Sea Angling* – produced by the Scottish Tourist Board in co-operation with the Scottish Council of Physical Recreation and the Scottish FSA. This is revised periodically. It costs 25p, post free, from the Scottish Tourist Board, 23 Ravelson Terrace, Edinburgh EH4 3EU.

In addition to much textual information it contains 24 charts specially prepared for anglers which, besides the usual chart features, show shore and boat angling marks and areas in which bait can be dug or collected.

The facts speak for themselves. In 1968 anglers fishing off the Causeway Coast in Co Antrim, which extends from Magilligan, Co Londonderry, in the west to Ballycastle in the east, landed 255 haddock each weighing over 5 lb, at that time the minimum 'specimen' weight acceptable by the Irish Specimen Fish Committee. The figure has since been raised to 7 lb.

In addition Strangford Lough, in Co Down, produced a new Irish record tope of 60 lb 12 oz and four more tope that topped the 40 lb 'specimen' mark. A Belfast Lough hake of 25 lb 5½ oz has held both the European and the Irish record since 1962 and a 7 lb plaice, taken at Portrush, Co Antrim, remains the best ever caught on rod and line in Irish waters.

The 250-mile coastline of Northern Ireland has much to offer the sea angler both from the point of view of the man who likes to keep his feet on dry land and for the boat angler, who wants to get out where he thinks the big ones are.

The visitor will find a growing awareness of the needs of the sea fishermen and most of the main resorts, and in particular those on the Causeway Coast and on either side of Belfast Lough, now have boatmen who are willing to take out parties or individuals for day trips.

In addition, regular boat competitions are held throughout the summer season and seats are always available for visitors, who are not affiliated to any of the local clubs.

Working round the coast from north to south, the first stop will almost certainly be for the impressive strands at Magilligan, Downhill, Castlerock and Portstewart. In recent years these have earned fame for the quality of their bass fishing.

The fish have not been plentiful but they make up in size what they lack in numbers. In fact Downhill gave up the heaviest Irish bass caught in 1965 (12 lb 1 oz), 1966 (12 lb) and 1967 (13 lb 15 oz). Portrush, Portstewart, Ballycastle and Portballintrae are the four main centres for the Causeway Coast and for fishing the Portstewart and Causeway Banks. This area provides the best mixed fishing in the Province, with the haddock taking pride of place.

The Causeway Coast boasts the finest haddock fishing in the British Isles. In addition there are cod, whiting, gurnard, both red and grey, coalfish, pollack, tope, skate and conger. One of the best conger marks is the wreck of the 14,000 ton cruiser,

HMS *Drake*, in Church Bay, Rathlin Island, five miles offshore from Ballycastle.

Shore fishing can produce good results in this area and the bay at Cushendun is particularly popular for codling, plaice and dabs. There is good pier angling at Carnlough, especially during the winter. Larne is convenient to the best fishing grounds in Belfast Lough and off the Maidens, a group of rocky islets, but suitable boats are scarce. Larne Lough holds big stocks of mullet but these are seldom fished for with rod and line.

Carrickfergus is an excellent centre for Belfast Lough and not far away from here a Belfast angler took a conger of 64 lb in July 1966, the second heaviest of its species ever landed from Irish waters.

Bangor, Co Down, best established of all the sea fishing centres in Northern Ireland, and Donaghadee, both make a special point of catering for the visiting angler, as does Groomsport. The Lough is famous for its big hake and fine plaice and also produces quality cod – the best in 1968 weighed 25¼ lb – whiting, haddock, pouting, gurnard, conger, herring and mackerel.

Moving on south in Co Down, we reach Ballywalter and then Strangford Lough. The villages of Strangford and Portaferry guard the entrance to the Lough and are linked by a modern ferry.

The bar mouth at Strangford, where there is a strong tide race, gives good results for cod while the more sheltered waters of the Lough have tremendous possibilities for big skate and tope.

The best Strangford skate so far weighed 175 lb and it was followed by one of 162 lb. Many more have been taken weighing between 100 and 125 lb.

Ardglass, Newcastle and Annalong all have something to offer the sea angler, as has Kilkeel, but it's not always easy to find boats. Warrenpoint is just starting to come into the picture and, like Rostrevor, is convenient to Carlingford Lough, which holds tope and countless dogfish.

FISHING IN THE REPUBLIC OF IRELAND

Ireland has always been famed for its sea fish. A few centres, notably Ballycotton, have been known to anglers for fifty years or more and have figured prominently in the big fish lists. Prior to 1958 there were few sea angling clubs in the country, and the few that did exist were concentrated mainly on the east coast, though the little fishing done on other coasts yielded remarkable results to anglers.

Since then the position has rapidly altered, for there has been a great surge of interest in sea angling and today there are many stations with first-class fishing catering for the visiting angler.

Local sea angling clubs, of which there are now over 140 affiliated to the Irish Federation of Sea Anglers, are usually open to visitors and can be counted upon to help the visitor to find sport.

Anglers contemplating a holiday in the Republic and requiring information and advice should write for details to the Angling Officer, Inland Fisheries Trust, Balnagowan, Mobhi Boreen, Glasnevin, Dublin 9 (a state-sponsored organization which develops all forms of sport fishing in Ireland) or to the offices of Bord Failte Eireann (the Irish Tourist Board), Baggot Street Bridge, Dublin 2.

Irish sea angling is a long way from being fully explored. More information becomes available every year, but many stretches of the coast are, as yet, virgin territory from the point of view of the angler.

The following stations are in costal order from north-east to north-west. Boats, boatmen and bait are available unless otherwise stated.

Carlingford (Co Louth)

Pollack, mackerel, codling, conger, dogfish and tope in Carlingford Lough. Some shore fishing.

Boyne Estuary (Co Louth)
Good bass fishing at times, especially drift lining from a boat in the tideway. Can be fished from Baltray or Mornington. Some beach fishing south of the Boyne at Bettystown.

Skerries (Co Dublin)

An angling charter service operates from here (sometimes from Howth). Boat fishing for pollack at the Rockabill, also codling, conger and coalfish. Some good fishing for tope and cod farther offshore.

Dublin Area
Northside

Bass from railway viaduct at Malahide. Bass and flatfish in the channel and sometimes good drift lining for bass and mackerel from small boats. At Howth there is pier fishing for small coalfish.

Southside

Occasional bass at Williamstown and Seapoint. School bass and flatfish in channels at Merrion Strand. Dunlaoire (West pier) small coalfish, dabs and mackerel in season and whiting in winter. Flounders, gurnard, occasional bass and small pouting and poor cod in autumn from a point halfway along the back of the pier. Mullet in the harbour. Boat fishing for codling (best in the autumn), wrasse, coalfish, mackerel with a chance of tope, skate and conger from Bullock Harbour and Coliemore Harbour (Dalkey). Thornback and blonde rays numerous and fair fishing for turbot, brill, dabs, plaice and gurnard on banks a long way out and only fishable by large motor craft. Some shore fishing for bass and flatfish at Killiney Bay (Co Wicklow) and boat fishing for dabs, gurnard and small pollack.

Fresh bait available from some Dublin tackle shops.

Bray (Co Wicklow)

Some pier fishing available for mullet, flounders and occasional bass. Rowing boats available for fishing mackerel, small coalfish, pollack and codling.

Greystones (Co Wicklow)

Beach fishing for flounders, plaice, small coalfish and occasional bass. Boat fishing for codling, pollack, coalfish, rays, skate and tope. This is the best fishing near Dublin and bait must be obtained from Dublin. There is fair fishing between Greystones and Wexford, at Arklow, Kilmichael Point and Courtown Harbour.

Wexford (Co Wexford)

Good bass and flounder fishing in river channel and beach

fishing at Curracloe and Raven Point. Rowing boats in town, and ragworm and lugworm available.

Rosslare (Co Wexford)

Wonderful bass fishing from small boats over the famous Splaugh Rock and in the Wexford Gut. It is quite common for one angler to take twenty to forty bass on one tide. Average weight 4 lb but plenty of bigger fish. Spinning with artificial baits is the usual method. Deep sea fishing at the Tuskar Rock for big pollack, cod, conger and tope. Shore fishing for bass at several beaches in the vicinity.

Kilmore Quay (Co Wexford)

Good beach fishing for bass with a chance of tope. Excellent fishing for tope from small boats just off the beach, also small skate, rays, turbot and other flatfish. Good pollack and general deep sea fishing farther out at the Saltee Islands.

Waterford Harbour (Co Wexford)

Good bass and flatfish fishing from the shore and boats in the estuary and good general fishing outside. Can be fished from Duncannon and Dunmore East.

Dungarvan (Co Waterford)

Good shore fishing for bass and good boat fishing for bass, pollack, mackerel, bream, gurnard and other species. Excellent fishing for blue sharks.

Ardmore (Co Waterford)

Good shore fishing for bass, pollack and flatfish. Good boat fishing for blue sharks, pollack, mackerel, bream, gurnard and other species, but only small boats available.

Youghal (Co Cork)

Deep sea fishing of the Ballycotton type and excellent fishing for blue sharks. First-class beach and estuary fishing for bass. Good fishing in small boats in the estuary for flatfish, bass, codling; good bass and pollack fishing outside.

Ballycotton (Co Cork)

This is one of the best-known sea angling centres in Europe and it has a long tradition of catering for anglers. There is an excellent harbour, tides are slack, deep water close in and a varied bottom. The boats are good, the boatmen know their grounds intimately, and have had long experience in dealing with anglers. Ballycotton figures prominently in the big fish lists and fishes consistently well. The Irish record skate (221 lb), cod (42 lb), pouting (4 lb 10 oz), and pollack (19 lb 3 oz) were caught here; and each year it produces a number of specimen fish. A great variety of fish can be caught – cod, ling, pollack, coalfish, conger, red bream, gurnard, pouting, whiting, tope and flatfish. It is noted for big skate and some good halibut have been taken. Blue shark are plentiful in the summer. Hake are not now common.

Big mullet can be caught in the harbour using fish gut as bait. Conger are taken at the end of the pier. There is good shore fishing for bass and sea trout on a small beach one mile from the town.

Ballycotton is popular and intending visitors should make arrangements well in advance. Boats can be booked through the hotel and guest houses.

Cork Harbour (Co Cork)

This is a large land-locked harbour with numerous islands, creeks and channels. Immense numbers of mullet and bass are to be found here and good shore fishing for bass can be had both by spinning and ground fishing. On the east side the best shore fishing places are Saleen, Eastferry, Belvelly and Dunkettle, and on the west side, Crosshaven. There is excellent boat fishing inside the very sheltered and extensive harbour for big skate, blonde and thornback rays, turbot, bass and tope. The fishing outside the harbour is of the Ballycotton and Kinsale type and the fishing for blue sharks is excellent. Good boats and boatmen are available at Cobh and Crosshaven.

Kinsale (Co Cork)

This is the most popular fishing centre in the country. The fishing in the open sea is exceptionally good and varied while in the estuary itself there is good boat and shore fishing. The Old Head of Kinsale juts out to sea for approximately three miles, and provides good shelter in the prevailing winds. There is very good fishing inside the Old Head, in the Race and the Lake for turbot, brill, cod, ling, skate, pollack, conger, whiting, big pouting, tope and huss. The 'Ling Rocks' some five miles off shore is possibly the best ground in Europe for big ling, pollack, cod, conger, red sea bream, pouting, tope and for big skate close to the rocks. There is excellent fishing for blue shark and the shark angler is catered for.

Inside the estuary there is good fishing for pollack, coalfish, flatfish, whiting, codling, bass and some skate, and there are several spots on the shore which provide good bass fishing.

Owing to its very sheltered position the angler can always get good fishing except in the worst conditions. A boat firm in Kinsale caters especially for anglers, and boats can be chartered, or a place in a boat booked. Both big powered boats and small craft with outboard engines are available, and it is advisable to book in advance. Tackle can be hired both for general fishing and shark fishing.

From Kinsale, west through Courtmacsherry and Clonakilty to Rosscarbery there is excellent shore fishing for bass, pollack and wrasse. The deep sea fishing is good but little explored. Boats are available at Courtmacsherry.

Rosscarbery (Co Cork)

This is a first-class shore fishing centre. Bass are very plentiful on the three beaches and in the estuary. Beach casting gear is essential for the beaches are shallow except near high water: spinning outfits can be used in the estuary. All the fishing is within three miles of the town, and there is always some spot at any stage of the tide which is just right for fishing. The deep sea angling is little explored, but small boats with outboard engines are available for fishing in the bay, and big pollack, coalfish, bass, codling, cod, tope and plaice are taken. (See note on bass in Rosscarbery Bay on page 90.)

Rosscarbery to Valentia

This area is little explored but there is good shore fishing in many places, particularly at Baltimore and Sherkin Island; in the Kenmare area and on the beaches at Waterville on Ballinskelligs Bay (excellent bass fishing). Generally this stretch of coastline is rocky and precipitous and the main shore fishing is for pollack and wrasse. There is excellent deep sea fishing out of Baltimore and Schull where boats are available. These two stations and Glandore also offer excellent fishing for blue shark. There is good inshore boat fishing at Bantry and Kenmare, the latter station being noted for large skate and tope. There is good mixed fishing at Castletownbere and Parknasilla.

Derrynane (Co Kerry)

Pollack, cod, ling, wrasse, turbot, skate and tope are plentiful and blue shark numerous, but few boats are available.

Cahirciveen/Valentia (Co Kerry)

Valentia had a reputation in the old days rivalling that of Bally-cotton. The fishing is of the same calibre for pollack, coalfish, cod, ling, red sea bream, conger, wrasse, gurnard, whiting, tope, huss, turbot, skate, halibut and blue shark. An Irish record halibut ($152\frac{1}{2}$ lb) came from here and other notable specimens are skate ($219\frac{1}{2}$ lb), conger (72 lb), tope (56 lb), turbot ($26\frac{1}{2}$ lb), gurnard (8 lb), mackerel (3 lb 6 oz), red sea bream (9 lb 6 oz) and whiting (4 lb $8\frac{1}{2}$ oz).

There is good bass fishing in the sound (within the harbour) and good general fishing in the whole harbour. The decline of Valentia in popularity was due to a fall in the standard of facilities for anglers, not a fall in the fish available. This has been put right to a large degree and the area is again becoming a great angling centre. Good boats and boatmen are available.

Valentia to Dingle

From Valentia east to the Dingle Peninsula there is good shore fishing for bass at Glenbeigh and Killorglin and excellent small-boat fishing at Cromane for tope, rays, huss and flatfish. The whole of the Dingle Peninsula provides excellent shore fishing. Particularly good is the bass fishing on the ocean surf beaches at Inch, Smerwick Harbour, and at Fermoyle, Kilcummin, and Stradbally on Brandon Bay. The bass fishing extends through the whole year and the October/November and February/March periods can provide the best of the fishing. There is first-class deep sea fishing for cod, ling, pollack, skate, rays, red sea bream, tope, huss, turbot, whiting, coalfish and conger. Boats catering specially for anglers are available at Dingle.

Fenit (Co Kerry)

Six miles from Tralee. Here an ocean pier runs far out into deep water (five fathoms at low tide). Apart from good bass and mullet some very big fish have been taken on rod and line from this pier, including skate of 137 lb and others over the 100 lb; a sting ray of $35\frac{1}{2}$ lb; five monkfish in one day, weighing respectively 48 lb, 45 lb, 43 lb, 40 lb, 38 lb. Heavy conger are common, and rays, dogfish, small pollack and pouting are numerous. Tope are occasionally caught. Shore fishing in the vicinity can also be good.

There is excellent boat fishing out of Fenit in Tralee Bay, the fishing for tope, monkfish, skate, rays, and huss being particularly good. Boats are available. North of Fenit there is excellent shore fishing in Barrow Harbour, Bannow Strand at Ballyheigue, and at Ballybunion. Apart from good bass and flatfish, tope can be taken from the shore in many places along this stretch of coast.

Shannon Estuary

Little is known about the angling here but there is good shore fishing in many places and bass are known to run as far as Kildysart. At Tarbert, on the Co Limerick side, several skate of over 100 lb have been taken from the pier, as well as good tope. Kilrush, on the Co Clare side, has good bass and general shore fishing, and there is mixed boat fishing, small skate, and pollack and tope being plentiful.

Shannon to Galway Bay

The Atlantic coast of Co Clare from Loop Head at the mouth of the Shannon north to Black Head at the entrance to Galway Bay is mainly rocky and precipitous. There is excellent rock fishing in many places for big pollack, mackerel, wrasse, tope, huss, rays, cod, conger – and in places porbeagle sharks have been caught from the shore. There are a number of good beaches on this coast which provide bass and flatfish. Porbeagle sharks are found in numbers off the coast of Clare and there is good general deep sea fishing. Liscannor, near Lahinch, is the best station. Boats are available.

Galway Bay

Porbeagle sharks are also plentiful in Galway Bay and are taken close inshore in depths of 10 fathoms or less at times. It is an excellent centre for porbeagle fishing and there is also good general fishing for tope, pollack, rays, common and white skate, huss, gurnard, etc. Boats are available at Galway.

Very little is known about boat fishing on the west coast from Galway north to Westport, but some deep sea angling is done out of Clifden and Cleggan. There is rock fishing for pollack, wrasse and mackerel on this coast and beach fishing for flatfish and the occasional bass.

Westport (Co Mayo)

Situated on Clew Bay, Westport has become one of the famous names in sea angling in recent years. It holds the Irish record for monkfish (69 lb), and for white skate (165 lb). Several monkfish of more than 50 lb and many large skate of over 130 lb have been taken. Smaller skate, rays, pollack, tope, gurnard, turbot, conger and whiting are plentiful, as are spur dogs, rough hounds and huss. There is good shore fishing at Bertraw, where several bass of over 14 lb have been caught. Clew Bay is dotted with islands and provides very sheltered fishing. The angler can always get afloat and is very well looked after. Good boats and boatmen are available.

Clare Island

Situated in Clew Bay, this is a good station for deep sea angling. There is excellent general fishing of the Achill type for a large variety of deep water species. Boat available.

Achill Island (Co Mayo)

The waters of Keem Bay, Achill Island (which is connected by a bridge to the mainland) produced the remarkable catches of porbeagle sharks made in the 1930s, when little was known about sporting shark fishing in British waters. There is excellent general

224

fishing of the Ballycotton type and the average size is big for each species. Blue shark are plentiful and a male blue shark of 206 lb established the Irish record in 1959. There are boats available for sea angling at Purteen and Darby's Point, and also at Bullsmouth at the northern end of the Sound dividing the island from the mainland. There is excellent inshore fishing for tope, rays and huss at Bullsmouth as well as deep sea angling off the northern side of the island.

Belmullet (Co Mayo)

In recent years some of the best deep sea angling on the Irish coast has been found in the Belmullet area. Big cod, ling, halibut, pollack, coalfish, conger, red bream, tope, huss, gurnard and a variety of other species are present in these rich waters, and the average size is in all cases big for the species. The Irish record halibut (156 lb) was caught here in 1972. In the shallow sheltered bays, particularly Broadhaven, there is excellent inshore fishing for turbot, plaice, dabs, a variety of rays, tope and dogfish. Boats are available.

The coast eastwards from Belmullet to Sligo is mainly rocky and provides good rock fishing. Killala Bay in the centre of this stretch gives good general deep sea and inshore fishing for a great variety of species, the tope fishing being particularly good. There is always the chance of a porbeagle. The bay can be fished from either side, the stations being Enniscrone and Killala. Boats are available.

Sligo

Excellent fishing for big pollack, gurnard, coalfish and huss. Tope are exceptionally plentiful. Two rods took 43 tope (average 28 lb) here in three hours. Best fished from Rosses Point or Sligo. Few boats available.

Donegal Bay

Good fishing for a variety of fish around Innismurrey Island. Best fished from Mullaghmore. Tope are very plentiful in the Bundoran area, and Killybegs on the northern side of the bay holds a big and well-attended annual angling festival.

From Donegal Bay round to Lough Foyle little angling has been done. Deep sea angling is available out of Bunbeg; quality and quantity excellent. There are boats also at Downings and in Lough Swilly. The latter is a long narrow, shallow inlet of the sea which yields exceptional fishing for tope. This still leaves a good deal of coastline about which little is known. The prospects are good and the waters await the adventurous angler.

Moville (Co Donegal)

Situated at the entrance to Lough Foyle this centre is noted for its big red gurnard, which seem to occur here in greater numbers and size than elsewhere in Ireland. Pollack, codling, huss, rays, flatfish, gurnards (tub, red and grey) and skate are plentiful. Tope are also numerous, and big sharks are occasionally hooked. Boats are available and the angler is well looked after.

The National Anglers' Council

CODE OF CONDUCT AND SAFETY AT SEA FOR ANGLING

1. The following minimum lengths of boats are recommended:

   (a) up to 12 ft overall – two persons
   (b) not less than 14 ft overall – three persons
   (c) not less than 16 ft overall – four persons
   (d) not less than 18 ft overall – five persons
   (e) not less than 20 ft overall – six persons

2. Boats up to 12 ft overall limited to three miles from shore.

3. The following safety requirements are for boats up to 16 ft overall:

serviceable engine; two distress (five-star) flares; one life-jacket per person; built-in buoyancy; approved type rescue quoit; one bailer; one set oars and one spare; compass; first-aid outfit; ample ropes; fog signal; sea anchor; powder or foam fire extinguisher; steering rowlock; masthead radar disc.

4. Boats from 16 ft to 20 ft overall:

serviceable engine; one set oars and one spare; two bailers; bilge pump; compass; anchor; sea anchor; one life-buoy per two persons; one life-jacket per person; six distress (five-star) flares; first-aid kit; fire extinguisher; bag or box of sand; ample ropes; fog signal; blanket; steering rowlock; masthead radar disc.

The Code of Conduct

It is also recommended that:

   (a) No angling boat proceeds to sea without informing someone on shore of this intention

(b) the boat accepts the ruling of some responsible person whether or not to proceed to sea in bad weather

(c) individual anglers should wear reliable life-jackets at all times when afloat

(d) boats at sea must conform to the Board of Trade rules of the road and during the hours of darkness must carry adequate lights

(e) where gas cylinders are carried these should be provided with an overflow to the sea.

French and German Names of Fish

English	French	German
Angler Fish	Baudroie	Seeteufel
Bass	Bar commun	Wolfbarsch, Seebarsch
Brill	Barbue	Kleist, Glattbutt
Coalfish	Lieu noir	Köhler, Seelachs
Cod	Morue	Kabeljau, Dorsch
Comber	Serran cabrille	Sägebarsch
Dab	Limande franche	Kliesche
Dogfishes:		
Lesser spotted	Petite roussette	Kleingeflechter Katzenhai
Greater spotted	Grande roussette	Grossgeflechter Katzenhai
Smooth hound	Émissole commun	Glatthai
Spurdog	Aiguillat	Gemeiner Dornhai
Dolphin (fish)	Coryphène équiset	Gemeine Bramen
Eel, freshwater	Anguille	Aal, Flussaal
Eel, conger	Congre	Meeraal
Flounder	Picard, leflet	Flunder
Garfish	Orphie	Hornhecht
Gurnard, Grey	Grondin gris	Gauer Knurrhahn
Red	Grondin rouge	Knurrhahn
Tub	Grondin perlon	Roter Knurrhahn
Haddock	Églefin	Schellfisch
Hake	Merlu	Seehecht
Halibut	Flétan	Heilbutt
Herring	Hareng	Hering
John Dory	Dorée	Heringkonig
Ling	Lingue	Leng
Mackerel	Maquereau	Makrele
Monkfish	Ange de Mer	Meerengel

English	French	German
Mullet:		
Thick-lipped	Muge noir	Grosskopfige Meerasche
Thin-lipped	Mulet	Kleinkopfige Meerasche
Golden grey	Muge dore	Goldmeerasche
Pilchard	Sardine	Sardine
Plaice	Plie, Carrelet	Scholle, Goldbutt
Pollack	Lieu jaune	Pollack
Poor cod	Capelin	Zwengdorsch
Pouting	Tacaud	Franz, Dorsch
Rays (see Skates, Rays)		
Rockling	Motelle	Seequappe
Salmon	Saumon	Lachs, Salm
Sand Eel	Equille	Kleiner Sandaal
Sea Breams:		
Common, red	Rousseau	Nordischerm Meerbrassen
Black	Canthare	Seekarpfen
Sea trout	Truite de Mer	Meerforelle
Shad, Allis	Alose	Maifisch
Twaite	Caluyau (male) Finte (female)	Finte
Shark: Basking	Squale Pèlerin	Reisenhai
Blue	Requin bleu	Blauhai
Porbeagle	Taupe	Heringshai
Thresher	Renard de Mer	Fuchshai
Skates and rays:		
Blonde	Raie douce, blonde	
Bottle-nosed (white)	Raie blanche	Bandroche
Common	Pocheteau	Glattroche
Cuckoo	Raie fleurie	Kuckucksroche
Electric	Torpille	Zitterroche
Shagreen	Raie chardon	Chagrinroche
Sting	Pastenague	Stechroche
Thornback	Raie bouclée	Nagelroche
Smelt: Sand	Souclet	Ahrenfisch
True	Eperlan	Stint

English	French	German
Sole	Sole commun	Tunge
Spanish mackerel	Maquereau espagnol	Kolios
Sprat	Sprat	Sprott
Tope	Milandre	Hundshai
Tunny	Thon	Thunfisch
Turbot	Turbot	Steinbutt
Weever, Greater	Grande vive	Petermann
Lesser	Petite vive	Kleiner Petermann
Whiting	Merlan	Wittling
Wolf Fish	Loupmarin	Seewolf
Wrasse, Ballan	Vieille commun	Gefleckter Lippfisch
Corkwing	Crenilabre taureau	Schwarzaugiger Lippfisch

General Index

An index of Fishing Stations follows the General Index

235

Index of Fishing Stations

Alan Young
Sea Angling for Beginners 50p

Sea angling remains basically the problem of getting the fish to take a
baited hook – by following the author's expert advice the new
fisherman will avoid much disappointment. The book deals in a practical
way with all the many aspects of fishing – what fish you may catch, what
are the best baits to use, and there is a full coverage of tackle and
techniques.

Trevor Housby
Boat Fishing 60p

An experienced professional charter-boat skipper describes the most
productive boat fishing techniques for saltwater species, described
here, together with a wealth of practical hints.

Shark Fishing in British Waters 40p

Many varieties of shark may be found and fished within easy distance
of Britain's coastline. Trevor Housby draws on a fund of shark-fishing
expertise and experience to show how the use of light-tackle
techniques and a sound knowledge of each individual species can place
shark fishing at the top of the big-game fishing league, with its demands
upon courage, endurance and skill.

T. C. Ivens
Still Water Fly-Fishing 80p

'Another great classic . . . Long regarded as the standard work on still
water fly-fishing . . . confirms its position as one of the world's best
textbooks on angling' SCOTSMAN

'A very good book by a good, experienced and thinking fisherman.
It contains much of value for the skilled and novice alike, from flies and
tactics to boat handling and clothing' THE FIELD

Two excellent handbooks,
edited by Kenneth Mansfield

Coarse Fishing 60p

Seven authors, each well known for their writing on angling topics,
provide the complete handbook on coarse fishing for every angler.
All the main species are dealt with individually, together with full
descriptions of tackle and techniques. Baits – how to find, clean and use
them – are covered in the same comprehensive manner, and there is a
wealth of other useful information.
'Very good value' EASTERN DAILY PRESS

Trout Fishing 70p

Seven articles about all aspects of trout fishing, written by
acknowledged experts, and edited to eliminate any duplication of
coverage. Supplemented by an appendix on tackle and knots, they make
up nearly three hundred pages of solid, no-nonsense advice and help
for all trout fishermen.